100 Edible Mushrooms

100 Edible Mushrooms

Michael Kuo

with John David Moore,
Darvin DeShazer, and Others

THE UNIVERSITY OF MICHIGAN PRESS   Ann Arbor

Copyright © by the University of Michigan 2007
All rights reserved
Published in the United States of America by
The University of Michigan Press
Manufactured in the United States of America
⊗ Printed on acid-free paper

2024   2023   2022   2021   9   8   7

A CIP catalog record for this book is available from the British Library.

Library of Congress Cataloging-in-Publication Data

100 edible mushrooms / Michael Kuo . . . [et al.].
     p.   cm.
  Includes bibliographical references and index.
  ISBN-13: 978-0-472-03126-9 (pbk. : alk. paper)
  ISBN-10: 0-472-03126-0 (pbk. : alk. paper)
  1. Mushrooms, Edible—Identification.   I. Kuo, Michael,
1963–   II. Title: One hundred edible mushrooms.

QK617.A12   2007
635'.8—dc22   2006038418

While every effort has been made to provide accurate
information in this book, neither Michael Kuo nor the
University of Michigan Press accepts responsibility
for any decision made by anyone on the basis of the text
and illustrations herein.

This book is for Kate,
who actually ate
Gyrodon merulioides.

Contents

Recommended for Beginners   75

Experience Required   111

Difficult   237

Recipes   303

Introduction

I love mushrooms. When I see one in the woods, I drop to the ground to admire it. When I see one from the car, I slam on the brakes. I can spend hours crawling around on hands and knees in my yard while my neighbors shake their heads. I touch them, sniff them, draw them, take their pictures, make them the stars of home movies, study them, put them under my microscope, dry them, keep them in my living room, give presentations about them, write books about them—and sometimes I eat them.

Most of the best meals I've eaten in my life included wild mushrooms. A creamy sauce of chanterelles (p. 139) over toast in an Italian restaurant in Durango, Colorado (see chef Vincent Ferraro's recipe on p. 305); veal cutlets with porcini (p. 32) in the Italian Alps; ravioli made from scratch and stuffed with *Boletus pallidus* (p. 129; recipe on p. 307); a mess of sautéed yellow morels (p. 87) over steaks . . . my taste buds think of these as the high points of my life.

But the truth is (and I want you to know this right away), I don't eat a lot of wild mushrooms. About once a month I cook up some fresh or dried morels, chanterelles, or porcini, but that's about it. For one thing, wild mushrooms scare me. Even when I am 100 percent sure of a

Hericium erinaceus (edible; p. 102)

mushroom's identity and the species has been eaten safely by thousands of people, my intellect has trouble communicating the certainty to the rest of me. The two times I have suffered from relatively minor mushroom poisoning ("gastrointestinal distress" is a nice euphemism for the symptoms), it was not pleasant. Once, I had correctly identified and eaten a mushroom (an orange-capped *Leccinum*; see p. 55) that, at the time, was widely reported as a safe edible. The other time, I ate *blueberries* that I had stupidly not washed after I had coated them with spore dust from poisonous puffballs (*Scleroderma citrinum*; see pp. 96–98) in the woods, stomping on them again and again like a madman in order to show a friend how they dispersed their spores.

So my goal with this book is only partly to give you the means to collect and cook up edible wild mushrooms. The bigger goal is to get you *interested* in mushrooms—edible or not. They are so fascinating, and so little is known about them! If you love the woods, as I do, think about this: the forest would not be there without mushrooms. The trees and woody plants require mushrooms for survival (see the Focus Point "Mycorrhizal Mushrooms," p. 108). Stumps and fallen logs would never rot away (see "Wood-Rotting Parasites and Saprobes," p. 82). Dead leaves and needles would pile up until the forest choked on its own debris (see "Litter-Decomposing Saprobes," p. 257). Instead of tilting as a result of the activity of a gazillion generations of enterprising earthworms, that tower in Pisa would be engulfed by dead grass that never decomposed (see "Grass-Loving Saprobes," p. 93). The fungi are integral to life on earth, and mushrooms deserve our respect and admiration!

Yeah, okay—not quite a Vince Lombardi halftime speech and definitely not Prince Hal's "We few, we happy few, we band of brothers" the night before battle. Maybe you just want to find some edible mushrooms and enjoy a good meal—you have, after all, purchased a book called *100 Edible Mushrooms*, not *Mushrooms Will Save the Planet*. So I have some good news for you and a little piece of bad news.

First, the good news. I have asked two mushroom experts who are also experts on *eating* mushrooms to help me out. John David Moore has written most of the "In the Woods" and "In the Kitchen" entries in the book, as well as some material in the section "Collecting, Preparing, and Eating Wild Mushrooms." John David introduced me to the world of mushrooms, many years ago, and we have been collecting mushrooms together ever since. This guy knows his mushrooms—and he can cook like nobody's business. Darvin DeShazer is scientific advisor for the Sonoma County Mycological Association. He can identify just about any mushroom you put in front of him in about two seconds, and he is also a wonderful cook; he has written the entries on picking and cooking western mushrooms. Shannon Stevens and Ken Gilberg of the Missouri Mycological Society have helped with some rarely eaten mushrooms, as has my wife, Kate Klipp.

The further good news is that there are well over 100 edible mushrooms included in these pages. Many of the individual entries actually represent two, three, a dozen, or even more species as they are currently defined by mycologists. *Hundreds of Edible Mushrooms*, however, wouldn't have made for a catchy title.

The bad news is that while there are indeed hundreds of edible mushrooms in North America there are not 100 *good* edible mushrooms. We were definitely scraping the bottoms of the edibility and palatability barrels to come up with 100 entries. If you want to eat the devil's urn (p. 94) or pickled stinkhorn eggs (p. 197), have at it, by all means. But don't say I didn't warn you!

How to Use This Book

The idea behind this book is to put mushrooms in your hand right away so that you can study their features and experiment with cooking them. Then, after you have begun to get a sense of how mushrooms are identified (and what the dangers are!), the plan is to go into the woods and begin bringing wild mushrooms home—*not,* at first, with the intention of eating them but rather to study them and continue learning how mushrooms can be identified with the kind of certainty that is required if you want to cook them up for dinner.

If you follow my advice in this book, you may be eating a few wild mushrooms from the "Recommended for Beginners" section in the first year—but this will depend on whether or not the mushrooms appear in your area and whether you find and identify them with certainty *at least two or three times.* I do not recommend that beginners (or experts for that matter) eat wild mushrooms they have not collected, scrutinized, poked, sliced, sniffed, and identified several times.

Focus Points

Since the goal is to have mushrooms in hand to serve as examples, I have included "Focus Points" throughout the book to illustrate mushroom features as you hold them. But there is an obvious problem with this approach: what if you do not find the example mushroom in your woods—and how would you know, anyway, if I'm not going to tell you "everything you need to know about identifying mushrooms" before you start trying to do it? To be honest, these problems are likely to pop up. However, I have put as many Focus Points as possible in the "From the Store" section, so that you can start developing a working knowledge of mushroom identification with mushrooms that have already been identified by others. I have also crammed the "Recommended for Beginners" section with Focus Points so that the example mushrooms do not require advanced skills to identify.

I have been teaching writing and literature to college freshmen for over fifteen years, so I suppose that "teacher mode" has become a part of my personality. I hope you do not feel patronized by my teacherly method in this book; the Focus Point approach is a bit like saying, "Class, get out your books and read along while we pass around the visual

Table of Focus Points

aid." But a hands-on approach (sometimes called kinetic learning) is experiential rather than merely intellectual—and it usually works better, in my experience. I do promise not to patronize you by creating Focus Points for things that anyone with a tenth-grade education could figure out—terms such as *cap* and *stem*, for example, or descriptors such as *convex* and *smooth*.

The "Table of Focus Points" lists the Focus Points found in the book for easy reference.

The Mushrooms

Each of the 100 edible mushrooms in this book—except those that are featured only in the "From the Store" section—is provided with a section entitled "Distinguishing Features." The mushroom is described from top to bottom, and I have tried to make the descriptions more or less parallel. I have also included information about the *absence* of features; every description of a gilled mushroom, for example, indicates whether there is a sack around the base of the stem—even though only *one* of the edible mushrooms in the book has such a sack, and it is not even a mushroom with gills. I have done this because it can be frustrating to read mushroom descriptions and be forced to *assume* that because something is not mentioned it is not present on the mushroom.

The distinguishing physical features are followed by a paragraph on the ecology of the mushroom. Some of the material in the ecology paragraph, such as geographic range or the types of trees associated with the mushroom, is essential to identification. Other information, such as the ecological role played by the mushroom, is admittedly not crucial to identifying mushrooms—though it is at the very heart of *understanding* them.

A paragraph entitled "Poisonous Look-Alikes" follows the ecology paragraph. If there is a known poisonous mushroom that could be reasonably mistaken for the edible mushroom, it is listed there and described in detail in the "Poisonous Look-Alikes" section of the book (p. 41).

Topics in the "Comments" section, which follows the list of poisonous look-alikes, range from further information on identification to general interest items that are not crucial to identification but may help to fill out the picture.

Information on how to collect each mushroom "In the Woods" follows—but here the assumption is that you know which edible mushroom you are looking for and how to recognize it. If this is the case, you will want to go about collecting the mushrooms differently than you would if you were trying to identify them. For example, some of the "In the Woods" paragraphs suggest that you slice off the stems of gilled mushrooms and place the caps gill-side down in your collection bag. But, while this is a great idea if you want to keep hard-to-clean dirt out of your mushroom's gills, it is a *terrible* idea if you still have to identify the mushroom (so terrible that potentially fatal mistakes could result). See pages 11–12 for information on collecting unknown mushrooms with the goal of identifying them.

The last paragraph for each mushroom is labeled "In the Kitchen," and it contains recommendations for cleaning, preparing, cooking, and preserving the mushrooms—as well as an assessment of their quality as edibles. Finally, recipes are recommended when a mushroom is particularly suitable; the recipes themselves can be found at the end of the book.

Terminology and Names

Few things irritate me more than useless jargon. There is simply no good reason for anyone, even a mycologist (a scientist who studies fungi), to call a mushroom's cap a "pileus" when speaking to anyone but another mycologist (and even then I have my doubts). I assume you want to learn about mushrooms rather than learn how to talk like a mycologist, and I have steered clear of mycological terminology as much as possible—to the point, even, of creating a little confusion if you attempt to compare my mushroom descriptions with the ones found in other mushroom books. But I want to keep the focus on the mushrooms, not the terminology, so I will write "gills that run down the stem" rather than "decurrent gills" and "a sack around the stem's base" rather than "a volva." However, I have included the more technical terms used by other authors in the "Glossary and Index," where they are translated from Mycologese into English. There is a cutoff point, of course, for using common language instead of mycological terms. It would make for a very thick and repetitive reading experience if I were to explain what a polypore, bolete, or gilled mushroom is every time I use one of those terms. If you find a term you are not familiar with, please look it up in the "Glossary and Index," where I have included definitions (or page references for definitions elsewhere in the book) for your convenience.

It may seem as though I am contradicting myself if I now tell you that I am not a fan of "common names" for mushrooms and that I think learning the scientific, Latin names for species is the best way to proceed. But it is accuracy and your safety that I have in mind. Some common names (shaggy mane, for example) are so widespread and universally recognized that I have included them. But many other common names are not so common—or even refer to different mushrooms when used by different people. Beefsteak, for example, is a common name of both a poisonous species of *Gyromitra* (p. 55) and the edible *Fistulina hepatica* (p. 154), depending on who is doing the talking. Many times, "common names" are simply the result of field guide editors holding guns to their mushroom authors' heads and forcing them to come up with something.

We may someday develop a system of common names for mushrooms in English and get everyone on the same page—though, to be honest, the project sounds impossible (especially that last part, about getting people to *use* the system). But why bother if we already have a naming system that is as universal as any system is likely to get? Scientific names do not get confused the way common names do. If you are new to the use of scientific names, the concept is easy enough to understand. Each name has two parts: the genus and the species. The genus (which is always capitalized) represents a group of related organisms; the species (which always begins with a lower-case letter) represents the specific organism within the group. Thus, your dog is *Canis familiaris*—where *Canis* represents the genus (which also includes the coyote, *Canis latrans*) and *familiaris* represents the species within the genus. Both names are required to name the organism, and since the names are in Latin italics are required. It's a bit like last names and first names, but you put the last name first: *Kuo michael*, for example, would indicate that within the Kuo family I am the Michael.

I suppose now is as good a time as any to tell you that mycologists change the scientific names of mushrooms frequently. As far as I know, I have used the most current scientific names for the mushrooms in this book, but by the time you read this some of them will be "wrong." In fact, some of them are undoubtedly wrong already if you ask a mycologist who disagrees with my choices. This is probably not the place to attempt an explanation of how and why mycologists change the scientific names of mushrooms, but it *is* frustrating for those of us who are trying to remember what's what or compare mushrooms in different sources. The good news is that the *species* name (the second name of the mushroom—the one beginning with a lower-case letter) does not change very often (accounting for changes to the last few letters that are sometimes dictated by the rules of Latin agreement). Thus, *Macrolepiota americana* (p. 278) may be found in other mushroom books as *Lepiota americana*, which is its former name. Wouldn't it be nice if mushroom books were to index the mushrooms by species as well as by genus? Yes, it would—and many of them do, this one included. You will find *Macrolepiota americana* in the "Glossary and Index" under *americana* and *Macrolepiota americana*, making it easier to cross-reference the mushrooms with those of other books.

Incidentally, do not worry about how to pronounce the Latin names. Who cares? Find a pronunciation that works for you, and if some snippity mushroom experts laugh, maybe you can think of some other names, in clear English, to pronounce for them.

Identifying Wild Mushrooms

Mushroom identification is occasionally easy. More often, however, it is difficult or *incredibly* difficult—and sometimes it is quite literally impossible. Many people do not know this and assume, with potentially tragic results, that the mushrooms they find in the woods can be safely eaten once they have been successfully compared to photos of edible mushrooms in field guides.

But mushrooms are not like, for example, trees. There are something like two to three hundred species of trees in North America, and a decent field guide can help an amateur identify most of them successfully, with some patience; fairly intense observation of such things as leaves, twigs, and winter buds is sometimes necessary—as is the use of scientific "keys," which ask sequential questions designed to help one eliminate identification possibilities (see the Focus Point "Identification Keys," p. 37).

By contrast, the total number of North American mushroom species is not only unknown but is hotly debated among mushroom scientists. Estimates range from five or ten thousand to over thirty thousand. Some scientists contend that as many as a third of our North American mushrooms have yet to be studied and named.

As for identification, it almost always depends on *very* rigorous observation of the physical features of a mushroom—and in many cases the use of a microscope. This does not mean that a microscope will be required to successfully identify the 100 edible mushrooms included in this book (with the possible exception of *Lyophyllum decastes*, p. 275). But mushrooms are simply not like trees or birds or the other organisms usually found in field guides, which is why the following complaint, included in an online review of another book of edible mushrooms in North America, does nothing but reveal the ignorance of the reviewer.

> I went to the woods and picked a bunch of different mushrooms—each one was different and tried to use the Guide to identify them. Out of about 14 visibly different species of mushrooms that I picked—the guide gave positive ID on ONE (!) mushroom only. Other 13 were not even included in the book.

All of the assumptions this reviewer makes are wrong. It is simply impossible to pick mushrooms in the woods and identify them all with a

Agaricus pocillator (poisonous; see p. 70)

field guide or a book on edible mushrooms. The task could easily be impossible for a *mycologist* armed with scientific equipment and a library full of scientific literature on mushrooms. Even the assumption that the reviewer found "14 visibly different species of mushrooms" is ludicrous. It might not take a specialist long to find pairs of mushrooms in the reviewer's woods that look very different but represent the same species—or that look the same but are actually distinct.

I am constantly amazed at the e-mails I receive from people who have found mushrooms, compared them to pictures in field guides, and want to eat them—or, worse, have already eaten them. I even have an e-mail folder labeled "I Ate This; What Is It?" . . . and the photos attached to the e-mails include shots of unknown *Amanita* species (see p. 43), unidentifiable little brown mushrooms (p. 61), false morels (p. 55), and what appears to be a moldy piece of old carpet.

The point is, would-be identifiers who are used to comparing things in the natural world to photos and descriptions in field guides must *lower their expectations* when it comes to mushrooms. Any mushroom guide will tell you that the cardinal rule for eating wild mushrooms is *When in doubt, throw it out*. I hope I have made it clear that this will happen much of the time—and that "doubt" cannot be erased with comparisons to photos.

One reason that photos are so unreliable in the identification process is that they do not display enough of a mushroom's physical features. A mushroom should be examined from top to bottom, inside and out, with more observational rigor than one might expect. In fact, there are so many details to observe in one little mushroom that I recommend writing them down—especially if you are new to mushroom identification. Not only will the process of carefully recording a mushroom's details help you to be as thorough as you need to be; it will also help ensure your objectivity, as I will explain in a moment.

Picking Mushrooms for Identification

Mushrooms belong to ecosystems and have evolved in carefully balanced relationships with other organisms. While some mushrooms appear to be quite cosmopolitan, able to adapt to a wide variety of ecosystems, others occupy more limited niches. Thus, you will need to take note of your surroundings—and the mushrooms' surroundings—when you pick them.

Is the mushroom growing from wood? If so, is the wood dead or living? If the tree is still alive, where on the tree is the mushroom growing—near the base of the tree, around the roots, or higher up? If the wood is dead, is it a log or a stick? Is the bark still attached to the wood or has it been decaying for a long time?

What kind of tree is (or was) it? No, successful mushroom identification does not usually depend on the ability to identify living and long-dead trees with 100 percent certainty, but this information can often make the process much easier. You may want to purchase a good tree identification book (see "Suggested Readings"). At a minimum, record whether you are under hardwoods or conifers. However, you must also realize that an old, dead log in a hardwood forest may have been a conifer (and vice versa), especially since much of the continent has been logged within the past century and a half. It is often possible to determine whether a fallen tree was a hardwood or conifer by observing the way the tree's branches were arranged; many conifers develop branches in "whorls" (radiating clusters aligned at roughly the same point on the trunk) each year.

If the mushroom is terrestrial, is it *really* terrestrial, arising from the soil, or is it actually attached to a buried root or stick? Or is it loosely attached to leaves or needles on the forest floor (in which case there is often—though not always—a pale, moldy-looking mass of material surrounding the mushroom's base and binding the leaves or needles together)? What trees are in the vicinity of the mushroom? (If you are collecting in a yard or another setting where humans may have influenced things, be sure to consider the possibility that a tree has been recently removed.)

What is the growth habit of the mushroom? Is it growing alone or in clusters with others? If there are clusters, are they tightly packed so that the bases of the stems are touching or even fused? If the mushroom is growing from a log, does it stick out laterally from the log (in which case it may lack a well-developed stem), does it sit on top of the log, or does it have a curved stem that comes out of the side of the log but aligns the cap so that it is perpendicular to the ground?

By now it should be obvious why I recommend writing things down. We have not even brought the mushroom home yet or begun to examine its individual features! Now imagine that you have picked several different mushrooms in different locations (or "14 visibly different species of mushrooms") and you are trying to remember accurately all of these details, many of which are crucial to identifying the mushrooms. Successful mushroom identification is a laborious, painstaking process, and cutting corners is not a good idea when your life hangs in the balance!

If you are picking unknown mushrooms, your chances of identifying them later are greatly increased if you use a knife to dig them up carefully. Telltale features—the "root" of a *Xerula* species (edible; p. 234), for example, or the sack covering the stem base of a deadly *Amanita* (p. 43)— are sometimes found beneath the ground or at the base of the mushroom; these details can be lost when mushrooms are picked casually. Put the mushrooms in separate paper bags and label them with a marker since you will need to remember which mushroom was which. You will also need to make sure it will be possible to figure out which field notes correspond to which mushroom; I often write my notes on the paper bag itself.

Since mushrooms, like people, can change dramatically in physical appearance over the course of their lifespans, you should collect several specimens representing various stages of development. Include immature, "button" specimens as well as mature ones. Sometimes it is impossible to do this, since mushrooms often pop up alone—but do not be surprised if identifying these lone soldiers with certainty turns out to be impossible later, as crucial information may be missing.

Working with Mushrooms at Home

You will want to work with your mushroom collections as soon as possible when you return from the woods. Mushrooms decay fairly quickly, especially in warm weather, and you may be surprised at what you find in your paper bag if you wait too long. Begin at the top of the mushroom and work downward, recording the details you observe. It is not, of course, imperative that you use this top-to-bottom approach, but since most mushroom guides describe their subjects in this order, comparing your description to other descriptions will be easier if you quell your rebel urges and follow the convention.

The mushroom guides listed in "Suggested Readings" (p. 313) include reliable, detailed texts and illustrations designed to help you observe and record the physical details of mushrooms; I highly recommend that you purchase them (or borrow them from your library) and study the chapters and sections on mushroom identification. The strategy I have used in this book is to put off the discussion of specific mushroom features and identification characters until you have mushrooms in hand. I hope that beginners will go to the grocery store, buy some mushrooms, bring them home, and study them—so that the experience is experiential rather than merely intellectual and illustration based (see "How to Use This Book," p. 4). But here I must emphasize two important parts of the observation process: thoroughness and objectivity.

At the risk of sounding like a broken record, let me say again that it takes a lot of mental energy and patience to observe a mushroom with the kind of rigor required for successful identification. Each detail is potentially crucial, from the spacing of the gills to the sliminess of the stem or the color of the spore print. It typically takes me about half an hour to observe and record the physical features of a single mushroom—and, while my goals are usually scientific rather than culinary, consider that what a mycologist risks when he or she cuts corners in the observation process is merely misidentification of the mushroom, which is safely dried and packaged in a scientific collection; what a "pot hunter" risks is a trip to the hospital or, worse, the cemetery.

After you have recorded the features of your mushroom, refer to the keys, photos, and descriptions in your mushroom guides. Years of experience helping beginners learn to identify mushrooms have convinced me that compromised objectivity is one of the top causes of misidentification. People often read descriptions of edible mushrooms first and then turn to the mushrooms themselves. The result is that the mushroom's details are filtered through preconceptions, the power of suggestion, and often the simple desire to match the scrumptious mushroom described in the field guide.

If you are a beginner, you will probably find that your initial written descriptions of mushrooms lack some crucial details. A *Lactarius*, for example, cannot be accurately identified without reference to the color of its latex—a milky or watery juice exuded when the gills are damaged or the mushroom is sliced. Who knew? Obviously, there will be a certain amount of going back and forth between your description, descriptions in field guides, and the mushroom. However, as you gain experience describing more and more mushrooms your descriptions will become more complete—and the potential for subjective errors will diminish.

Mushroom identification is a lot like fingerprint analysis, in which "points" of comparison are matched by forensic scientists or, these days, software programs. The mushroom you picked in the woods, like the fingerprint lifted carefully from a crime scene, must be matched to an individual in your "database." Obviously, your database will need to consist of thorough and reliable descriptions of mushrooms—the more the better. This is why I recommend using as many mushroom guides as possible. You can't get up on the witness stand and proclaim your identification to God and country if your supporting evidence consists of a single, quick comparison to a brief description or photo in one field guide. You'll be obliterated on cross-examination, which might have to be conducted in the hospital instead of the courtroom. However, if your supporting evidence involves careful, point-by-point comparison to descriptions in twelve authoritative sources, your case will be airtight.

It is a little-known fact that there are no national standards for fingerprint analysis and that different crime labs set their own standards based on their assessment of what constitutes professionalism. Thus, in one courtroom a defendant may be found guilty on the basis of a fingerprint matching nine points of comparison—while a defendant in another courtroom is found guilty on the basis of a fingerprint matching five points. However, since your mushroom identification will need to be without doubt (otherwise, of course, you will throw it out), you will need to match *all* the points of comparison in *all* the sources.

Many features of mushrooms vary substantially, depending on growing conditions and the like. Good field guides try to account for this variation, presenting a range of possibilities. The gills are "close or crowded" or the cap is "slimy when fresh but soon dry." Thus, deciding whether your mushroom matches a described character may involve some interpretive license. Just remember, however, that your final proclamation must be beyond a reasonable doubt—and I have now dropped the extended courtroom metaphor and mean this quite literally. Do not pin your certainty on one or two variable features, and do not ignore any features that clearly do not match.

I refuse to eat any mushroom that I have not collected and identified *several times*—and this is a practice I recommend you adopt, especially if you are a beginner. The identification process I have described here—taking notes in the field, then bringing the mushroom home and carefully writing down its features for comparison with keys and descriptions in multiple mushroom guides—is a slow one, and it may take several mushroom seasons of collecting before you can confidently eat any but the most easily recognized mushrooms (see the "Recommended for Beginners" section). But patience and experience are the best antidotes to mushroom poisoning, and, while it may be disappointing to throw away a mushroom you have tentatively identified as a choice edible, recall that there is no medicinal antidote for the toxins found in the world's deadliest mushrooms.

Learning from Experts

None of the mushroom experts I know gained his or her experience alone. Consulting others with more experience is crucial to learning how to identify mushrooms, and an afternoon in the woods with a mycologist or experienced amateur is worth more than a gazillion hours spent reading mushroom field guides and looking at photos.

The best way to get help from experienced mushroomers is to join a mushroom club. These groups can be found across North America (an Internet search will supply information on the ones nearest you) and provide excellent opportunities to gain mushroom experience. Most mushroom clubs and mycological societies sponsor regular "forays," in which members collect mushrooms and bring them back to a central location, where they are laid out on tables and identified by mycologists or the more experienced members of the group.

In fact, many mushroom clubs hold weekend forays, combining mushrooming with cocktails, great cooking, cocktails, lectures and slide shows by mushroom experts, cocktails, campfires, and (I nearly forgot to mention) cocktails. Top-name mycologists and expert amateurs can be found at many of these forays—a scenario one is unlikely to find outside of the mushroom world. Imagine Lee Iacocca coming to serve as an expert at your car club's next meeting or Toni Morrison showing up to share her thoughts at the next meeting of your writers' group and you have approximated the kind of experience you can easily have at a mushroom foray.

The mycologists and expert amateurs I know are patient and kind—and *very* good at teaching. Last year I watched Gary Lincoff, author of the *National Audubon Society Field Guide to North American Mushrooms* and many other great mushroom guides, as he circulated among the collection tables and answered questions at a foray in California. Now, I know a thing or two about patience, since I've taught freshman English

Suillus granulatus (edible; p. 218; photo by Mark Davis)

for nearly seventeen years, but I was floored by Gary's ability to answer mushroom questions he has heard countless times as though he had never heard them before and by his ability to teach the basics of mushroom identification. One timid man held up a large *Russula* and then, in his nervousness, dropped it to the floor, where it shattered into a million pieces. He was crushed. Gary, however, knelt down to examine the mess. "Ahhh," he said. "See how this thing shattered when you dropped it. That tells us it's a *Russula* since their flesh crumbles easily."

While there are more mushroom clubs and mycological societies in North America than you might think, it is quite possible that there is no such group in your immediate area. In this case, seeking the help of experts may be more difficult. Planning a vacation to attend one of the annual national mushroom forays is one option. But you may need to consult the Internet directory of your local university or community college to see if there are any mycologists or mushroom experts in the biology department.

Bear in mind, however, that mycologists are not paid to tell you whether every mushroom you find is edible or not. Any mycologist is used to having mushrooms, or photos of mushrooms, thrust in his or her face with the question, "Can I eat this?" But imagine how tiresome that might become, especially when the questioners show no interest in *learning* anything that might help them answer such questions in the future.

In the end, there is no way around the fact that mushroom expertise takes hard work and practice: years of collecting mushrooms, observing their features, and attempting to identify them; patient study of mushroom guides; and diligent learning from experts. The rewards, fortunately, are wonderful. Few things are more satisfying than arriving at a positive identification of a difficult mushroom (edible or not)—to say nothing of the time in the woods, the great meals, the friendships developed with other mushroomers, and the satisfaction that comes with beginning to understand the natural world.

Collecting, Preparing, and Eating Wild Mushrooms

In the Woods

If you are absolutely sure you are collecting known, edible mushrooms for the table, you won't want to collect them the same way you would collect mushrooms for identification (see pp. 11–12). But, since one of the things I'm going to recommend for "pot hunting," for example, involves slicing off the base of the stem—often one of the defining features of a deadly *Amanita*—allow me to stress, one last time, that you should be 100 percent certain of your identification. The scenario I am anticipating is that you have collected and successfully identified the mushroom in question *several times*, using the methods described in the previous section. You have taken careful notes in the woods, recorded the mushroom's physical features, and used multiple keys and mushroom guide descriptions to arrive at your identification. If you are a beginner, you may have consulted a mushroom expert. In short, you have complete confidence in your ability to recognize the mushroom.

Now your goal is different: you want to get your mushrooms home free of dirt and forest debris and in good shape for the kitchen. Many mushroomers use large, open baskets to collect edible mushrooms. A basket is easy to carry, and it allows air to circulate between the mushrooms. Yes, you will look a bit like the perfect model of a Modern Major Mushroomer, but if you skip the knickers and suspenders you can probably still retain your dignity—unless you are collecting in the Midwest.

Whatever you choose to carry your mushrooms around in, don't let it be a plastic bag from Wal-Mart (or anywhere else). Plastic bags do not let air circulate, and they tend to promote condensation, especially on warm days, when you are likely to find more *mush* than mushroom in your bag when you get home. Some people advocate the use of mesh bags, like the kind used for onions and potatoes, on the theory that the mushrooms will spread spores through the woods and repopulate. The assumptions behind this theory are flawed, however (see my book *Morels* for details), and mesh bags tear mushrooms apart, leaving you with a collection of crumblies rather than a mountain of munchies.

It is amazing how the slightest bit of dirt or debris—one tiny piece

Field Equipment for Hunting Edible Mushrooms

By John David Moore

- A good, sharp, pocketknife with a blade strong enough for digging up soil and cutting wood or bark. It's a good idea to have your knife attached to a belt or belt loop with a cord or chain since it's easy to lay a knife down and forget about it when the excitement of a massive morel fruiting grips you.
- Brown or white paper lunch bags. Avoid plastic; it doesn't breathe. Paper bags can be written on to record any crucial information about environment and other details that help in identification or in finding a particularly fruitful spot again.
- A pen or marker.

- A basket or backpack for holding your bagged collections.
- A soft-bristled brush for field cleaning your finds before bagging them. One filthy mushroom in a bag means cleaning all the rest eventually.
- A long, sturdy, walking stick for poking around in leaf litter, keeping your hands out of poison ivy, and fighting off hungry dog packs. It's also handy for removing mushrooms such as oysters (p. 202) and *Hericium* species (p. 102) from high spots on tree trunks.
- Insect repellent. You'll definitely be journeying in the favored realms of mosquitoes, blackflies, and ticks in your forays. For the purpose of tick detection, light clothing is also recommended.

of a leaf, for example—can manage to cover every mushroom in your basket by the time you have left the woods. It is well worth your time to clean mushrooms carefully in the woods. Use a knife to slice mushrooms off above ground and trim away any adhering piece of dirt or debris. Use a soft-bristled brush, as well, for hard-to-reach areas. Beyond these steps, certain mushrooms require other tactics; see the "In the Woods" sections for the individual mushrooms included in this book.

You will no longer want to collect specimens in all stages of development, as you did when collecting for identification purposes. Now you want only fresh, firm mushrooms that are completely free of decay. Young specimens are usually the best mushrooms for the table, which is why the cultivated mushroom most commonly sold in stores, *Agaricus bisporus* (p. 28), is packaged in the button stage, while the partial veil still covers the gills. Mature specimens are also worth collecting, provided that they are still firm and meaty. Bear in mind, however, that mushrooms may continue maturing after you have collected them; one mushroom that has decayed in your basket by the end of the day can ruin an entire afternoon's effort.

Consider the Substrate

By John David Moore

Most hunters of edible mushrooms would not gather their culinary ingredients near interestingly colored ponds at the equivalent of the abandoned Toxico Chemical Plant—but it's also worth thinking twice or thrice about some less obviously threatening environments. The verdant expanses of neighborhood lawns and parks, the lush grass of highway borders—all home to many delectable species of mushrooms—can conceal an unappetizing and possibly dangerous assortment of fertilizers and weed killers. Likewise, areas downwind of heavily sprayed cropland (think Roundup) should be approached with caution. Public woodlands can also present dismal surprises for mushroom gathering. I recently had to dispose of a substantial collection of edibles after realizing that the numerous dead shrubs in an area of state park were not due to a hot, dry summer but were the calculated result of spraying to eliminate a prolific invasive shrub species. When possible, try to be informed about your gathering areas. When it comes to lawns and parks, it may be advisable to seek out the look of neglect and indifference since the patchy lawn and dandelion meadow may be the best bet for safer edibles.

Yet another environmental caution involves trees—specifically locust, eucalyptus, and buckeye species, be they alive, dying, or dead. Edible mushrooms such as chicken of the woods (p. 79) and the honey mushrooms (p. 244), which grow on these trees, are sometimes reported as causing varying degrees of gastrointestinal distress. Why this is remains one of many mycological mysteries—and there is some anecdotal evidence that long cooking may correct the problem. Still it's advisable to leave the mystery alone and, erring on the side of caution, avoid eating any otherwise edible mushroom growing on, or even in the vicinity of, these potentially "toxic" trees.

In the Kitchen

Generally speaking, wild mushrooms should be prepared soon after you return from the woods. In some cases this is a necessity; the shaggy mane (p. 148), for example, is likely to turn into black, gooey ink if you wait more than a few hours before cooking it. On the other hand, yellow and black morels (pp. 87 and 84) will last for several days in the refrigerator. You can consult the "In the Kitchen" sections of this book for recommendations on individual mushrooms, but your experience with the mushrooms themselves will be your best guide for determining how long they are likely to last before cooking.

Despite your efforts in the woods, you are likely to find that your mushrooms need to freshen up a bit before going to the prom. Trim away any unsavory parts that you missed and discard any mushroom that didn't travel well. Remember that simple food poisoning is still a possibility—even when you are sure your mushrooms are not, in and of themselves, poisonous—and that inspectors from the Food and Drug

Yellow morels (edible; p. 87)

Administration were (probably) not with you in the woods. And consider this: if there is visible mold on one part of a mushroom, it is entirely likely that the mold is present on the *rest* of the mushroom, even though you can't see it without a microscope. (Though if the visible mold is crusty and bright reddish orange and your mushroom is a *Russula* or *Lactarius*, see the lobster mushroom on p. 267!)

Slice your mushrooms so that you can inspect their insides for worm holes, hidden decay, and so on. Many tiny woodland critters like to eat mushrooms just as much as you do, and I doubt you want to invite them to your table. Be sure to inspect the interior of the mushroom's stem, since this is the first course for many of these uninvited guests, which then move into the cap for the rest of their meal. Occasionally it is possible to salvage some of a mushroom thus invaded by trimming off sections that have not yet been ravaged—for example, in the case of large boletes or chanterelles—but I do not recommend eating sloppy seconds. Truth be told, your average mushroom-loving grub is probably harmless if accidentally consumed, so my hesitation has more to do with squeamishness than anything else. I have seen people cook and enjoy slices of *Boletus edulis* (p. 123) that were riddled with wormholes . . . but I have also seen my buddy Eric, in high school biology class, eat a live goldfish with no apparent ill effects.

In general, washing or rinsing mushrooms is not the best idea from a culinary perspective—but sometimes it has to be done. In fact, wild mushrooms should be washed more often than not, despite what purists say. Morels (pp. 84 and 87), cauliflower mushrooms (p. 108), and species of *Hericium* (p. 102), especially, have so many tiny, dirt-susceptible crevasses that immersion is a necessity; fortunately, these mushrooms are sturdy and not particularly absorbent.

Some mushrooms can be stored in a cool location for a day or two before being prepared for the table. If you live in an area where nighttime temperatures are cool during mushroom season, you may be able to store fresh mushrooms on your porch or in your garage overnight (or longer). Otherwise, we're talking about your refrigerator, and experience will tell you what you can get away with. However, the more separated your mushrooms are, the more likely it is that they will survive prolonged storage. Mushrooms in a basket or bowl filled to the brim will not fare as well (especially those at the bottom of the pile) as mushrooms that have been stored with plenty of breathing space.

Keep one specimen apart from the others, untrimmed and unwashed, and store it in your refrigerator until a few days after you have had your meal. This is a very important precaution, since the mushroom could be your safety net if something goes wrong and you develop symptoms of mushroom poisoning. A mycologist or amateur mushroom expert may need to examine what you ate, at the request of your doctor, who may be struggling to determine what treatment is required. The toxins in poisonous mushrooms differ substantially, though the symptoms they cause are often similar—which means that effective treatment could depend on reliable identification of the mushroom. I hate to say it this directly, but if the scenario I'm describing were actually to unfold, the doctor and mycologist could not rely on your description of the mushroom, since you obviously would have missed something important, and would need to examine it themselves. On a brighter note (brighter for your mushroom ego, if not your stomach), another potential scenario involves the expert determining that the mushroom you ate was entirely edible and safe and that the doctor should search elsewhere for the source of your ailment—an equally important discovery, as far as your treatment is concerned.

For the most part, wild mushrooms should not be eaten raw. Most of us have stomachs that are used to cultivated and domesticated foods, and raw food from the wild can result in minor gastrointestinal distress. Thus, while many mushrooms require brief cooking techniques, they should not be cooked *too* briefly. A few wild mushrooms are eaten raw with some regularity; these are noted in the "In the Kitchen" entries.

If you are eating a mushroom you have never tried before, try only a few bites. No matter how delicious it is, refrain from eating more until a few days have passed and you have suffered no ill effects. Not only are you hedging your bets against an untreatable or even fatal dose of any potential toxins; you are also limiting your digestive system's exposure to a mushroom that may be comfortably consumed by most people but not you. Individual "allergic" reactions to edible wild mushrooms are fairly common, and, while they are not typically "serious" from a medical perspective, the gastrointestinal distress (vomiting, diarrhea, cramps, and so on) can be quite unpleasant. The hen of the woods (p. 163) affects me this way, despite the fact that it is a delicious, popular, edible mushroom regularly consumed by avid collectors across the continent. In fact, while I don't mean to suggest that you should ignore the Few Bites Rule for other types of mushrooms, the polypores appear to create more than their proportional share of these "allergies."

In the course of working on this book, John David Moore and I discovered that the subtle tastes of wild mushrooms are more easily detected and compared when they are cooked alone, without any competing ingredients. The traditional method for sautéing wild mushrooms is to fry them briefly but thoroughly in butter or oil—but this can make many mushrooms taste like . . . well, butter or oil. A nonstick frying pan solves this problem; if you want to experience the taste of the mushroom, the whole taste of the mushroom, and nothing but the taste of the mushroom, try cooking some slices without anything else in the pan. In fact, this is a great way to try a new mushroom for the first time, since you are getting a good culinary sense of the mushroom but have not wasted your time and ingredients on a recipe that you should only eat a few bites of anyway.

At this point I must sound a bit like Polonius, in *Hamlet*, who tries to give his son a lifetime's worth of patronizing fatherly wisdom in a few short moments as he sends him off to college. So rather than droning on with more little tidbits of mushroom-safety wisdom, I have created a list entitled "Safety Precautions for Trying New Mushrooms" (p. 24), which includes items I have discussed here, as well as a few other safety measures worth considering. But did I mention that money can come between friends? Neither a borrower nor a lender be . . .

Safety Precautions for Trying New Mushrooms

- Collect and identify a species *two or three times* before eating it.
- Keep one specimen aside, uncleaned and unaltered from its natural state, in your refrigerator.
- Know your doctor's phone number and your area's poison center number.
- Prepare only fresh, firm mushrooms.

- Cook a small amount and eat only one or two bites.
- Cook the mushrooms thoroughly.
- Do not combine the consumption of alcohol with trying a new wild mushroom.
- Do not eat a bunch of other things your stomach is not used to.
- Never "pig out" on wild mushrooms; eat them in moderation.
- Eat more only after a few days have passed.

Preserving Wild Mushrooms

By John David Moore

Drying is the best method for long-term preservation of the inevitable overflow in some of your edible harvests. However, some people suffer respiratory problems or allergic reactions to drying mushrooms; be sure to ascertain whether you are one of these people before drying large quantities of mushrooms in your living quarters. While some argue that there are limits to how long dried mushrooms remain palatable, I've found that the dried morel crop of 1999 still makes a topping meal six years later. The best modern approach involves the wonders of the electric food dehydrator set at a medium temperature and filled with loosely arranged, thinly sliced, fresh specimens. Make sure the mushrooms reach a brittle state before removing them and store them in mason jars with tightly fitting caps. Taking my mother's sage advice on keeping flour, cornmeal, and other dried foodstuffs free of weevils and other miniscule menaces, I put a bay leaf in each jar with the mushrooms. It has worked so far. Small mushrooms such as black trumpets (p. 99) and *Marasmius oreades* (p. 283) can be dried whole. Hollow species such as morels (pp. 84 and 87) can be dried whole or cut in half lengthwise.

Without a food dryer, you can dry mushrooms whole or sliced by threading them with a needle on fine string and then hanging them above a stove or heater or in a sunny window. As this method takes longer, you'll want to be sure you enjoy the mushroom scent that can permeate your domicile for the time (days) this procedure can take. In predictably sunny, dry weather, you can dry mushrooms outside on a cloth-covered rack or anything else that lets air circulate around them. Finally, there's the oven—where you may be able to dry mushrooms on

Drying the king bolete (edible; p. 123)

racks at low temperatures, preferably with the door open. With ovens and food dehydrators, be sure the temperature never exceeds 140 degrees or your harvest will cook, blacken, lose flavor, or simply become something extremely unpleasant.

Although dried mushrooms lose their shape in various ways, they retain, and in some cases increase, their flavor and texture. The standard method for reconstituting dried mushrooms is to soak them in a bowl of warm water for twenty to thirty minutes. You can also use wine, cream, or even beer. You can keep the mushrooms submerged by placing a plate over them in the bowl. The soaking liquid, strained free of any dirt and debris through cheesecloth or paper towels, can be used as broth or in a sauce. If you're using dried mushrooms in a stew or soup, you can add them directly, without rehydrating.

Freezing is a good method for short-term preservation—a month is about the limit. Since frozen raw mushrooms lose flavor and can sometimes become a watery mess upon thawing, the best procedure is to sauté the mushrooms in butter or stew them in a small amount of water before freezing in tightly sealed bags or other plastic containers.

I do not recommend canning as a method of preservation, especially when it involves pressure cookers or boiling water baths. Mushrooms are a nonacid food, and pressure canning with extreme care is the only method that can prevent the deadly presence of *Clostridium botulinum*, which can't be detected through odor or any physical changes in the canned material. I've read somewhere that one ounce of this joyful germ can kill several million people. If you insist on canning your mushrooms, consult clear, authoritative instructions such as those in *Joy of Cooking* and other culinary compendiums. For short-term canned preservation, you can clean your freshest mushrooms extremely well, blanch them, and put them in tightly sealed jars with a good vinegar or oil, together with peppercorns, garlic cloves, and two or three bay leaves. Keep an eye on your jars for any sign of moldiness and discard any collections with moldy contents. After you open a jar, keep it in the refrigerator and use the contents fairly quickly.

Salting, along with drying, is the oldest method of preservation. It works well for mushrooms—especially if you don't want to salt anything you cook with them. It's important to use the cleanest and freshest mushrooms. Use one part salt to three parts mushrooms and layer the mushrooms and salt alternately, with salt completely covering the final mushroom layer. It's best to use sterilized jars with noncorrosive, tight fitting tops. Before cooking your salted mushrooms, wash them thoroughly. You will probably find that salt will not be needed in any meal you prepare with salted mushrooms.

From the Store

*T*he safest place to hunt for mushrooms is in your grocery store. The button mushroom (p. 28), which is cultivated primarily in Pennsylvania and California, is found in virtually every grocery store in the United States and Canada. It is usually sold, as its common name suggests, in the "button stage," but mature versions of it are also found in most grocery stores packaged as "portobellos." Oyster mushrooms (p. 36), enokis (p. 34), and shiitakes (p. 38) are increasingly popular, and many grocery stores feature them as well. These are also cultivated by mushroom farmers. The only *wild* mushrooms sold in stores across the continent are porcini (p. 32), which are harvested from the woods by commercial collectors (see the Focus Point on "Commercial Mushroom Picking" on p. 299).

All of these mushrooms are good to eat, though some are better than others (enokis are rather tasteless, while porcini are among the best foods on earth). But they all serve as good demonstrators of mushroom features, and there is no better place to start learning about mushrooms than at your kitchen table with a pile of store-bought specimens. While the button mushrooms, oyster mushrooms, enokis, shiitakes, and porcini go a long way toward covering "the basics" of mushroom identification, however, they certainly do not go *all* the way. There are no polypores in the group, for starters, and the boletes are only represented by the dried and sliced porcini, which are perfect for eating but not so perfect for demonstrating what a bolete is.

Other mushrooms are sold in stores, especially in big cities, college towns, California, and other places where delicacies and rare foods are popular. Asian food markets such as those in San Francisco's Chinatown often sell an incredible array of diverse mushrooms, both fresh and dried (including the jelly ear [p. 119] and *Hericium erinaceus* [p. 102]). But these are not widespread markets, and I have opted to include here only mushrooms that pretty much anyone can find with a little shopping around.

Incidentally, the mushrooms I've just described are not the only fungi you can find packaged and ready for sale in your grocery store. They are in the bread, beer, and wine—and if your grocery store is one of those monstrous, Vatican-sized, "one-stop shopping" behemoths the pharmacy shelves are chock-full of fungal derivatives. If you find fungi in the meat department, however, you should probably have a word with the manager.

1 The Button Mushroom and the Portobello: *Agaricus bisporus*

Edibility Rating: Great.

Comments: The button mushroom is the easiest of all mushrooms to identify—when found in your supermarket, packaged nicely, and ready to eat. However, the species can also be found in the wild, where it occurs in both native and "escaped" populations. Outside the grocery store, the button mushroom is extremely difficult to identify with certainty, and it should *not* be collected for the table by beginners. For a feature-by-feature description of the button mushroom and its ecology, see page 239, where the wild and escaped versions are re-presented with a "difficult" rating. Here, however, we will trust the mushroom farmers and take identification of the button mushroom for granted. The average American consumes 2.2 pounds of *Agaricus bisporus* a year—an impressive number when you consider how little a mushroom weighs. The color

of *Agaricus bisporus* ranges from white to brown, as is evident in the grocery store; "cremini" mushrooms, which were developed by commercial growers, are merely brown strains of the more familiar white strain. "Portobello" mushrooms represent buttons that have been allowed to mature. Since *Agaricus bisporus* is available anywhere, at any time of the year, it is the perfect mushroom for demonstrating many of the physical features used in the identification process. Eight Focus Points follow. You will need both the classic white buttons *and* a portobello or two in order to observe all the features discussed.

In the Store: (John David Moore) Stalking and collecting cultivated mushrooms involve techniques that differ radically from those used in the woods and fields. The whole matter of parking alone deserves a discussion too lengthy to be included here. Other challenges, such as shopping cart maneuvers, checkout line choice, and bag selection, are best managed through

Focus Point
Gills, Gilled Mushrooms

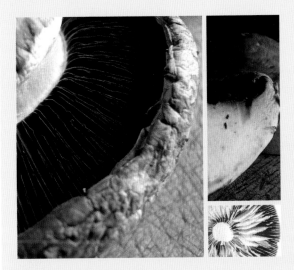

The button mushroom has gills, though they will be covered by a partial veil (see "Partial Veil," p. 30) if you have purchased the classic white button mushrooms rather than portobellos. The gills (called "lamellae" in Mycologese) are the many platelike or bladelike structures attached to the underside of the cap, and they represent an ingenious reproductive strategy. Like all mushrooms, the button mushroom is a spore factory created for the sole purpose of manufacturing microscopic spores that would have been carried away by air currents (if the mushroom growers had not interrupted the process) and, with any luck, have landed in a suitable location to germinate and start a new organism. The odds of any individual spore having this kind of luck are so low, however, that the mushroom produces *millions* of spores to compensate. The gills are assembly lines, and they dramatically increase the number of spores the mushroom can produce. Both sides of *each gill* are covered with microscopic spore-producing machinery. Imagine the difference if the underside of the cap were simply a flat production surface—in fact, try using a toothpick or knifepoint to separate some gills, lay them out flat, and make the comparison. When I do it, it appears that about fifteen gill faces would do the job. But I count roughly five hundred gills on the button mushroom I'm examining; multiplying by two to account for the fact that each gill has two spore-producing sides, I get one thousand assembly lines for the spore factory—which means that using gills to make spores has increased the mushroom's productive capacity by a factor of sixty-seven (one thousand divided by the fifteen assembly lines the factory would have with a flat surface).

Focus Point
Short Gills

If you attempted the calculation just discussed for yourself, you quickly discovered that I neglected to mention that the gills are not all equal in length and many of them do not span the full distance from the edge of the cap to the stem. I did my best to calculate some averages and account for these "short gills" (called "lamellulae" in Mycologese), but you may discover that you're better at math than I am. Using only margin-to-stem gills would leave huge areas of the factory floor empty—so the short gills fill the gaps. The button mushroom struggles to fill every available space, but not all gilled mushrooms are this production oriented. Some mushrooms have no short gills; others have only a few near the edge of the cap. Though mushroom identification never hinges on a precise determination of how many short gills can be counted, the presence or absence of short gills is occasionally a feature that can help in the identification process.

Focus Point
Free Gills

The way a mushroom's gills are attached to the stem is often a crucial identifying feature. In the case of the button mushroom, however, the gills do not touch the stem at all, which means they are "free." It may take some squinting to observe this if you are looking at classic buttons, but if you are examining a portobello there should be a noticeable gap between the ends of the gills and the stem. The deadly mushrooms in the genus *Amanita* (p. 43) also tend to have free gills, so this is an important feature to learn. Some mushrooms have gills that are attached to the stem (see the enoki, p. 34), some have gills that are attached by a "notch" (see the matsutake, p. 297), and others have gills that run down the stem (see oyster mushrooms, p. 36).

Focus Point
Close Gills

If you're not sick of looking at the button mushroom's gills yet, take note of how they are spaced. The spacing is called "close" by mycologists, and it should be compared to "distant" spacing (see *Marasmius oreades*—edible; p. 285) and "crowded" spacing (see the shaggy mane—edible; p. 150). Gradations in gill spacing can be dramatic, but more often than not the assessment is more or less a judgment call, at least between adjacent positions on the three-point verbal scale. Reasonable descriptions usually indicate a range of possibilities, and a description of the button mushroom might indicate that its gills are "close or crowded."

Focus Point
Partial Veil

The button mushroom has a partial veil, which is clearly in evidence in the classic white buttons we slice for pizzas and salads. The veil is a covering that protects the young gills until the mushroom is mature and the spore factory is ready for production. In *Agaricus bisporus* this covering is substantial and tissuelike. It is whitish, and often it is just beginning to detach from the edge of the cap when the mushroom is purchased. As the mushroom grows, the partial veil is stretched and eventually breaks free of the cap's edge, collapsing against the stem to form a "ring" (see the next Focus Point).

Focus Point
Ring

You will probably need portobello mushrooms to see the ring on the stem of *Agaricus bisporus*—and since portobellos are often sold as sliced sections of a mature cap you may need to search around for a grocery store that sells whole ones with the stems intact. The ring is the remainder of the partial veil, and it hangs fairly high on the stem. In *Agaricus bisporus* the ring is a bit fragile, and it is not *always* in evidence. Rings on mushrooms in nature sometimes fall off, even on species that have sturdier, more reliable rings; this is another reason to collect multiple specimens, representing all stages of development, when you are trying to identify mushrooms. The button mushroom's ring hangs like a skirt; in other mushrooms the ring may look more like a bracelet, or it may collapse completely against the stem. *Annulus* is the term for a ring in Mycologese.

Focus Point
Bruising and Discoloring

The flesh and surfaces of *Agaricus bisporus* usually bruise and discolor slightly pinkish, at least in places. Slice a mushroom in half to see the bruising: the flesh is whitish but turns slowly pinkish in some areas when exposed to air. The stem surface, when rubbed with your thumb, may also bruise pinkish—and even the cap surface, especially along the edge, will often bruise. After some time, the pinkish areas turn brownish. Bruising and discoloring are not always dramatic and pronounced with button mushrooms, but fresh specimens usually manage to "blush" a little when rubbed (just like you and me). Determining whether a mushroom bruises or discolors is often *very* important in the identification process; see "Poisonous *Agaricus* Species" (p. 70) and "Poisonous Boletes" (p. 53) for two examples.

Focus Point
Spore Print

Although a mushroom's spores are too tiny to be seen by the naked eye, they can be seen en masse with a spore print. You will need a brown-gilled portobello in order to obtain a spore print from *Agaricus bisporus,* since the classic white buttons with pinkish gills are immature and have not yet begun to produce spores. Slice a section from the cap, and place its gills down on a piece of white paper. Cover the slice with a cup or glass and wait several hours. When you return, you should find the paper covered with spore dust arranged in the radial pattern of the gills. The color of a mushroom's "spore print" is often one of the most crucial identifying features; in *Agaricus bisporus* it is a rich, chocolate brown. I suggested a piece of white paper in order to show off this color—but since many mushrooms have pale or white spore prints, white paper is not always the best choice. I use a piece of glass, which I can then set against various backgrounds in order to see the color clearly. You may have noticed that the spore print of *Agaricus bisporus* is roughly the same color as the mature gills. Although this is sometimes the case in the mushroom world, it is *not* universally true; gill color is not a reliable shortcut to spore print color.

repeated experience. But the most relevant concern is mushroom choice. The button mushroom will be found packaged in puzzling variety: small and white, small and brown (the cremini), small brown or white and sliced, large brown caps with dark brown gills (the portobello), or the same large caps sliced. What secrets need be known to sort out this array of choices? First of all, check for freshness. The veggie boys in the stockroom seem to place bets on how far an item can deteriorate and still be bought by some sucker. White *Agaricus bisporus* should be firm and *white*. Avoid those with brown and possibly slimy blotches. Also check for any damp, slimy spots on the brown cremini. If possible, check the gills on portobello caps to be sure they're not starting to deteriorate into goo. Of course, they're usually packaged gill-side down to keep you from being nosy. The sliced mushrooms of any variety should have firm, undiscolored flesh. They are more easily inspected since you can see the gills, but they will not keep as long as whole mushrooms. If possible, find a market that sells mushrooms unpackaged so you can make your selections with more assurance.

In the Kitchen: (John David Moore) Since the button mushroom and its variant, the so-called portobello, are exceptions to the rule about not eating any fungus raw, it's best to take advantage of the exception and enjoy this tame species uncooked for dipping or in marinades and salads. In those dark, nonfungal times of year, of course, *Agaricus bisporus* can be relied on to fill in somewhat adequately for fresh wild mushrooms in most recipes. If it makes you feel better, you can even arrange your market finds in your yard and then forage for them to the astonishment of watchful neighbors. But whether they arrive on your countertop via the backyard or direct from the grocery store, it's best to trim the stem bases and wash them thoroughly before cooking or using them in any raw preparation. They are, after all, "cultivated," and that often suggests chemical applications. Although I find button mushrooms inferior in taste to the closely related, wild meadow mushroom (p. 114), in its portobello form the firm, meaty texture makes up for what it lacks in flavor.

Recommended Recipes: Jaeger Sauce for Schnitzel or Steak (p. 306), Marinated Mushrooms (p. 306).

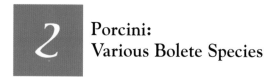

2 Porcini:
Various Bolete Species

Edibility Rating: Great.

Comments: Porcini are served in restaurants worldwide and are increasingly found for sale in North American grocery stores and specialty

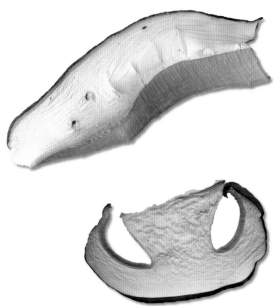

shops. They are boletes—usually the king bolete (p. 123) or species that are similar. Although the mushrooms are occasionally sold fresh, the porcini most frequently encountered in North America are sliced thinly and dried. Even in this state, however, porcini display a central bolete feature: the layer of tubes that is found on the underside of the cap. Search among your porcini pieces for one that resembles the top slice in the illustration. I am assuming, of course, that you have purchased porcini at your grocery store; if you are getting out a flashlight and magnifying glass in your local restaurant, you should prepare yourself for some strange looks. The darker area of tiny, parallel lines (you may have to squint hard) underneath the confluent, pale area is the tube layer. To make sense out of what you are seeing, refer to the Focus Point on boletes on p. 78—later. Now you should probably stop playing with your food and *eat* it instead since porcini are among the very best edible mushrooms.

In the Kitchen: Dried porcini must be reconstituted in liquid and cooked before they are any good; don't try eating "porcini chips" or you will definitely wonder what all the fuss is about. However, it is a common culinary mistake to soak porcini too much before cooking, and the result can be disappointing unless you like eating slugs. If your porcini are headed for any recipe in which they will be thoroughly cooked and soaked (e.g., most sauces), I recommend adding them without reconstituting them beforehand. But if your recipe is not likely to expose them to high heat and liquid (e.g., in the stuffing for Mushroom Ravioli [p. 307]), soak them in white wine for a few minutes, until they are soft, before cooking. Do not be put off by the funky smell (not quite unpleasant but not pleasant either) that a bag of dried porcini emits; you will be surprised at how good they taste—and (I have seen this happen to myself and many others) your sniffer may eventually learn to associate the smell of the dried mushrooms with the wonderful taste that comes later and register the odor as pleasant.

Recommended Recipes: Mushroom Quiche (p. 307), Mushroom Ravioli (p. 307), Porcini Sauce for Pork Roast (p. 309).

3 The Enoki: Cultivated *Flammulina velutipes*

Edibility Rating: Good.

Comments: These long-stemmed, gilled mushrooms are found throughout North America but only in grocery stores. They are the cultivated

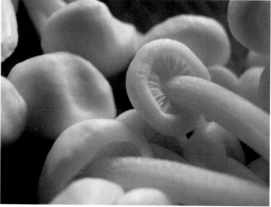

Focus Point
Attached Gills

To examine the gill attachment of the enoki, you may need a razor blade, which you will use to slice the tiny caps in cross section. If you are a middle-aged squinter in need of bifocals, like me, you may find it easier to use a magnifying glass. The tiny gills are not free from the stem, like the gills of the button mushroom (p. 28). Instead they are attached to the stem but do not begin to run down it, as in the oyster mushroom (p. 36). Also compare them with the "notched" gills of the matsutake (p. 297). Mycologists separate what I am calling "attached gills" into the more finely tuned labels "adnate" and "adnexed." Adnate gills are broadly attached to the stem; adnexed gills are attached about halfway. Never, in over fifteen years of identifying mushrooms, have I found the difference to be very useful in the identification process.

Focus Point
Clustered Growth

Even though the enoki is impossible to examine as it is growing without touring a mushroom farm, it is still possible to see that it grows in dense clusters, since it is packaged with the stem bases intact. Although natural clusters are usually not as densely packed as those of the enoki, clustered growth is sometimes an important identifying feature (see the honey mushrooms on p. 244 for an example). Mycologists call clustered mushrooms "caespitose" or, in an alternate spelling, "cespitose." Often when mushrooms are packed so tightly together, the stem bases are narrowed as they are in the enoki.

form of *Flammulina velutipes* (edible; p. 262), but they look nothing like their natural counterparts. Since this mushroom does not occur in nature, it would be a very bad idea to gather similar-looking mushrooms in the woods and eat them. Before eating the enoki, however, beginners might benefit from closely examining its features; for this, see the two Focus Points above.

On the Space Shuttle: If you have unlimited cash at your disposal, you might try this experiment: pay the National Aeronautics and Space Administration a gazillion dollars to take your little enoki friends on the space shuttle to see how they act in a low-gravity environment. The fact that this has already been done, in 1993, should not deter you, since the mildly interesting results will engage your mind for at least, oh, five or ten minutes. It seems the enoki doesn't know which way is up when gravity is absent, and the long stems grow any which way, including *upside down*. Whether or not this result might have been predicted by any tenth grader and whether or not the funding for this experiment came from public sources are questions I will leave to you. I will simply point out that at about the same time the United States decided to "end welfare as we know it" because it was too expensive, leaving thousands of poor people to fend for themselves.

In the Kitchen: (John David Moore) The stem bases of the enoki should be trimmed to remove dirt and bits of woody habitat. Wash well and trim. The stems can then be separated or, if one prefers a more chewy texture, left in small clumps. Overcooking should be avoided, since overcooked enokis take on the appearance of clinically depressed bean sprouts and the flavor and texture of very wet and thin noodles. They are best added to soups and stir-fries in the last minute of cooking to preserve their appearance and texture.

Recommended Recipe: Five-Spice Beef with Enokis (p. 305).

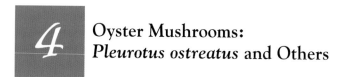

4 Oyster Mushrooms: *Pleurotus ostreatus* and Others

Edibility Rating: Great.

Comments: Some experience identifying mushrooms is probably required if you are going to pursue the various oyster mushrooms in the

Focus Point

Gills That Run Down the Stem

Oyster mushrooms have rudimentary, lateral stems that are sometimes nearly absent—but the gills are not only attached to the stublike stem; they run down it. Mycologists, and many mushroom guides, call such gills "decurrent." Compare this method of attachment with the free gills of the button mushroom (p. 30), the attached gills of the enoki (p. 35), and the notched gills of the matsutake (p. 299).

Focus Point

Identification Keys

Mycologists and mushroom experts rely on "keys" to identify mushrooms; the keys present alternatives and narrow down the identification possibilities through the process of elimination. Using keys—in field guides and more technical mycological publications—is unavoidable if one is going to identify mushrooms. While it takes a little practice to use keys successfully, the concept is easy enough once one has studied an example. The sample key presented here identifies oyster mushrooms (and a few other things) in your grocery store.

1) Object(s) packaged and shelved, available for purchase 2
1) Object(s) not as above 4

2) Package labeled "oyster mushrooms" . . . . Oyster Mushrooms
2) Package not so labeled 3

3) Package, when spilled, covers the floor with long, skinny pieces of pasta . . . . Spaghetti
3) Package not as above when spilled 5

4) Object with four wheels and a kiddy seat . . . . Grocery Cart
4) Object with conveyer belt and scanner . . . . Checkout Counter

5) [Etc.]

woods; see the additional entry on oysters on page 202. Here I will use the oyster mushroom found in grocery stores to communicate several Focus Points for mushroom identification and will rely on the "key" to determine its identity. I think oyster mushrooms have a peculiar and distinctive smell, but I would be hard pressed to describe it. An "oyster mushroom smell" is about all I can come up with, but the not unpleasant odor seems fairly distinctive in the mushroom world. The commercially produced oyster mushrooms found in grocery stores have the same odor as their wild counterparts in my experience. See the Focus Point "Odors" (p. 206) for more on mushroom odors.

In the Kitchen: (John David Moore) The virtues of the cultivated oyster mushroom are that the most labor it exacts involves standing in a checkout line and, when it comes to cleaning it, you don't have to chase any beetles around your countertop (as you do with the wild oyster mushroom). When it comes to flavor, I find it inferior to the wild variety, even though the texture is sometimes more tender. As with other cultivated mushrooms, you can't be sure what chemicals they have been fraternizing with. Wash them and drain them well even if the package doesn't tell you to. I find they do best in dishes in which texture, not flavor, is the important contribution.

Recommended Recipe: Artichoke Shiitake Pizza (p. 303), substituting oysters for shiitakes.

5 The Shiitake: *Lentinula edodes*

Edibility Rating: Good.

Comments: The shiitake, *Lentinula edodes,* is an Asian species that is widely cultivated in Asia and, increasingly, North America. It does not grow in the wild on our continent, so you will only find it in grocery stores, specialty shops, and certain markets (in San Francisco's Chinatown, for example). It is sold both dried and fresh.

In the Store: (John David Moore) The shiitake has become a fairly regular feature in the vegetable sections of mainstream grocery stores. You can find it both fresh and dried, but if you're shopping for the former, be sure it is fresh. The off-white gills should not be discolored or slimy, and the caps should be free of any soft-looking, dark areas. Even if your shiitakes are as fresh as possible, it's best to eat them within two or three days. Dried versions, however, will keep indefinitely if stored in airtight containers.

In the Kitchen: (John David Moore) On the label of the package I'm currently examining, some folks in Watsonville, California, tell me to "wash before using." The advice should be heeded, as with any other cultivated mushroom. Before or while washing your shiitakes, you may want to trim off the stems, which can be rather tough. Drain and dry the mushrooms off before cutting them into slices about a quarter inch wide. Sautéed shiitakes will absorb whatever oil, fat, or butter you're using and become rather greasy. For this reason many people prefer them

Focus Point
Gill Edges

The gill edges of the shiitake are jagged, like the edge of a finely serrated knife. You may have to use a magnifying glass to see the edges clearly. Although aberrant growth conditions can make the gills of just about any mushroom jagged—for example, when a cap has been "pinched" between logs or when the gills are very old and beginning to erode—some species feature serrated gills with regularity regardless of growing conditions. The edible train wrecker (*Neolentinus lepideus,* p. 195) is another example of a mushroom with jagged gill edges. Although it is not a feature that helps to define any of the mushrooms in this book, another identification characteristic involving the gill edges has to do with whether the edges are colored the same as the faces. Gills with differently colored edges are called "marginate" gills by mycologists, and they can be quite striking, as in eastern North America's *Mycena leaiana* (edibility unknown; not treated in this book), whose gills have pale orange faces and dark orange to red edges. More often, however, marginate gills are merely whitish or brownish and demonstrate the color difference only at maturity. Marginate gills frequently represent the naked-eye manifestation of microscopic, sterile cells on the gill edges called "cystidia" (see the Focus Point "Cystidia," p. 288).

baked with a filling of breadcrumbs and herbs. Their flavor is slightly nutty, and the texture is meaty and pleasantly chewy. Dried versions can be tough if they are not soaked long enough (twenty to thirty minutes should do it), but they have a more distinct and concentrated taste, which means that only a few mushrooms can thoroughly flavor a sauce, soup, or stew.

Recommended Recipe: Artichoke Shiitake Pizza (p. 303).

Poisonous Look-Alikes

The mushrooms included in this section are poisonous mushrooms that I think could reasonably be confused with the 100 edible mushrooms in this book. I have *not* included every poisonous mushroom in North America, so it would be a very bad idea to assume that if a mushroom is not included in this section it is edible. *Conocybe filaris*, for example, contains deadly amatoxins (see p. 43), but it is not included because none of the 100 edible mushrooms could "reasonably" be confused with it.

Yes, I am putting the poisonous mushrooms here, before you head for the woods in the "Recommended for Beginners" section, to scare you. I strongly recommend that you learn how to recognize an *Amanita* (p. 43) and *Galerina marginata* (p. 46) before picking any edible mushroom. Collect these deadly mushrooms (don't worry about touching them; no mushroom is so poisonous that it will hurt you to handle it), bring them home, and get to know them well. The other poisonous species should also be learned before collecting edibles, though most of them are not likely to be *fatal* for healthy adults.

Clockwise from upper left: The death cap, *Amanita phalloides* (photo by Pam Kaminski); the destroying angel, *Amanita bisporigera* (photo by Pam Kaminski); patches on an *Amanita* cap; deadly *Amanita* buttons with sacks around the stem bases; an *Amanita* emerging from its sack; a button sliced open to reveal the mushroom inside; *Amanita thiersii*; warts on an *Amanita* cap.

Amanita Species

Toxins and Effects: The destroying angel (*Amanita bisporigera*) and the death cap (*Amanita phalloides*) are two of the deadliest mushrooms on the planet, containing enough poison to kill you with a few bites. The toxins in these (and several other) amanitas are called "amatoxins," and there is no known antidote. Initial symptoms usually develop within twenty-four hours of ingestion and include vomiting and bloody diarrhea. In many cases these symptoms are followed by a period of apparent remission, during which the victim feels better. But the remission is a cruel hoax; in the meantime, the victim's liver and kidneys are being destroyed. Death, which occurs in 10 to 60 percent of amatoxin cases, takes anywhere from three to seven days. Treatment is symptomatic, though medical professionals have begun to report some success with a combination of penicillin G and silibinin—an extract derived from milk thistle that is currently not approved for use in the United States. See the Focus Point "The Meixner Test for Amatoxins" (p. 48) for information on chemical testing for amatoxins. Many other *Amanita* species contain other awful toxins, including ibotenic acid (in *Amanita gemmata*, *Amanita muscaria*, *Amanita pantherina*, and other species), which can produce vivid dreams, hallucinations, and delusions—but also terrible nausea and vomiting and/or, in some cases, deep sleep. The toxins in some other species of *Amanita* have yet to be identified, but they are clearly dangerous and in some cases potentially fatal.

Distinguishing Features: Species of *Amanita* are gilled mushrooms that grow on the ground in woods or, more rarely, in grassy areas where trees are absent. Their caps are oval or convex when young and expand to broadly convex or flat in maturity. The cap colors vary widely, from bright reds and yellows to pure, stark white. Many species have distinctive warts or patches on the cap surface. The gills are free from the stem, or just barely attached to it, and are usually white—though in a few species the gills are grayish, yellowish, or orangish. When young the gills are covered with a tissuelike partial veil. The stems are usually fairly long proportionally. There is typically a ring on the upper stem (those species that lack rings, with some exceptions, have strongly lined cap edges and feature sacks around the stem bases). The stem base is almost always distinctive in the genus *Amanita*. Many species, including the deadliest, develop from an egglike button that leaves a sack around the stem base when the mushroom matures. Other species have concentric scales around the stem base, or a basal bulb, or a distinctive "rim." Species that have indistinct stem bases, ironically, are distinctive within the genus *Amanita*. The flesh is whitish or pale yellowish, and in a few species it changes color (usually to pinkish red) when sliced. The spore print is white.

Ecology: *Amanita* species are mycorrhizal partners with trees, with a few rare exceptions— notably, *Amanita thiersii*, which is apparently a saprobe and grows in grass whether trees are present or not. They grow alone, scattered, or gregariously in summer and fall—or in winter and spring in warmer climates. The various species are distributed throughout North America, and deadly poisonous species should be expected in all areas of the continent.

Comments: All beginning mushroom hunters should learn to recognize the genus *Amanita*, and none of the species should be eaten. While many species are poisonous—even fatally so—the deadliest amanitas are the destroying angel, the death cap, and closely related species. The destroying angel, *Amanita bisporigera*, is a stark white woodland species. Its stem base is enclosed in a white sack, and its cap rarely has warts or patches. It has a large and prominent ring on the upper stem. Some field guides also treat "*Amanita virosa*" and "*Amanita verna*" as destroying angels, but *Amanita* experts have recently begun to synonymize these species with *Amanita bisporigera*. The western destroying angel, *Amanita ocreata*, is often a little stockier than its eastern counterparts, but it shares other physical features. The death cap, *Amanita phalloides*, has a greenish to yellowish or brownish cap that often features one or more whitish patches and does not have a lined edge. Its stem base is enclosed in a white sack, and it has a large and prominent ring on the upper stem. Its distribution in North America is uncertain, but it has been documented on the West Coast and in the Southwest, and it is suspected to occur in the Northeast. I have found it in California and Pennsylvania. Thrill seekers and mystics who pursue the infamous *Amanita muscaria* (which has a bright red or bright yellow cap adorned with white warts and a swollen stem base that features concentric, shaggy rings) should be advised that the North American varieties of this species are not only psychoactive but also seriously poisonous for many people. *Amanita thiersii*, which appears on lawns and in other grassy areas, is a potential danger for those who assume that amanitas are absent where trees are absent. Its cap and stem are densely shaggy with soft, white scales that come off on one's fingers when the mushroom is handled. Its stem base

Focus Point

Universal Veils, *Amanita* Eggs, and Stem Sacks

Many species of *Amanita*, including the deadly destroying angel and death cap, feature a sack around the base of the stem. The sack is called a "volva" in Mycologese and is the result of a "universal veil." Unlike a *partial* veil (see the Focus Point "Partial Veil," p. 30), which covers only the gills or pores, a universal veil covers the entire mushroom when it is in the button stage. Thus, many species of *Amanita* appear as pale "eggs" before the universal veil is broken by the growing mushroom. When sliced open, *Amanita* eggs reveal the mushroom-to-be developing inside—which is one reason collectors of edible puffballs (p. 189) should slice open their finds and inspect the interior flesh. As an *Amanita* grows, the universal veil is split apart. Remnants are some-times left as warts or patches on the cap surface (see the Focus Point below), and the bottom portion of the universal veil may be variously disposed. In some species it turns into flakes, scales, or shaggy zones on the base of the stem. In the deadly poisonous species the universal veil remains as a (usually whitish) sack around the stem base. The sack is often prominent and easily seen, but it is also often submerged under the ground and difficult to detect if you have not carefully dug up the base of the stem with your pocketknife. For this reason beginning collectors should *always* dig up the stem bases of the gilled mushrooms they collect. Occasionally, universal veils create stem sacks elsewhere in the mushroom world. Of the mushrooms treated in this book, only the stinkhorns ("edible"; p. 197) have universal veils and stem sacks—and they are not likely to be confused with gilled amanitas, even in the "egg stage" (stinkhorn eggs are filled with chambers of dark goo).

Focus Point

Warts or Patches on the Cap

Warts or patches on the caps of some *Amanita* species are remnants of the universal veil (see the Focus Point above). "Patches" are large sections of veil material adhering to the cap surface; "warts" are small. The red form of the infamous *Amanita muscaria*—the classic "toadstool" of fairy tale illustrations—has many prominent warts on its cap, while the death cap typically features a large central patch. Warts and patches (especially patches) are subject to the elements, how-ever, and rain may wash them away. Additionally, aberrant specimens in which the cap has managed to pop out of the universal veil without adhering remnants are not infrequently encountered. Since warts and patches are not scales, which develop from the surface of the cap itself, they can sometimes be removed with relative ease. But they are also tightly adherent in many cases, and discerning the difference between warts and patches, on the one hand, and true scales, on the other, is a matter of careful observation and understanding how the scales, warts, or patches developed.

Focus Point
Amanita Bravado

"Amanita Bravado" is not a rare species of *Amanita;* it's a behavioral disorder. Sometimes mushroom hunters with considerable identification skills are able to successfully identify and eat some of the nonpoisonous amanitas—such as *Amanita rubescens* or *Amanita novinupta* (neither of which is treated in this book)—without experiencing ill effects. However, amanitas are poorly known in North America, and the true *Amanita rubescens,* for example, may not even occur on our continent, despite its inclusion in field guides. People who eat amanitas, in my humble opinion, are exercising poor judgment—though I concede that there are several distinctive and harmless species, especially on the West Coast. The real problem, however, occurs when *Amanita* eaters begin to brag about it. In some mushroom clubs and mycological societies, experienced mushroomers love to engage in Amanita Bravado, and daring to eat amanitas can become almost a rite of passage for new and inexperienced club members. This is a dangerous state of affairs for obvious reasons, and the people involved have made little social progress since high school. If you have enjoyed a nice meal of amanitas, keep it to yourself. Bragging about it only creates social pressure on others, with less identification experience, who could make a potentially fatal mistake.

is indistinct, but like other amanitas it features gills that are free from the stem and a white spore print. *Amanita thiersii* appears to be increasing its range rapidly, moving from Mexico and Texas to areas where it was previously unseen, including Kansas, Illinois, and Kentucky.

Galerina marginata and Similar Species

Toxins and Effects: These deadly mushrooms contain amatoxins—the same poisons found in some species of *Amanita;* see "Toxins and Effects" (p. 43) for details about the effects of amatoxins and the Focus Point "The Meixner Test for Amatoxins" (p. 48) for information on chemical testing for amatoxins.

Distinguishing Features: *Galerina marginata* is a fairly small gilled mushroom that grows on logs and stumps, often in clusters but not infrequently alone. The somewhat greasy or sticky cap is convex, broadly bell-shaped, or nearly flat. Its surface is smooth and brown to tawny brown or cinnamon. However, the color often changes markedly as the mushroom dries, becoming pale tan or even whitish. Two-toned specimens, caught between color stages, are frequently encountered. The

edge of the cap is finely lined. The gills are attached to the stem or begin to run down it—but in old age they can pull away from the stem and appear to be free of it. They are yellowish at first but become rusty brown as the spores mature. When young they are covered with a tissue-like (or nearly cobwebby) partial veil. The stem is thin (rarely more than half a centimeter wide), and its surface is smooth or finely shaggy. A braceletlike ring is usually present on the upper stem; it is whitish at first but soon becomes rusty brown as it catches spores that fall from the gills. Specimens are not infrequently found, however, in which the fragile ring has disappeared. The stem surface is whitish or, near the base, dark brown to blackish. There is no sack around the stem's base. The flesh is insubstantial and watery brown. The odor is not distinctive or, in some collections, a little mealy. The spore print is rusty brown.

Ecology: *Galerina marginata* is a wood-rotting saprobe found on the deadwood of fallen hardwoods and conifers. It typically grows in clusters, but solitary and scattered specimens are common. It prefers cooler temperatures and is usually found in spring or fall (or in winter in warm climates)—but it is not afraid to show itself in summer as well. It is widely distributed in North America.

Comments: Along with the death cap and the destroying angel (see p. 44), this deadly mushroom should be earnestly studied by anyone who considers collecting wild mushrooms for the table. A study in 2001

Focus Point
The Meixner Test for Amatoxins

The Meixner Test is a relatively simple (but not infallible) test that can be used to determine whether amatoxins are present in a mushroom. Note, however, that there are plenty of other serious toxins found in mushrooms, and the Meixner test does *not* test for "edibility" (no such test exists). To perform the Meixner test you will need concentrated hydrochloric acid, a newspaper, mortars and pestles, a pipette, rubber gloves, and a laboratory hood under which you will perform the test (and, if you are performing the test on dried mushrooms, you will need some 70 percent ethanol to rehydrate your mushrooms). In short, you will need the chemistry lab at your local high school, junior college, or university—and you will probably also need some help from someone who handles the chemicals and equipment regularly.

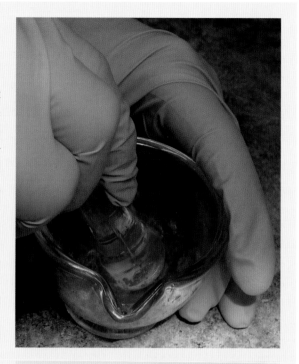

Always perform the test with positive and negative controls to be sure that your results are actually informative. In addition to the mushroom in question, test a mushroom known to contain the toxins (I use *Galerina marginata* since it occurs in large quantities in my area every spring and fall), as well as a mushroom you are certain does not contain them—say, a species of *Russula*. With controls, you can be more sure that you have performed the test correctly and do not have a "false positive" or "false negative" result.

Put a small portion of each mushroom in a mortar and grind it to a paste with a pestle. Be sure to use separate mortars and pestles for each mushroom in order to avoid contamination. You will probably want to label the mortars in order to avoid confusion about which paste corresponds to which mushroom since they all look more or less the same after grinding. Fresh mushrooms will

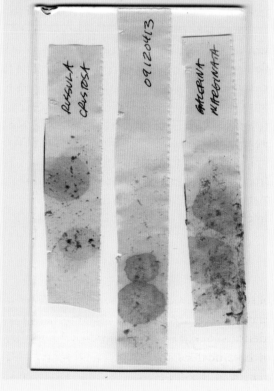

turn into paste easily with grinding, but if you are working with dried mushrooms you will need to add a few drops of 70 percent ethanol to rehydrate the material.

Cut strips from the margins of newspaper pages, where no ink is present; you will need one strip for each mushroom. Clearly label each strip near one end, leaving plenty of room to perform the test without interference from ink or lead. Newspaper has high lignin content and works much better for the Meixner test than other types of paper, which may produce false results.

Using the pestles, your fingers, or any tools that seem appropriate, spread some paste from each mushroom sample on its corresponding strip of newspaper. If you use your fingers, or use one tool for this process, be sure to avoid contamination by washing thoroughly between samples. Scrape away any excess material so that the newspaper strips are soaked with the paste.

Place the strips under the laboratory hood, turn on the fan, and wait until they are completely dry. There is some evidence that exposure to heat or wind stress at this point (say, from a hair dryer) can influence your results, so the best idea is to be patient and wait. Once the strips are dry, put on rubber gloves and goggles. Using a pipette, place a tiny drop of concentrated hydrochloric acid on each newspaper strip where it absorbed the mushroom paste. Be careful! Hydrochloric acid is very dangerous.

After a few minutes, color reactions should begin to appear on the strips. The positive reaction is bluish, and the negative reaction is, well, something else; it depends on what you used as your negative control. The Meixner Test is known to produce reddish reactions for some mushrooms, though the significance of the reaction is apparently unclear. In the illustrations, *Russula crustosa* (edible; see p. 212) is the negative control, and the color change with hydrochloric acid is pinkish. *Galerina marginata* is the positive control in the illustrations. The mushroom under study is an unnamed species of *Amanita* I have called the "sand dune *Amanita*"—and it is clearly very toxic.

The color changes may take a while to develop, and reactions that look faint at first may become more noticeable over the course of an hour or two; be sure to wait a while before giving up on color changes. Once the hydrochloric acid has dried, you can take the strips out of the hood, and away from the lab, fairly safely. Place them in separate envelopes and be sure not to touch the acid droplet (wash your hands thoroughly if you do so by accident). Within half a day or so the colors will begin to fade. I recommend taking photos in natural light within an hour or scanning the strips of paper in a flatbed scanner (wash the glass thoroughly when you're done).

of several dozen *Galerina* species found that *Galerina autumnalis*, *Galerina marginata*, and *Galerina venenata*, among others, are genetically identical despite minor differences in physical features. By the rules of botanical naming, the oldest valid name in the group, *Galerina marginata*, takes precedence and should be used for all of the former "species." In most field guides, this mushroom will be listed as "*Galerina autumnalis*."

Chlorophyllum molybdites

Toxins and Effects: This mushroom produces unidentified "gastro-intestinal irritants." Nausea, vomiting, and diarrhea develop within a few hours of ingestion and typically dissipate within a day or so. Serious cases can require hospitalization.

Distinguishing Features: This medium-sized to large gilled mushroom grows in grassy areas, often in arcs or fairy rings, across North America. Its cap is round at first but expands to broadly convex or nearly flat. The dry, whitish surface is adorned with large, soft scales that have brownish to pinkish-brown tips. The edge of the cap often features hanging white remnants of the tissuelike partial veil, which covers the young gills. The gills are free from the stem. Their color progresses from whitish to grayish green to darker (something in the neighborhood of "dark, dirty, brownish green")—but the white stage can last until the cap is quite large. The stem is long and features a prominent, double-edged ring. The surface of the stem is smooth and white, but it discolors

Center photo by Pam Kaminski

and ages brownish. The base of the stem is not enclosed in a sack. The flesh is white and does not change color when sliced—with the exception of the flesh in the base (*not* the apex) of the stem, which is pale orangish or reddish in some collections. The spore print is greenish.

Ecology: *Chlorophyllum molybdites* is a grass-loving saprobe, found in lawns, meadows, ditches (and so on) across North America. It grows alone, scattered, or in fairy rings and arcs in summer and fall.

Comments: This species causes more mushroom poisonings in North America than any other, probably because it is so attractive, "munchable looking," and readily available, popping up in lawns and parks. I suspect that many of the poisoning cases result from a kind of irresponsibility that is less reasonable than merely confusing *Chlorophyllum molybdites* with the parasol mushroom (edible; p. 281) and the shaggy parasol (edible; p. 253). Confusing *Chlorophyllum molybdites* and the shaggy parasol is easy enough to do, even when comparing fresh specimens to thorough descriptions; I know experienced mushroom hunters who have made this mistake. But the high number of poisonings is not likely the result of experienced mushroomers having correctly placed *Chlorophyllum molybdites* in a small group of closely related mushrooms, some of which are edible. Instead, people who have no business eating *any* wild mushroom are simply cooking them up, willy-nilly, without having the slightest idea what they are—or having compared their mushroom to a few photos on the Internet, deciding they have a "match." This summer, for example, I was consulted in a poisoning case that involved confusing *Chlorophyllum molybdites* with the shaggy mane (edible; p. 148). These mushrooms are similar only on *very* casual inspection! It is fortunate that the case was in Minnesota—which is, for the time being anyway, outside the range of *Amanita thiersii* (see p. 44), a potentially deadly species that is also large, shaggy, whitish, and fond of grass (and has been steadily widening its distribution over the past decade).

Poisonous Mushrooms in the *Lepiota* Group

Toxins and Effects: These mushrooms contain the same "amatoxins" found in the deadly species of *Amanita* (see p. 43).

Distinguishing Features: The deadly species in the *Lepiota* group are small to medium-sized gilled mushrooms that grow from the ground or forest debris in woods—or sometimes in lawns, ditches, gardens, compost piles, and so on. They have dry, convex caps that typically feature tiny scales on a pale background. The scales are often brown, or some form of "-ish brown" (reddish brown, for example), and are usually concentrated more densely toward the center of the cap, where the surface may be smooth and dark—though the cap may be differently colored (reddish, blackish, gray, white, or even bluish) overall. The edge of the cap may feature the hanging remnants of a partial veil, which covers the young gills. The gills are white or pale yellowish and are free from the stem. The stem is slender, and its surface is usually at least finely scaly or hairy. It features a fragile ring, but the rings of these species are notorious for disappearing. The stem base is not enclosed in a sack but may be attached to whitish strings or fuzz. The flesh is whitish or pale yellowish. The odor is often (but not always) fragrant or sharply unpleasant. The spore print is white.

Ecology: These species are litter-decomposing saprobes that are often found growing from forest debris on the ground and are attached to a whitish mycelium that can be discovered, with a little searching, binding together leaves, needles, small sticks, and so on. The mushrooms can also appear in disturbed soil, grass at the edges of lawns, gardens and compost piles, and similar locations. They tend to appear in summer and fall (or in winter in warm climates), and the various species are distributed across the continent.

Comments: *Lepiota josserandii*, *Lepiota castanea*, and *Lepiota helveola* are among the species known to be deadly—but I have written my description to encompass just about *any* small *Lepiota* since all of them should be avoided. They are extremely difficult to identify with certainty (I have watched *Lepiota* expert Walt Sundberg eagerly studying collections of little *Lepiota* species and I have to admit that my eyes glazed over after only twenty minutes at the microscope), and they are insufficiently documented. In short, the whole group constitutes a recipe for disaster as far as edibility is concerned. *Chlorophyllum molybdites* (p. 50) is a member of the *Lepiota* group but is treated separately here. It should be emphasized that edibility is not known for *most* of the species in the *Lepiota* group—even those that do not match my description very well—which means that only the tried-and-true edibles in the group should be considered for the table: the parasol mushroom (p. 281), the shaggy parasol (p. 253), and *Macrolepiota americana* (p. 278).

Poisonous Boletes

Toxins and Effects: Some red-pored species are reported to contain muscarine; see "Toxins and Effects" for species of *Clitocybe* (p. 58) for a description of this serious toxin. Unidentified "gastrointestinal irritants" are the culprits in other boletes known to be poisonous, causing nausea, vomiting, and diarrhea within a few hours of ingestion. If my experience with orange-capped *Leccinum* species is indicative, the symptoms are severe but dissipate gradually over the space of a day or so. There are reports of more serious poisonings from some boletes, however, and at least one fatality has been attributed to a red-pored bolete.

Distinguishing Features: See the Focus Point "Boletes" (p. 78) for help recognizing a bolete. Of the hundreds of bolete species in North America, only a few are known to be poisonous, and these can be separated into three groups.

Group One: Boletes with red or orange pore surfaces that bruise blue. *Boletus satanas* and species in the *Boletus erythropus/subvelutipes* group are the primary offenders, but all red-pored boletes should be avoided, especially since current bolete taxonomy is anything but comprehensive and reliable. Although following my advice will keep a few species known to be edible from your table—primarily *Boletus frostii* (not treated in this book) of eastern North America and Mexico, which has a dramatically netted and pocketed red stem—you will avoid venturing into

Above: Group One (photo by Dianna Smith); *lower left:* Group Two; *lower right:* Group Three

territory where species are not clearly defined and some mushrooms are known to be poisonous.

Group Two: Boletes with yellow pore surfaces that bruise blue—especially those with red to reddish-brown caps. *Boletus fraternus*, which can be nearly impossible to separate from *Boletus campestris* and/or *Boletus rubellus*, is the primary offender, but poisonings from *Boletus bicolor* and a few other species have been documented. The red-capped, yellow-pored, blue-bruising species of *Boletus* are poorly delineated at the moment, and the safest course is to avoid all of them. That said, a few clearly distinguished species (most of which turn blue only faintly if at all) can be safely tried by experienced collectors, providing they are identified with 100 percent certainty; *Boletus subglabripes* (p. 131) is an example. Blue-bruising boletes with other cap colors and/or pore surfaces should probably also be avoided by beginners, just to be safe, but experienced collectors may enjoy *Gyroporus cyanescens* (p. 169), *Boletus pallidus* (p. 129), and *Boletus zelleri* (p. 133), among others.

Group Three: Orange-capped *Leccinum* species. See page 182 for help identifying members of this bolete genus. Though it is a fact only recently finding its way into the mainstream of mushroom publications, it is a certainty that at least one or two of the orange-capped *Leccinum* species in North America is mildly poisonous. It is still unclear precisely which species is the culprit (and more than one species may be responsible), but all of them should be avoided.

Comments: Because the poisonous boletes can be so easily characterized and avoided, the bolete family is one of the safest groups of mushrooms for experimentation, and precise identification of individual species is not always necessary; see the unidentified *Boletus* species on page 249 for an example. However, excluding the mushrooms grouped here will only keep you out of the hospital (or from setting up camp in the bathroom) if you know what a "bolete" is and have some experience observing its features.

False Morels

False morels are common in springtime woods across the continent, and all collectors of morels (pp. 84, 87, and 192) should learn to recognize them. I have split the false morels into two groups.

Group One:
Gyromitra Species

Toxins and Effects: Gyromitrin is the toxin found in species of *Gyromitra*. The effects range from none to vomiting and diarrhea, kidney and liver failure, and (very rarely) death. Faced with the choice of writing many pages or a few lines about this poison and its presence in false

Upper left: Gyromitra montana; upper right: Gyromitra caroliniana (left) and Gyromitra brunnea (right); middle left: Interior of a false morel; middle right: Gyromitra esculenta; lower left: Verpa conica button (photo by Hugh Smith); lower right: Verpa bohemica (note cap attachment)

morels, I will opt for the latter and say only this: scientists do not know what the various North American species of *Gyromitra* are, whether they all contain gyromitrin, whether growing conditions or geography affect toxin levels, whether the cooking process always removes the toxin, whether there is a cumulative buildup of the toxin in individuals who eat false morels, whether this, and whether that. In short, they don't know much about gyromitrin and false morels—but *neither do you or I,* and we have no business eating these mushrooms. Farmer Bob and Logger John may have eaten false morels for years without ill effects, but they have probably done all kinds of other stupid things, too. For the pages-long version, see my book *Morels*.

Distinguishing Features: Species of *Gyromitra* have caps and stems and grow primarily from the ground (several species that grow on wood appear only in the fall and, along with a few other species that look like veined cups, are not likely to be confused with the edible mushrooms in this book). The caps are irregular in shape and can often be described as "wavy" or "lobed." They are *not* regularly pitted and ridged, with the possible exception of occasional *Gyromitra caroliniana* specimens, which are easily distinguished from true morels on other features. The cap color is usually reddish to reddish brown, though yellowish-brown versions are sometimes encountered. The stems are whitish or pale tan. The interior of *Gyromitra* species is *not completely hollow* as it is in the true morels. In many species the flesh is chambered and contains air pockets, but no *Gyromitra* could reasonably be considered truly hollow. The sizes range from fairly small to gargantuan (over five pounds!), depending on the species and growing conditions.

Ecology: Species of *Gyromitra* are officially saprobes, but I would not be surprised to discover that they are actually like morels and have a mycorrhizal stage. The species treated here grow alone, scattered, or gregariously in spring (account for elevation and geography in the timing of "spring") and occur under hardwoods or conifers across North America.

Comments: Identifying species of *Gyromitra* ranges from fairly easy to fairly difficult. The genus is poorly documented and will probably be turned on its taxonomic head once DNA studies begin to test the various species that have been defined on the basis of physical features. See my book *Morels* for a comprehensive treatment of the genus in North America and for a full discussion of its toxicity.

Group Two: *Verpa* Species

Toxins and Effects: Minor gastrointestinal distress (vomiting and diarrhea) is suffered by a fairly large percentage of people who consume *Verpa* species. Loss of muscle coordination is also reported occasionally.

Distinguishing Features: Species of *Verpa* grow on the ground in hardwood forests and occasionally under conifers. The brownish caps are shallowly to deeply wrinkled (*Verpa bohemica*) or fairly smooth (*Verpa conica*) and are attached to the rest of the mushroom only under the center, so that they hang free from the stem the way a thimble would sit atop a pencil's eraser. The stems are whitish or very pale brown, with smooth to wrinkled and/or grainy surfaces. *Verpa* stems are fairly hollow, but usually feature wispy, cotton-candy-like fibers inside.

Ecology: Like species of *Gyromitra*, *Verpa* species are officially saprobes, but they are probably mycorrhizal at some point in their life cycle. They fruit in spring, primarily in hardwood forests (but sometimes under conifers), and often begin to appear about a week before the true morels. They grow alone, scattered, or gregariously.

Comments: *Verpa* species are, I admit, consumed by many people and are even counted as "morels" in some morel-hunting championships. Still, given the established record of unpleasant experiences, they cannot be recommended for the table.

Poisonous *Clitocybe* Species

Toxins and Effects: Muscarine is the primary toxin found in poisonous species of *Clitocybe*. The effects are awful and too numerous to list comprehensively here (one mnemonic used by doctors and medical students

Left: Group Two (photo by Emilio Pini); *right:* Group One.

to memorize just a few of the symptoms is SLUDGE: Salivation, Urination, Gastric Upset, and Emesis)—but profuse sweating, irregular heart rate, breathing difficulty, and impaired vision deserve special mention. In severe cases hospitalization is necessary, and doctors sometimes use atropine as a treatment. Fatalities are rare and are generally limited to victims with preexisting health problems.

Comments: The genus *Clitocybe* is large and diverse—too large and diverse to cover comprehensively here. Instead I will focus on general, easily observed features that help to define the genus and on two poisonous species groups that could cause confusion with some of the edible mushrooms in this book. Species of *Clitocybe* are gilled mushrooms that:

- Grow on the ground or, if they grow on wood, have well developed, more or less central stems.
- Have spore prints that are whitish, pale yellowish, or pale pink—but if the spore print is pink, it should not be a dark, fleshy pink (be sure you are looking at a thick print).
- Have gills that are not thick and waxy and that begin to run down the stem or are attached to it by a "notch" (in which case the spore print will be pinkish rather than white or yellowish).
- Lack partial veils and thus do not feature rings on the stems or hanging remnants on the edges of the caps.
- Lack universal veils and thus do not feature a sack around the stem base.
- Have (often but not always) a sweet odor.

Edibility is not known for most of the several hundred species of *Clitocybe* on our continent. The only decent edible species of the lot is the Blewit (*Clitocybe nuda*; p. 255)—which, ironically, doesn't look much like the poisonous species described here (it's purple) and thus doesn't merit a reference to poisonous *Clitocybe* species in its look-alikes list. The rest of the genus should be avoided—even those species not accounted for in the two groups described here.

Group One: *Clitocybe dilatata* and Closely Related Species

Distinguishing Features: These mushrooms are fairly large and grow in dense clusters in disturbed soil—in ditches, on roadways, along paths, and so on—or in woods. They are saprobes and appear in summer or fall. *Clitocybe dilatata* is a common mushroom in the Rocky Mountains and the Pacific Northwest, but similar species are found in eastern North America. The caps are white to pale grayish and are often somewhat contorted as a result of clustered growth. The edge of the cap is rolled under at first; later it is often wavy or irregular. The gills are white and begin to run down the stem. The stem is smooth and white and lacks a ring. The stem bases are frequently packed so tightly that they appear to be fused together. The flesh is white. The spore print is white. The spores, under a microscope, are elliptical and smooth.

Group Two: *Clitocybe dealbata* and Closely Related Species

Distinguishing Features: These small species grow in grass or disturbed-soil settings (gardens, compost piles, ditches, and so on), but similar woodland species should also be avoided. The caps are broadly convex, flat, or shallowly depressed and have fairly smooth surfaces. The color is whitish, dirty cream, brownish, or very pale tan—sometimes with hints of pink. In a few species, long cracks occur with consistency on the cap surface in old age. The gills are whitish or dirty cream, and they begin to run down the stem. They are fairly closely packed together. The stem is smooth and colored like the cap. It lacks a ring. The flesh is thin and whitish and does not change color when sliced. The odor is not distinctive in some species but is somewhat mealy in others. The spore print is whitish. The spores, under a microscope, are elliptical and smooth.

Inocybe Species

Toxins and Effects: Muscarine is documented in many species of *Inocybe* and is suspected to occur with frequency throughout the genus. See the "Toxins and Effects" entry for species of *Clitocybe* (p. 58) for a description of muscarine's effects.

Comments: *Inocybe* is a huge genus of small to medium-sized gilled mushrooms—*all* of which should be avoided and some of which are seriously poisonous. Although identifying species within the genus is a

task so difficult that most *mycologists* take a bye, *Inocybe* species are so common that the features defining the genus should be studied by anyone who considers collecting wild mushrooms for the table. To wit, those features are:

- A brown spore print.
- Caps that are often pointed, at least in the middle, and often feature scales or silky, radiating fibers. In many species the edge of the cap splits, radially, with age.
- Gills that are some shade of brown when mature.
- Distinctive odors in many species. "Sweet," "fishy," "spermatic," "like green corn," and "mealy" are all in the batter's box.

Focus Point

LBMs (Little Brown Mushrooms)

Believe it or not, mycologists use this term all the time, though it is obviously not very scientific. I should probably mention that LBMs don't have to be brown unless you are a terminology fundamen-talist (in which case you could switch the acronym's middle object to *boring* instead of *brown*). Boring little mushrooms featuring drab yellows, tentative tans, dirty whites, and gloomy grays . . . and all of them qualify for LBM status in my book. (Wait! This *is* my book!) More to the point, LBM's *should not be eaten* since they are incredibly difficult to identify and contain within their ranks some seriously poisonous little buggers.

- Terrestrial growth—usually in woods but sometimes in grassy areas where trees are present.

One fairly small group of *Inocybe* species features purple or lilac shades, but the vast majority are yellowish or brownish—and unspeakably boring. *Inocybe* species are mycorrhizal partners with hardwoods and conifers and are distributed across the continent.

Cortinarius Species

Toxins and Effects: The genus *Cortinarius* is suspected of harboring several unidentified and potentially serious toxins, but the most serious known *Cortinarius* offenders are kidney toxins such as orellanin, which can cause kidney failure or death. Transplants may be required, and recovery can take up to six months. Orellanin is particularly insidious in that it can take up to three or four weeks to produce symptoms.

Comments: *Cortinarius* is the largest genus of mushroom-producing fungi. Thousands of species have been described, and some mycologists believe there are hundreds, or even thousands, that remain undescribed. Obviously, the genus is too large to characterize adequately here. How-

Upper right: photo by Dianna Smith

ever, the entire genus should be avoided, with the sole exception of *Cortinarius caperatus* (edible; p. 260), which, with its tissuelike (rather than cobwebby) partial veil and true ring, is the only known exception to the first of the three features that help to define the genus *Cortinarius* and other, closely related genera.

- A cobwebby "cortina" covers the young gills (see the illustration). The cortina is a partial veil. Cortinas are often quick to disappear but can usually be found if you have button-stage specimens at your disposal. The cortina sometimes collapses against the stem as the mushroom grows, and in many cases it creates a "ring zone" of adhering fibers on the stem surface.
- The spores are rusty or rusty brown when viewed en masse, as in a spore print.
- *Cortinarius* species grow on the ground—a result of the fact that they are mycorrhizal partners with trees.

None of the three features by itself is necessarily indicative of *Cortinarius*, but the triple combo is pretty much infallible—further evidence that identification often hinges on collecting multiple specimens that represent all stages of development, since observing the cortina requires a button and observing the spore print requires mature gills. *Cortinarius* species are most diverse and numerous during cool weather and under conifers (a mind-numbing array of species appears, for example, in the spruce-fir zone of the Rocky Mountains during the fall monsoon season), but plenty of species can be found under hardwoods and during warm weather.

 Warning: *Cortinarius* Species with Purple or Lilac Shades

Distinguishing Features: These species grow under hardwoods and conifers across North America. They share, of course, the three universal features emphasized above—but beyond this they differ widely and do not form a coherent taxonomic group, scientifically speaking. However, the purplish shades can cause confusion with several edible mushrooms. The entire mushroom may be purple or lilac, or the color may be limited to the cap, gills, or streaks in the flesh (especially the flesh in the stem base). Species that demonstrate faint lilac shades in limited locations often lose their lilac credentials as they mature. The purple or lilac color in the gills of *Cortinarius* species, when present, changes to rust or rusty brown as the spores mature. The rusty spore print and the presence of the cortina (on buttons) will serve to separate these species from the edible look-alikes in this book.

Entoloma Species

Toxins and Effects: Various unidentified gastrointestinal irritants, ranging from the relatively benign (causing nausea, vomiting, and diarrhea) to the fairly serious (requiring hospitalization) are documented in some species of *Entoloma* and suspected in many others. The entire genus should be avoided, from a culinary perspective, with the possible exception of the "aborted" form of *Entoloma abortivum* (edible; not treated in this book), which is unappetizing and mealy smelling.

Comments: *Entoloma* is a large genus (or family of genera, depending on the mycologist) that includes hundreds of species worldwide. The mushrooms are too diverse and numerous to treat comprehensively

Photo by Dianna Smith

here, but they share three easily observed features that will help to separate them from most of the edible look-alikes in this book.

- Dark, fleshy pink spore prints
- Gills that are attached to the stem (often by means of a notch) or rarely begin to run down it but are not free from it
- Terrestrial growth (with a few, very rare exceptions)

Many species of *Entoloma* qualify as LBMs (see the Focus Point "Little Brown Mushrooms" on p. 61) and are not likely to attract the interest of pot hunters. Other species are larger and look more appetizing. Since the genus (or family) is known to contain several poisonous species, and since *Entoloma* taxonomy in North America is anything but comprehensive, beginners should avoid *any* truly terrestrial mushroom with attached gills and a pink spore print. Advanced collectors should make exceptions to this rule only when 100 percent certain that they have correctly identified a species known to be edible (including, in this book, the Blewit [p. 255] and *Clitopilus prunulus* [p. 258]).

A special note of caution is in order for springtime morel hunters who are desperate to eat wild mushrooms but are not finding morels. A group of species centered around *Entoloma vernum* appears with some regularity in the springtime woods. I have seen this mushroom fruiting by the hundreds in one of my favorite morel spots—when morels were frustratingly absent. *Entoloma vernum* has a pointed brown cap and a straight, narrow stem—and, of course, attached gills and a pink spore print. I can't imagine anyone mistaking it for a morel, but I do receive dozens of eager e-mails every spring from morel hunters who have picked *Entoloma vernum* and want to eat it. This group of related species is decidedly poisonous, however; a case I was consulted on last year involved the hospitalization of several healthy adults. Thwarted morel hunters should stick to the devil's urn (edible; p. 94), *Polyporus squamosus* (edible; p. 204), and the jelly ear (edible; p. 119).

Jack O'Lantern Mushrooms: *Omphalotus* Species

Toxins and Effects: Generic "gastrointestinal irritants" are suspected in *Omphalotus* species, as well as muscarine—a more serious toxin, which

Photo by Pam Kaminski

can require hospitalization (see "Toxins and Effects" for species of *Clitocybe*, p. 58).

Distinguishing Features: These fascinating mushrooms are medium-sized to large gilled mushrooms that grow in dense clusters on stumps and buried roots. The caps are convex at first but are soon flattened. The surface is smooth. The color is bright orange—or, in western North America, *orangish* with hints of olive green. The gills run far down the stem and are colored more or less like the cap. There is no partial veil covering the young gills, though the edge of the cap is often curled under at first to protect them. The stem is also colored like the cap, and its surface is smooth. It lacks a ring, and the base is usually tapered. There is no sack around the stem's base. The flesh is pale orange and does not change color when sliced. The odor is not distinctive. The spore print is whitish to pale yellow.

Ecology: *Omphalotus* species are wood-rotting saprobes. They grow in dense clusters on dead stumps of hardwoods—primarily oaks in eastern North America and primarily oaks and eucalyptus in western areas. The eastern jack o'lantern mushroom appears in summer and fall, while the West Coast species appears in fall and winter.

Comments: The eastern species, *Omphalotus illudens*, is bright orange, while its western counterpart, *Omphalotus olivascens*, is dingy olive orange. Both have often been given the name *Omphalotus olearius*, which is a European species that may (or may not) encompass our North American jack o'lantern mushrooms. Although I described the jack o'lanterns as "fascinating," careful readers may have wondered what on earth was fascinating in the ensuing description. Well, nothing . . . except that I left out the part about gills that glow in the dark. Fresh specimens will sometimes demonstrate this amazing phenomenon—though I admit that it took more than ten years of collecting jack o'lanterns and hovering in dark closets before I finally saw it. The trick, which I finally discovered with help from members of the Missouri Mycological Society, is to wrap the mushrooms in damp paper towels when you collect them. Then study some other fungi (particularly those that are used to ferment alcoholic beverages) as thoroughly as you can. If you follow this process, the luminescence is undeniable.

 ## Poisonous *Russula* Species

Toxins and Effects: Unspecified gastrointestinal irritants, causing NADIVO (Nausea, Diarrhea, and Vomiting) within a few hours of ingestion and passing (and passing and passing) over the course of a day or so.

Comments: *Russula* is a large genus, and its members are fairly easily recognized through a combination of features.

- Terrestrial growth under trees
- Caps that are convex, flat, or centrally depressed (never conical or bell shaped)
- Stems that are fairly short and often about as long as the cap is wide
- Crumbly, brittle flesh
- Brittle gills that are attached to the stem or begin to run down it
- Absence of a partial veil covering the young gills, absence of a ring on the stem, and absence of a sack around the stem's base
- Whitish, yellowish, or orange spore prints
- Tissues that do not produce a "juice" or "milk" when damaged

While recognizing a russula is usually easy enough for mushroom hunters with a little experience in the woods, identifying the many species is one of mycology's more frustrating challenges. The edible russulas treated

Upper left: Group One; *upper right:* Group Three; *bottom row:* Group Two

in this book have fairly distinctive features, which help to separate them, but this scenario is not par for the course at Country Club *Russula*. Although I am tempted to launch a chapter-length tirade on this topic, I will restrain myself and say only this: the characters used by mycologists to separate *Russula* species are often ridiculous. Can you peel the "skin" of the cap one-quarter of the way from the edge toward the center, or one-half the distance? Is the taste "slightly acrid" or "acrid"? Is the cap "pale isabelline" or "rosy avellaneous"? Is the spore print "warm buff" or "pale creamy yellow"? Are the spores "partially reticulate" (don't ask) or "completely reticulate in most collections"? In short, nearly the whole genus is composed of dubious species separated on the basis of silly differences, and it is often a waste of one's time to attempt to identify russulas beyond the fairly distinctive species and species groups included in field guides.

No russula is known to be dangerously, fatally toxic (with one possible exception in Group One), but many of them are mildly poisonous—causing gastrointestinal distress—and many are simply too acrid, bitter, or otherwise unpalatable to consider eating. The poisonous (or potentially poisonous) groups that could be confused with the edible mushrooms in this book are characterized as follows.

Group One:
Blushing and Blackening Russulas

These species vary substantially in cap color, but all have flesh that turns reddish or grayish when sliced. The color change can be fairly slow to manifest itself, however, so be sure to wait at least fifteen or twenty minutes. Often the cap, gills, and/or stems of these species will also demonstrate the color changes when bruised. The species that bruise and discolor reddish *then* blackish are the most dangerous (*Russula subnigricans*—not treated here—has even been implicated in a fatality), but I have collected specimens from this group that lacked the reddish stage they were supposed to display, so I am including the straight-to-black species as a precaution, with the exception of *Russula claroflava* (edible; p. 291), which is easily separated on the basis of its yellow cap and habitat in conifer bogs or subalpine hardwood forests.

Group Two:
Maraschino Cherries Gone Bad Russulas

These species have a distinctive, sweet odor that is hard to describe but fairly easy to recognize once you have smelled it. I think it smells like maraschino cherries that have been left out on the counter for a few weeks. Others describe the smell as "sweetly spermatic" or similar to that of benzaldehyde. The caps are often sticky when fresh and young and range in color from pale dirty yellow to rusty orange or brown. It is unclear whether any of the mushrooms in this species complex is "truly" poisonous, and a good lawyer would easily make mincemeat out of a mycologist on the witness stand who claimed a "scientific certainty." But the group is fairly frequently reported as causing gastric distress and should be avoided.

Group Three:
Red Russulas

A handful of russulas known to be mildly poisonous (*Russula emetica* is the primary offender) have red caps—and since red russulas are for the most part ridiculously difficult to separate, they should all be avoided in the absence of other, clearly distinctive features (such as the shrimplike odor of the edible *Russula xerampelina*, p. 295). *Russula rubescens* (not treated in this book), of eastern North America's hardwood forests, has the unique distinction of belonging in both this group and Group One since it has a red cap *and* flesh that turns reddish when bruised.

Poisonous *Agaricus* Species

Toxins and Effects: The toxins in poisonous species of *Agaricus* fall into the broad category of "gastrointestinal irritants." Symptoms develop fairly promptly, within a few hours of eating the mushrooms, and include nausea, vomiting, and diarrhea. In today's medical jargon, the symptoms might be labeled HFS (Human Faucet Syndrome). Fortunately, HFS rarely requires hospitalization for healthy adults, and it usually disappears within a day or so. Some people are apparently unaffected by the irritants in poisonous *Agaricus* species, but the number of reported poisonings and unpleasant experiences is so high that you should definitely not find out whether you are one of them.

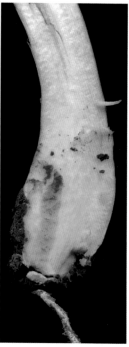

Distinguishing Features: Species of *Agaricus* are gilled mushrooms that grow on the ground, in woods, or in grassy areas. The caps are convex when young (or, in some species, squarish or blockish), but by maturity they are usually broadly convex or nearly flat. The cap surface is dry and is either smooth or fibrous to somewhat scaly. In many species the fibers, when present, are denser toward the center of the cap. With a few fairly rare exceptions, the cap colors range from whitish to brownish, yellowish brown, golden brown, or cinnamon brown. In some species the cap does not bruise or discolor; in others it bruises pinkish, reddish, or yellow. Cap bruising is best tested by rubbing the soft edge of the cap with your thumb (be persistent). The gills are free from the stem and are covered with a tissuelike partial veil when young. They are chocolate brown when mature, but in youth they are pale. In some species, the gills pass through a pinkish stage on their way to becoming brown; in others the pink stage is absent or substituted with a gray stage. *Agaricus* stems are fairly variable in stature, ranging from short and squat (often with a tapered base) to long, thin, and fragile. In most species the partial veil leaves a ring, or fragile ring vestiges, on the upper stem. The stem surfaces range from smooth to shaggy. In some species the base of the stem forms a bulb, but there is never a sack enclosing the stem base. The stem may bruise like the cap, especially near the base. The flesh is generally whitish, but it may change color when sliced (either slowly or promptly). The flesh *in the base of the stem* is yellow in some species. The odors in *Agaricus* range from "not distinctive" to "mushroomy" (the common button mushroom sold in stores is an *Agaricus*; see p. 28), strongly almondlike, aniselike, or unpleasant and "phenolic" (like creosote or ink). Odor is best tested by crushing the flesh in the stem base between your thumb and finger. The spore print is chocolate brown.

Ecology: *Agaricus* species are terrestrial saprobes. Many grow in grass or disturbed soil, often in urban settings. The woodland species can be found just about anywhere in the forest, but many appear to prefer disturbed-soil settings such as path edges and clearings. *Agaricus* species grow alone, scattered, or gregariously in summer and fall (or in the winter in warm climates) and are distributed throughout North America.

Comments: While there are no universal tests to determine which mushrooms are poisonous and which are edible, species of *Agaricus* offer a small subset of mushrooms that those of us without toxicology degrees can "test" in order to experiment with relative safety, even when precise species identification eludes us. The species of *Agaricus* known to be poisonous demonstrate one or all of the following.

- Yellow staining. Rub the edge of the cap and the base of the stem repeatedly.
- Yellow flesh in the base of the stem.
- An unpleasant, phenolic odor. Crush the flesh in the base of the stem.

Strict avoidance of any *Agaricus* that demonstrates one or more of these characters is the best rule—though some edible mushrooms (e.g., the horse mushroom, p. 238) may be taken out of consideration. Advanced collectors should learn the individual species that are exceptions and return to the rules when an *Agaricus* collection cannot be identified to species. The unidentified *Agaricus* species on p. 242 is an example of how an advanced collector might proceed to the table with an unknown *Agaricus*—but note that you must be *100 percent sure* you have collected an *Agaricus* species before deciding to eat it (after eliminating the features just discussed). This kind of certainty takes years of experience identifying mushrooms, and beginners should *not* experiment; there are plenty of gilled mushrooms that look somewhat like *Agaricus* species, do not have yellowing flesh, do not smell of phenol, and are poisonous (*Hebeloma sinapizans* comes to mind as an example). The most widely distributed and common poisonous *Agaricus* is *Agaricus xanthodermus*, which demonstrates all three of the no-no characters. It grows in grass and often crops up in large numbers in lawns, gardens, parks, and meadows. Another group of commonly collected poisonous species includes *Agaricus placomyces*, *Agaricus praeclaresquamosus*, *Agaricus pocillator* (see the photo on p. 10), and others. These species—which are primarily woodland—are generally tall in stature and demonstrate one or more of the no-no characters.

Gymnopilus Species

Toxins and Effects: The toxins are psychoactive; see "Comments" for further information.

Distinguishing Features: Species of *Gymnopilus* are mostly found growing from wood (often in clusters), but a few can grow from buried wood and appear terrestrial (and one or two are apparently "truly" terrestrial).

Above: Gymnopilus spectabilis (photo by Tim Zurowski); *below:* Gymnopilus liquiritiae

The convex to flat caps are fairly dry. Many species feature a partial veil, which covers the young gills and leaves a ring or "ring zone" of adhering fibers on the stem. The gills are attached to the stem (sometimes by means of a notch) or begin to run down it. The stem is central and well developed. The spore print is bright orange to bright rusty brown (a character that by itself will eliminate confusion with most of the 100 edible mushrooms in this book). Other features vary fairly widely between the species.

Ecology: *Gymnopilus* species are primarily wood-rotting saprobes found on the deadwood of fallen hardwoods and conifers. They grow alone, scattered, gregariously, or in clusters in summer and fall (or winter in warm climates). The species are widely distributed in North America.

Comments: Edibility is not known for many *Gymnopilus* species, and a few contain psychoactive toxins. Although they are more likely to provoke a trip to the moon than a trip to the hospital, these species should not be hunted by thrill seekers who do not have years of mushroom identification experience under their belts. I wish I had a dollar for every e-mail I have received from someone who wants to "do mushrooms," has heard a scientific name or two and visited a few Web pages, and now wants to pick psychoactive mushrooms in the wild. As I hope I have convinced you elsewhere in this book (see pp. 9–17), mushroom identification is *very difficult*, takes *lots of work*, and can result in *fatal mistakes* if approached casually. The people who send these e-mails usually have no interest in such diligence and are likely to kill themselves. Compare the illustrated mushrooms, for example, to *Galerina marginata* (deadly; page 46), which also grows on wood, has a ring, and features a rusty brown (rather than bright orange to bright rusty brown) spore print. Just as there are no shortcuts to certainty when it comes to identifying mushrooms for edibility (short of looking for them in your grocery store), there are no shortcuts for determining psychoactive species other than trusting a drug dealer. Go ahead: Trust a drug dealer.

Recommended for Beginners

T he mushrooms in this section are fairly distinctive and will serve as a good introduction to collecting wild mushrooms for the table. Some of them are *very* good to eat, such as the black and yellow morels (pp. 84 and 87); others, to be brutally honest, are terrible—but they do have the virtue of being comparatively easy to recognize. Most of the mushrooms in this section can be collected across the continent, though some have limited geographic ranges. The twelve mushrooms in the section span the mushroom season in most areas, appearing from early spring to late fall. In warmer climates, at least one or two of them can be found whenever mushrooms can be expected.

Aside from building your repertoire of edible species, I hope you will build on your knowledge of mushroom identification by adding bricks to the foundation you built with mushrooms from the store. With this in mind, I have included many Focus Points in this part of the book.

6 The Old Man of the Woods: *Strobilomyces floccopus*

Edibility Rating: Fair.

Distinguishing Features: This odd-looking bolete grows on the ground in woods in eastern North America. Its distinctive, soft cap is covered with woolly black or grayish scales. The edge of the cap often features clinging remnants of a partial veil, which covers the young pores when the mushroom is in the button stage. The pore surface is whitish or grayish at first but is soon dark gray. When bruised, it turns reddish and then black. The stem is somewhat tough, and its surface is shaggy, with black or grayish scales and fibers. It has a fragile ring, but the ring often falls off or becomes hard to distinguish from the scales. The flesh is whitish but turns pinkish red when sliced (sometimes slowly) and eventually black or grayish (the black stage may take as long as half an hour to

Left: photo by Pam Kaminski; *upper right:* photo by Dianna Smith

develop). The cap turns yellowish when a drop of ammonia is applied. The spore print is black or dark blackish brown.

Ecology: Species of *Strobilomyces* are mycorrhizal partners with hard-woods—especially oaks. They grow alone or scattered in summer and fall in eastern North America.

Poisonous Look-Alikes: None—but consult "Poisonous Boletes" (p. 53).

Comments: This distinctive mushroom is admittedly not very appe-tizing looking, but it has the advantage of being fairly easily distin-guished from other mushrooms. I have never discovered the origin of the common name old man of the woods, but the old man must be Old MacDonald, since *someone* has to tend to the menagerie of mushroom monikers represented by the hen of the woods (edible; p. 163), chicken of the woods (edible, p. 79), sheep polypore (edible; p. 117), and others. The most commonly encountered old man of the woods is *Strobilomyces floccopus*. A few other species of *Strobilomyces* have been described in North America, but they are virtually indistinguishable and micro-scopic analysis is often required to separate them definitively. *Tylopilus alboater* (edible; p. 227) and a few other species of *Tylopilus* are also black or dark gray, but they lack the woolly scales of the old man.

In the Woods: (John David Moore) In late summer to early fall in east-ern North America, head to your nearest hardwood or mixed hardwood and conifer forest and look on banks along trails and roads, as well as in any shady area. The old man of the woods is hard to spot and tends to grow alone or scattered, its dark color blending in with soil and shadow. It is common, but it's rare that one finds many in a single spot. Young individuals are the best, but if you need older specimens to fill up the pan, remove the tough stems in the field. Brush the caps off before bagging them, since the shaggy surface easily retains and camouflages debris.

In the Kitchen: (John David Moore) Clean your collection with care. The charcoal gray to black tufted cap makes it difficult to distinguish dirt from mushroom. Rinse your mushrooms and drain well unless you plan on stewing them. Some people recommend removing the tufted "skin" of the cap, but I've never noticed that it makes any difference in taste or texture. Besides, if the cap skin is removed in addition to tubes and stem, you're not left with much more than a mysterious-looking

Focus Point

Boletes

The old man of the woods serves as a good introduction to some of the features that define and help to identify boletes—although it is a lousy introduction to the culinary pleasures of boletes since it is mediocre at best, while *Boletus edulis* (p. 123), *Xanthoconium separans* (p. 232), and others are among the very best edible mushrooms. I owe an apology to western readers, however, since the old man of the woods is limited to areas east of the Rocky Mountains. While there are two exclusively western boletes in the book (*Boletus zelleri*, p. 133; and *Suillus pungens*, p. 225) and many that are found in both eastern and western areas, none of them is as easily recognized as the old man of the woods, and some experience is required to identify them. However, beginning western collectors can still learn about boletes by examining the photos and reading what follows—and some bolete features can be learned through careful examination of dried porcini slices (p. 32), which are frequently sold in grocery stores and specialty shops. Like all boletes, the old man of the woods has a central stem and features a layer of tubes on the underside of the cap. Boletes are spore factories, and the tubes are the assembly lines. The microscopic, spore-producing machines are located on the inner surfaces of the tubes. Imagine taking the cardboard tube from a roll of paper towels and affixing a lot of seeds to the inside of the tube. Then repeat the procedure with many other tubes and glue them together. Suspend all the tubes from a board, so that they hang downward, then wait for the seeds to fall out. This, more or less, is a bolete's strategy, and the spores fall from the tube mouths into air currents. The tube layer is soft and can usually be peeled away from the cap *as a layer* fairly easily. The ends of the tubes create a "pore surface," which in the old man of the woods changes color when it is scratched with a knifepoint or the end of a stick. Whether the pore surface of a bolete bruises or not (and what color change results from the bruising) is often an important character in bolete identification. The old man of the woods has soft flesh, like all boletes. In this species, however, the flesh changes color when sliced. Experimenting with this mushroom's "blushing" is a good way to get acquainted with such color changes—and the length of time you may need to wait before the changes are evident. Many boletes have color-changing flesh, and assessing this character is important since most of the boletes known to be poisonous have flesh that changes to light or dark blue when exposed to air. The old man of the woods also features a partial veil and a (fragile) ring on its stem; these features, which are not uncommon among boletes, are discussed with the button mushroom on p. 30. Boletes are almost exclusively mycorrhizal partners with trees and are thus found growing from the ground (with *very* few exceptions). Terrestrial polypores (e.g., species of *Albatrellus*—edible; p. 117) may resemble boletes but can be easily distinguished when you try to remove the adherent tube layer or slice the leathery flesh. The following list summarizes the central features of boletes.

- Terrestrial growth
- Central stem
- Pore surface and tubes
- Removable tube layer
- Soft flesh

morsel resembling discolored tofu. Sautéed slowly for ten minutes (especially if the stems are included), the old man of the woods has a pleasantly chewy texture but rather bland flavor. Charles McIlvaine, a virtual fungal omnivore, describes a "strong woody taste, sometimes musky, sometimes faintly of anisette." This all sounds quite tasty, but I regret that it has not been part of my experience with *Strobilomyces floccopus*. Flavor may vary with environment, however, and with other species of *Strobilomyces*, which are confusingly similar but luckily all edible. If your finds are on the bland side, they are best put into dishes where they can absorb other flavors and add a somewhat meaty texture.

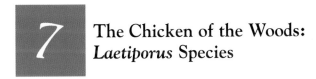

7 The Chicken of the Woods: *Laetiporus* Species

Edibility Rating: Good.

Distinguishing Features: The chicken of the woods is a large polypore that grows from the wood of standing trees or fallen logs or from roots at the bases of trees. The various species are distributed across the continent. The entire "chicken" is a large cluster (up to 60 cm across or more) of large, overlapping individual caps that are fan shaped, tongue shaped, or roughly semicircular. They are fairly soft and fleshy and are yellow, orange, cinnabar red, or (rarely) whitish with hints of one of these colors. The surface is finely velvety and usually somewhat wrinkled. The pore surface, beneath the cap, is bright sulphur yellow or orangish in most of the species but whitish in one species. It does not change color when bruised with a knifepoint. The pores are tiny and nearly invisible to the naked eye when the chicken is a chick. The flesh is white, soft, and somewhat stringy. It does not change color when sliced and exposed to air. In older specimens it can develop a tough, leathery consistency, especially in the area farthest from the edge of the cap. The spore print (which is often hard to obtain and certainly not crucial for identification) is white.

Ecology: Species of *Laetiporus* are parasites on living trees and saprobes on deadwood. They cause a reddish brown, cubical heart rot in the wood, with thin areas of white mycelium visible in the cracks. The mushrooms do not appear until well after the fungus has attacked the tree; by the

Upper: Laetiporus cincinnatus; middle: Laetiporus coniferi-cola (photo by Hugh Smith); *lower: Laetiporus cincinnatus* pore surface (photo by Dianna Smith)

time the chickens appear on standing trees, they are definitely coming home to roost as far as the tree's health is concerned. They fruit in summer and fall in most areas but appear in fall and winter in warmer climates. The distribution and wood preference for the most common North American species are discussed under "Comments."

Poisonous Look-Alikes: None.

Comments: Beginners should probably avoid the rare chickens with whitish upper surfaces until they are familiar with this wonderful edible mushroom; white specimens increase the look-alikes list to include many other polypores. Admittedly, most of these are so tough or otherwise unpalatable that no one would consider eating them—and none is known to be dangerously toxic—but since edibility is unknown in some of these cases it's best to be conservative until you are a chicken whiz. There are about a dozen species of *Laetiporus* currently described from North America. They are "biological species," which means that mycologists have defined the species on the basis of whether or not they will "mate" and produce offspring—more or less the same concept we usually use to define species of large animals. Trust me: you do not want to know what mycologists do in their labs to get fungi to "mate" (though I will say that one prominent mycologist has made a movie of the process and added a soundtrack of cheesy love songs—and that some fungi have *hundreds of genders*). The end result of these experiments, as far as *Laetiporus* is concerned (you're still chewing on that "hundreds of genders" thing, aren't you?), is that some species that *look* identical refuse to mate with one another, so that those of us who are not myco-porn producers have no way of telling them apart. Fortunately, the major species of *Laetiporus* in North America can be roughly separated with reference to their preferred woody substrate and geographical distribution. They include *Laetiporus sulphureus*, which fruits above the ground on the dead or living wood of hardwoods in eastern North America (cap and pore surface both yellow); *Laetiporus gilbertsonii*, which fruits above the ground on the wood of oaks or eucalyptus on the West Coast (cap and pore surface both yellow); *Laetiporus conifericola*, which fruits above the ground on the wood of conifers in western North America (cap and pore surface yellow); and *Laetiporus cincinnatus*, which fruits at the trunk bases of oak trees (or from their roots, appearing to be terrestrial) in eastern North America (cap yellow, orangish, cinnabar red, or rarely whitish; pore surface white). The eucalyptus-loving version of *Laetiporus gilbertsonii* should probably be avoided (see p. 20). Since the chicken of the woods is a polypore, be sure to follow the precautions on p. 24 when you try it the first time; "allergic" reactions and minor gastrointestinal distress occur in some people.

Focus Point

Polypores

The chicken of the woods is a "polypore," which, like other mushrooms, is a spore factory designed to release microscopic spores into air currents. To increase its production capacity, a polypore uses tubes for its assembly lines (see the entry for the old man of the woods, a bolete [p. 78] for an explanation of tubes). Unlike boletes, which have a tube layer that can be removed from the mushroom *as a layer* with relative ease, polypores have tightly adherent tube layers that are difficult or nearly impossible to separate. Polypores are stingy architects when it comes to designing the spore factory, and they create only the structures they absolutely need to arrange the tubes so that spores will fall out of their ends and into the air. Some polypores, such as *Ischnoderma resinosum* (edible; p. 171), only create caps when they have to and merely spread a pore surface along the bottoms of fallen logs that are not pressed into the ground; then, when the mushroom begins to grow up the side of the log, caps are required in order to align the tubes properly. Stems only enter the picture when they are required to separate individual caps and/or when the polypore is growing on top of the log or on the ground. The vast majority of polypores grow from wood, though a few grow from the ground (including species of *Albatrellus* [edible; p. 117], which are mycorrhizal partners with trees). Some polypores grow on the root systems of trees or at the butt of the trunk and can thus appear to be terrestrial; one such species is *Laetiporus cincinnatus*. Polypores tend to hang around longer than gilled mushrooms or boletes, and as a consequence they are often quite tough (some even seem to be harder than the wood from which they are growing). The area of growth in a polypore is at the edge of the cap, and this zone is usually the softest. Older specimens of the chicken of the woods have leathery or corky flesh in the stem area but softer, more palatable flesh near the cap edge. The chicken of the woods is annual (until the mycelium runs out of nutrients to digest) but some polypores are perennial and develop a new zone of growth at the edge of the cap every year. Perennial polypores are too tough to consider for the table, but you may be interested in examining them closely since the growth zones can be counted like tree rings to determine the age of the mushroom.

Focus Point
Shelflike Clusters

Many polypores, including the chicken of the woods, develop clusters of shelflike caps that overlap. Mycologists call this growth pattern "imbricate clusters." In some species the mycelium seems to figure out in advance where to place the shelving caps so they will be adequately spaced to allow spores to catch air currents; in other species, such as the chicken of the woods, the mushroom itself seems to do the thinking, developing lateral stems that keep the pore surfaces separated from the caps below them.

Focus Point
Wood-Rotting Parasites and Saprobes

The chicken of the woods is homicidal, as forest managers across the continent will tell you. Its parasitic mycelium begins to develop in wounds in the tree's bark and quickly spreads through the wood, rotting it and eventually killing the tree; it is thus referred to in forestry circles as a "forest pathogen." The chicken is also apparently "saprobic," meaning that it can feast on deadwood as well. After the chicken's mycelium has plowed through the wood, digesting yummies, the wood becomes rotted and breaks up into brownish, vaguely cubical chunks. Many wood-rotting fungi create this kind of rot; others create whitish or straw-colored, stringy rots. One wood-rotting species, the train wrecker (edible; p. 195), does its job so efficiently that it is reported to have rotted railroad ties sufficiently enough to cause derailments. Mycologists do not often attempt to identify mushrooms on the basis of the type of rot caused by their mycelia (the plural of mycelium), but paying attention to rot is obviously a crucial factor if one wants to *understand*, rather than merely eat or identify, wood-rotting fungi. However, it is not always possible to find recognizable rot in wood where mushrooms are growing, and, absent a clearly observed physical connection between mycelium and mushroom, only a scientist armed with a DNA sequencer could guarantee that a mycelium in the wood corresponds to a given mushroom. This ambiguity is the result of the fact that *many* fungi are typically involved in the decomposition process. When a tree falls, the wood-rotting fungi don their napkins and get out the silverware. Interestingly, many wood rotters appear to take turns, feasting on different nutrients in the deadwood and waiting in line for their turn to sit down at the table—a process that rots the wood (and at first the bark) in stages and eventually returns its components to the soil. Several of the wood rotters in this book are parasites: some of the honey mushrooms (edible; p. 244), at least one species of *Hericium* (edible; p. 102), and the cauliflower mushroom (edible; p. 108) are examples. Other wood rotters are benign saprobes and merely decompose deadwood; these include the deer mushroom (edible; p. 287) and oyster mushrooms (edible; p. 202).

Focus Point
Mycelium

If you spend some time inspecting the log that your chicken of the woods is slowly devouring, you may be able to find evidence not only of the rot created by the mushroom but of the mycelium itself. A mushroom's mycelium is actually the main part (or stage) of the organism; what we call a mushroom is merely the spore factory constructed by the mycelium when it reproduces. Under a microscope, a mycelium typically appears as a tangled web of tiny, stringlike cells; to the naked eye, it often appears as whitish, moldy-looking fuzz. You can sometimes find this fuzz on a chicken's log, working its way through cracks in the wood—though, as I noted earlier, there is really no guarantee that the mycelium you're looking at corresponds to that of the chicken since other fungi are also at work in the wood. This is why mycologists—and you—identify species by looking at the spore factories (the mushrooms), which display many physical differences that can be observed. It's a bit like identifying apple trees on the basis of their seed factories (apples) without looking at the trees themselves. Mycelia are often nearly impossible to find, but they are sometimes visible if you are willing to put in some effort. Saprobes that decompose litter (see the Focus Point "Litter-Decomposing Saprobes," p. 257) are often visibly attached to litter-binding, whitish mycelia. The rhizomorphs of some honey mushrooms (edible; p. 244) and *Stropharia rugosoannulata* (edible; p. 213) constitute mycelia. And the fairy rings found in lawns and meadows (see the Focus Point "Fairy Rings," p. 285) indicate a mycelium's presence, even when mushrooms are absent, with a ring of darker grass. In a few species, such as *Laccaria ochropurpurea* (edible; p. 269), part of the mycelium can even be found as a fuzzy coating on the base of the mushroom's stem.

In the Woods: (John David Moore) Once you locate one of these colorful fungal arrangements, color and texture will determine its freshness. Fresh, appetizing specimens are soft, fleshy, and squeezable. An analogy to tofu has often been applied. Older *Laetiporus* species fade to buff and eventually to chalky white, becoming dry and crumbling easily. Although you can remove the whole fungus from its host, it is only the more tender outer edges of the shelves that are desirable. If you trim off one to two inches from the margins, the mushroom will keep growing and you can return for a later harvest, provided some other fungiphile doesn't beat you to it.

In the Kitchen: (John David Moore) The chicken of the woods can usually be wiped clean with a damp cloth. Washing or soaking it will cause it to absorb useless liquid, and young, fresh specimens will have plenty of moisture already. For cooking, it's best to cut it into small squares or strips while trimming any discolored areas. Often the chicken can engulf debris, growing around grass and stray bits of bark or sticks. Watch out for these intrusive odds and ends when cutting up your harvest for the pan. More often than not you will harvest more than you can immediately use of this frequently sizable fungus, and you will want to preserve the excess for future feasts. Freezing briefly sautéed or stewed *Laetiporus* preserves the flavor and texture well for the short term. For long-term preservation, drying is preferred. The dried fungus, although it keeps indefinitely, takes long rehydration to resurrect the tender, poultrylike texture that helps make the chicken so palatable.

Recommended Recipe: Chicken of the Woods with Lemon Cream (p. 305).

Black Morels: *Morchella* Species

Edibility Rating: Great.

Distinguishing Features: Like most yellow morels (edible; p. 87), black morels fruit from the ground in spring—or even in summer in high-elevation conifer burn sites in western North America. They feature a *completely hollow*, egg-shaped to somewhat pointed cap that has a pitted and ridged surface. While the pits and ridges are not symmetrical, they are fairly regular (and often arranged in more or less vertical channels), and the surface cannot be adequately described as wavy or merely wrinkled. When young, the ridges are pale brown (or nearly whitish) and packed fairly tightly together. As the mushroom matures the ridges darken to black or dark brown. The pits are brownish at maturity, but in some western versions they have a definite greenish or pinkish (though *not* reddish or reddish-brown) cast. There is a shallow "rim" where the cap meets the stem (like a little racetrack for ants if you were to hold the mushroom upside down), but the two parts of the mushroom are decidedly joined together and the edge of the cap does not create a substantial, overhanging flap. The stem is whitish and may be smooth, finely dusted, or a little wrinkled. It is *completely hollow*, and

Upper left: photo by Hugh Smith; *upper right, lower left, and lower right:* photos by Pam Kaminski

no flesh or little wisps of cotton-candy-like fibers are found in its interior. The spore print is whitish, yellowish, or pale orange.

Ecology: Black morels are mycorrhizal partners with various trees, but the mushrooms appear in large numbers when the host tree is dead or dying—at which point they don a different ecological hat and become saprobes. Although they *can* appear just about anywhere as long as there is a living or dead tree in the vicinity, black morels are found in greatest numbers under ash trees in eastern North America and in conifer burn sites in western North America in the spring following the fire. These are not the only places to find black morels (plenty are found elsewhere), but they are probably the most prolific producers. Black morels appear in early spring and are usually the first of the morels to appear. At high elevations in western burn sites, "spring" can mean July or August—a few weeks after the last snowbanks have melted. Black morels grow alone, scattered, or gregariously.

Poisonous Look-Alikes: False morels (p. 55).

Comments: Compare black morels carefully with the false morels (p. 55), which are not completely hollow and have wavy to convoluted, reddish-brown to brown caps. Also compare them with the yellow morel (edible; p. 87), which has pale ridges, and the half-free morel (edible; p. 192), which is colored like the black morel but features a substantial overhanging flap where the cap meets the stem. In rare instances black morels have been known to cause "allergic" reactions, especially when combined with alcohol, so be sure to follow the precautions on page 24 when you try them for the first time. At this point in mycological time, it is probably a good idea to abandon any attempt to pin scientific species names on our North American morels. Ongoing DNA studies support the idea that we have at least five genetically distinct black morels—and that they are not necessarily "morphologically" distinct, which means we can't tell them apart by looking at them. Ecological factors such as distribution, forest type, mycorrhizal host, and so on are likely to become our only recourse for identification short of a DNA sequencer, but the lines have not yet been drawn with anything approaching certainty. To make matters more confusing, the existing scientific names for black morels are pretty much worthless from a scientific standpoint. See my book *Morels* for an extensive discussion of morel classification. Fortunately, your taste buds don't care, and black morels are fairly easily recognized, as a group.

In the Woods: (John David Moore) When you come upon the black morel, make note of the trees and their condition. Tree species can give you clues on where else to hunt, and dying, diseased trees will often indicate the possibility of future harvests for a few years. Spotting black morels takes patience and a keen eye, especially since young ones may hide amid the leaf litter. Cut them carefully so as not to end up bagging a lot of dirt from the base; once dirt gets into the pitted caps, it's a major challenge to get it out. As black morels age, they become crumbly and are best left to go about their reproductive business in peace. Brushing your finds off in the field is pointless considering the nature of the pitted caps. It's best to save the cleaning for the kitchen.

In the Kitchen: (John David Moore) Being hollow, the morel makes a perfect hideout for slugs and larvae. Even if the pitted exterior seems clean and free of invaders, you should slice your mushrooms lengthwise or into rings to hunt down pests before further cleaning under running water followed by thorough draining in a colander or on paper towels. Some people soak morels overnight in salt water to get rid of pests. I find that this pretty effectively destroys the texture and reduces the flavor. If I have specimens that appear clean inside and out, I prefer to keep them away from water altogether. If I'm going to dry any of my finds, I'll cut them into rings or keep them whole and let the dirt and dried wildlife come off when they're soaked back into shape. For short-term preservation, you can sauté your finds in a bit of butter and then freeze them after placing them in freezer bags in portions suitable to future use. The black morel, prepared purely by sautéing for two to three minutes, has a flavor that some people describe as nutty with a smoky quality. Black morels have a stronger taste than yellow morels but lack the latter's meaty, chewy substance.

Recommended Recipes: Bigos (Polish Stew) (p. 304); Jaeger Sauce for Schnitzel or Steak (p. 306).

9 Yellow Morels: *Morchella* Species

Edibility Rating: Great.

Distinguishing Features: Yellow morels fruit from the ground in springtime woods (with the exception of one West Coast and Mexican Gulf Coast species, which appears in the winter in lawns and gardens; see "Comments"). They have *completely hollow* caps that are egg shaped to somewhat pointed. The surface features pits and ridges that are not arranged symmetrically but are also not arranged in a way that could be

Upper left and upper right: Morchella rufobrunnea (photos by Hugh Smith); *middle left:* "esculentalike" morel (photo by Mark Davis); *middle right:* "deliciosalike" morel puffing spores on a flatbed scanner; *lower left:* photo by Dianna Smith; *lower right:* "esculentalike" morels (photo by Mark Davis)

described as wavy. The ridges are pale yellowish brown (sometimes nearly white) and remain fairly pale throughout development; they are never dark brown or black. The pits may be blackish or pale at first, but at maturity they are usually more or less the same color as the ridges. In short, the pits may be darker than the ridges but not vice versa. The edge of the cap is attached to the stem directly without an overhanging flap; there is usually not even much of a "rim" at the point of attachment. The stem is also *completely hollow*, though it may have flaky "layers" near its base in older specimens. The spore print is whitish, yellow, or pale orange.

Ecology: Like the black morels (edible; p. 84), most yellow morels are mycorrhizal partners with trees and become saprobes when the tree dies. However, at least one species of yellow morel, *Morchella rufobrunnea* (see "Comments"), is capable of living without a mycorrhizal stage in its life cycle. Yellow morels, like their darker-capped cousins, can appear almost anywhere, but they are found in greatest numbers under ash, tulip trees, old apple trees, and dead elms. They are also frequently found under cottonwoods (eastern or western) in river bottoms. The various species of yellow morels are distributed across the continent. They appear in spring, usually about a week or two after the black morels appear, and grow alone (sigh), scattered, or gregariously.

Poisonous Look-Alikes: False morels (p. 55).

Comments: False morels (p. 55) are not completely hollow and have wavy to convoluted, reddish-brown to brown caps. Compare yellow morels with black morels (edible; p. 84), which have darkening ridges, and half-free morels (p. 192), which have darkening ridges and a substantial overhanging flap where the cap meets the stem. Also compare them with stinkhorns ("edible"; p. 197), which grow in lawns and gardens in summer and fall and feature a sack around the base of the stem, as well as cap surfaces that, until they are cleaned by greedy flies, are covered with a foul-smelling, brown to olive-brown slime. Since mycologists are currently investigating the morels, classifying them with scientific species names is difficult. However, the situation for yellow morels is a little better than that for the black morels, and we have a (probably) valid scientific name for one North American species, as well as a genetically supported means of dividing the yellow morels into two large groups. There are at least seven genetically distinct species of yellow morel in North America. *Morchella rufobrunnea* is a West Coast species that grows in landscaped areas and disturbed ground, often in the absence of nearby trees, from December to February. When young it has a pointed, sometimes twisted cap with long, longitudinal ridges and black pits; in age it is more or less egg shaped, with yellowish-brown pits and ridges. Its cap surface turns pinkish red when bruised. It also

Focus Point
Spore Puffing

Morels and other members of the phylum Ascomycota release their spores from microscopic structures called "asci" (see the Focus Point "Asci," p. 194), and, for reasons that are not completely understood, they often coordinate this release across all the assembly lines in the spore factory so that all the asci release spores simultaneously. If you have handled many morels, you may have been surprised when one of them began "smoking"; occasionally, morels are picked just before they are ready to release spores and something—a change in temperature or light perhaps—triggers the event. I have seen this happen with some frequency when I put morels and other members of the Ascomycota in my digital scanner; others have reported "puffing" when washing morels under cold water. Some claim to be able to *hear* the spore release as a hissing sound, but I must have a tin ear when it comes to morel spores.

grows on the Gulf Coast of Mexico. Our other yellow morels are not easily distinguished on the basis of their physical features aside from sorting them into two groups: the "*deliciosa* type" and the "*esculenta* type." The former type is apparently found only in eastern North America and has small, pointed caps with vertically elongated pits and ridges. The latter type is found across the continent (one species is clearly transcontinental) and has larger caps with rounded tops and more randomly arranged pits and ridges. The existing names for yellow morels (aside from *Morchella rufobrunnea*) are European and may or may not correspond to any of our North American mushrooms. All are delicious, however, so we will leave the matter to mycologists.

In the Woods: (John David Moore) Certainly the most common question asked about this icon of fungal fanaticism is simply where to find it. The vast discussion of the question, both written and oral, scholarly and folkloric, catalogs so many viable environments—from apple orchards to sandy shorelines, under ash trees, and the middle of ash pits—that it's tempting to just say, "Look everywhere." But in the interests of practicality let's narrow that to "Go find a bunch of trees." These include ash, aspen, tuliptree, apple, beech, maple, white pine, elm (live, dead, or in between), and, drawing on personal experience in northern climes, balm of Gilead. As far as I know, trees such as the date palm, mangrove, banyan, and baobab can safely be excluded. Once you've selected a wooded area, start looking around your trees of choice, moving into a wider radius. Check around roots, in hollows, along and on moist hillsides, and along forest edges. Sometimes simple aimless wandering does the trick when rigorous methods fail. Once you've flushed out a morel, check the area carefully for others, and if the resulting harvest is noteworthy remember the spot, as it may produce annually. Clean your finds in the field by trimming the dirty bottoms of stems and picking off any obvious debris.

In the Kitchen: (John David Moore) In my experience, yellow morels tend to be more prone than black morels to infestation by all manner of many-legged, nonlegged, and even winged critters. This may be because they appear later in the season when the warmer conditions inspire a great deal of hatching on all levels of life. This can of course make for extra labor in the kitchen, where you should follow the same procedures recommended for black morels (see p. 87). If you have critters that just won't abandon their territory amid the pits and crannies of the cap surface, even under the force of running water, you may want to try blanching the morels in boiling water so that the varmints float off under extreme duress. After this procedure, a rinsing under cold tap water should get rid of any undesirable elements still lodged in the cap pits. Yellow morels can be preserved and prepared with the same methods used for their black counterparts (see p. 87). Their flavor is more delicate and texture more meaty. They are suited to a wide variety of dishes but do best in preparations in which their quality is not overshadowed by other flavors.

Recommended Recipes: Asparagus Garnish with Mushrooms (p. 303); Shrimp-Stuffed Morels (p. 310).

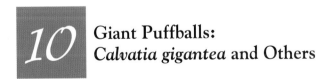

Giant Puffballs: *Calvatia gigantea* and Others

Edibility Rating: Good.

Distinguishing Features: Giant puffballs are easily recognized by their size and shape. Typical specimens are about the size of a soccer ball and more or less round. However, they can be much larger (a five-foot, fifty-pound specimen is on record!), and their shape can be more "bloblike" than round, especially when they attain enormous sizes. The whitish surface ranges from smooth to elaborately sculpted, depending on the species. Be sure to slice your puffball to make sure the flesh is white and firm; although the color of the mature, on-its-way-to-spore-dust flesh

Above: photos by Mark Davis

can be a useful character for precise identification (*Calvatia cyathiformis*, for example, develops a purplish interior in age), it is also an indicator that in terms of edibility your puffball is past its prime.

Ecology: *Calvatia gigantea* and similar species are saprobes found growing alone or gregariously in grassy areas across North America, occasionally forming arcs or fairy rings. They seem to prefer disturbed-ground settings and are frequently encountered in late summer and fall along the edges of fields and meadows, in grassy ditches, and in similar locations.

Poisonous Look-Alikes: None.

Comments: For puffballs that are smaller than a soccer ball, see "Puff-balls: *Lycoperdon* Species and Others" (edible; p. 189). If you have a conservationist bent, you might want to consider that a 30-cm specimen of *Calvatia gigantea* (roughly the size of the specimens in the photo) can produce an astounding seven trillion spores—a fact cited by mycologist Nicholas Money in "Why Picking Mushrooms May Be Bad Behaviour," a recent article in which he advances the idea that picking wild mushrooms may adversely affect their survival. Every *Calvatia gigantea* spore, he argues,

> is important. Frying slices of a puffball in olive oil means that none of its spores—had they been allowed to develop—stands any chance of producing a new colony. No chance is considerably different from a slim chance. Simple math.

Money's position is hotly debated, however; see the Focus Point "Commercial Mushroom Picking" (p. 299) and my book *Morels* for more information.

In the Woods: (John David Moore) Giant puffballs are a favorite for human interest photos in many a small-town newspaper, where small children commonly are shown cradling one of these huge fungal balloons. These mammoth mushroom balls can be spotted (usually when you're not looking for them) in fields, along roadsides, at the edges of woods, under hedges and bushes, and in either open or dense woodlands. In eastern North America and the Midwest, these monsters tend to appear in the late summer and fall. Out west they erupt in the spring

Focus Point
Grass-Loving Saprobes

The giant puffballs are good representatives of the many grass-loving saprobes in the mushroom world. Like all saprobes, these mushrooms subsist on dead organic debris; their mycelia chow down until the nutrients in the substrate are exhausted—at which point the fungus moves on hungrily, searching for more food. Many grass-loving saprobes produce mushrooms with regularity every year (or even several times a year), suggesting that the production of mushrooms is not a result of the mycelium's starvation and desire to escape the immediate vicinity (as is apparently the case with the morels, for example). In fact, the mycelia of grass-loving saprobes often expand outward every year, creating arcs and fairy rings (see the Focus Point "Fairy Rings," p. 285). Other grass-loving saprobes include the meadow mushroom (edible; p. 114) and *Marasmius oreades* (edible; p. 283)—as well as poisonous species such as *Amanita thiersii* (p. 43).

and early summer. Once you've found some, remember the spot or buy the acreage; puffballs will appear there again given the right conditions.

In the Kitchen: (John David Moore) After cutting away the dirty base of your puffballs, if you haven't already done so in the field, it's best to wash your finds under running water using a soft brush or cloth. Drain or wipe them dry before slicing. While slicing, check for any larvae and yellow or yellow-brown discoloration indicating your mushroom's slow loss of palatability. Some people prefer to remove the skin or rind, but I find this only makes sense with the tough-skinned puffballs. Texture trumps flavor in any puffball I've ever eaten, although they have a characteristic richness and absorb other flavors well. The most popular and perhaps the best way to prepare large puffballs is to treat the slices like eggplant. Dip them in egg, coat with bread crumbs, brown them in oil, and then bake them as a casserole with cheese, herbs, and a sauce of fresh tomatoes, garlic, and peppers. Once you start thinking of the puffball as a fungal eggplant, many culinary variations become possible. Puffballs keep well for a couple of days under refrigeration, but methods of long-term preservation are disappointing. Frozen and then thawed, they are soggy and unappetizing. Drying turns them leathery upon reconstitution in water.

11 The Devil's Urn: *Urnula craterium*

Edibility Rating: Mediocre.

Distinguishing Features: The devil's urn is a cuplike fungus that appears on sticks and buried logs in eastern North America's hardwood forests in early spring. It is shaped like a deep goblet whose mouth becomes wider with age. The outer surface is black or dark brown and often has a gritty or finely scaly texture, especially when the mushroom is young. The upper edge, around the opening, becomes torn and/or folded over with age. The inner surface is black and fairly smooth. The short, stemlike structure at the base of the goblet looks like the result of someone pinching off the bottom. It is usually blackish. The flesh is pliant and black.

Ecology: *Urnula craterium* is a saprobe, and its mycelium decomposes the wood of hardwood sticks (which may be buried, making the devil's

urn appear terrestrial). It is sometimes found growing alone but is more frequently found in dense clusters. It appears in early spring, before the morels, and continues fruiting during morel season. Its range is limited to eastern North America.

Poisonous Look-Alikes: None.

Comments: The devil's urn is not a tantalizing tidbit for your taste buds, but it has the advantage of being fairly easy to recognize—and it is often more common in the springtime woods than the elusive morel; it and *Polyporus squamosus* (edible; p. 204) can often provide disappointed midwestern and eastern morel hunters with *something* to bring home if morels are scarce. The devil's urn has been confused with black trumpet (edible; p. 99) by some collectors who evidently need calendars (black trumpets appear in summer and fall) and corrective lenses, but the mistake is harmless from an edibility standpoint (though black trumpets are *much* better to eat).

In the Woods: To be honest, I doubt you're going to try the devil's urn more than once, so you should probably just snip one or two off at the base, shake out any rainwater that has collected in the goblets, and brush away any adhering debris before putting the little guys in your paper bag or basket. If you turn out to be a devil's devotee, I'm sure you will adopt your own practices for collecting *Urnula craterium* in quantity.

In the Kitchen: Wash the mushrooms under running water; their texture is not absorbent and they won't suffer from immersion. I tried the devil's urn by sautéing it slowly in butter (while my friends made gagging sounds and watched the butter turn black). I ate two mushrooms, and what I will say is this: the devil's urn is not as bad as I thought it was going to be. It's not *good*, mind you, but it would be possible to eat it with a forced smile if your Aunt Wanda served it to you. I have a feeling the devil's urn would be quite a pleasant culinary experience if it were stuffed with crabmeat, cheese, and bread crumbs and baked for a good long time—but I admit I haven't done this, and mycologist Tom Volk has pointed out that *anything* would be good if it were stuffed with crabmeat, cheese, and bread crumbs and baked for a long time.

Recommended Recipe: Stuff with crabmeat, cheese, and bread crumbs. Bake for a long time.

 Boletus parasiticus

Edibility Rating: Fair.

Distinguishing Features: This small bolete is found in eastern North America and grows *only* as a parasite attached to the poisonous puffball *Scleroderma citrinum*. *Boletus parasiticus* has a dry, yellowish-brown to

Photo by David Work

Focus Point

Mycoparasites

The mycelium of *Boletus parasiticus* attacks the puffball and kills it. Poor puffball. To be honest, I have real doubts (which I'll detail in a moment) about whether *Boletus parasiticus* is actually a parasite, but it is the classic textbook representative for "mycoparasites"—fungal parasites that parasitize fungi. The other mycoparasite in the book is *Hypomyces lactifluorum*, the Lobster Mushroom (edible; p. 267), which is a relative of the whitish fuzz attacking the small *Boletus parasiticus* in the photo, *Hypomyces chrysospermus*—a parasite parasitizing a parasite! Fungi parasitize all kinds of things (every potato plant in Ireland in 1845, for example), but the mushroom-producing fungi that are parasites tend to attack other mushrooms, trees and woody plants, or insects. The latter case is particularly grotesque, and the principal practitioners are in the genus *Cordyceps* (inedible; not treated in this book)—including *Cordyceps militaris*, which re-creates that infamous scene from the movie *Alien* by erupting from the pupae of butterflies and moths. By far the most common parasites in the mush-

room world, however, are the species that attack living trees; see the chicken of the woods (edible; p. 82) for a discussion of these mushrooms. Now here's why I wonder about the putative parasitism of *Boletus parasiticus*. Shouldn't the parasitized organism die or at least get discouraged? In over fifteen years of searching, John David Moore and I have only found *Boletus parasiticus* in one location, which he describes on p. 98. There is never a shortage of *Scleroderma citrinum* in this place, even in the many years when the theoretically parasitizing bolete is absent. When populations of true parasites—the honey mushrooms (edible; p. 244) for example—move through victim populations, the victims are wiped out and the parasites move on to new ground. We have not tracked precise fruiting locations of the *Scleroderma* and *Boletus* within this small area, but the puffballs are everywhere, every year, and show no signs of victimization (except for the nearly illiterate message one of them scrawled on a log one year: "HeLp uZ PleeZ"). Our experience suggests some kind of mutualism between the two species—and it is interesting to note that both *Scleroderma citrinum* and most species of *Boletus* are mycorrhizal.

olive-brown cap, a yellow to olive-yellow pore surface that does not turn blue when bruised, a pale or brownish stem that is usually adorned with tiny brown fibers and lacks a ring, pale yellow flesh that does not turn blue when sliced, an olive spore print, and a cap that turns orange brown or reddish brown when a drop of ammonia is applied. The golden yellow puffball host (which you are *not* going to eat, since it is poisonous) is hard, has a prominently scale-studded surface, and features a black to purplish-black interior.

Ecology: *Boletus parasiticus* is one of only a few parasites in this book and is always attached to the puffball *Scleroderma citrinum* (which is a mycorrhizal partner with hardwoods and conifers). It appears in summer and fall throughout eastern North America, though it is, in my experience, rather rare.

Poisonous Look-Alikes: Poisonous boletes (p. 53).

Comments: Although the mushroom itself is rather nondescript, I am recommending it for beginners because of its habitat. If your putative *Boletus parasiticus* is *not* growing on a tough, scaly puffball, do *not* eat it as a beginner, since it is probably something else. No other bolete is known to grow on puffballs of any kind. Though *Boletus parasiticus* is not the most common of mushrooms, beginners who find it have a wonderful opportunity to learn how the features of boletes are described and used for identification (see the Focus Point "Boletes," p. 78) since the habitat alone identifies the mushroom and the features can then be described and compared to descriptions in field guides.

In the Woods: (John David Moore) This mushroom is worth finding if only because of its rarity and rather grotesque relationship with the inedible puffball, *Scleroderma citrinum*. The puffball inhabits a variety of environments, but the only place I have found it succumbing to the parasitic charms of the bolete is in a hemlock bog, growing on decayed stumps and in thick needle duff. Indeed, several sources mention hemlock (and sometimes pine) as part of this bolete's milieu. Although *Scleroderma citrinum* can be found in such bogs even in drier seasons, wet conditions appear to be required to produce *Boletus parasiticus* in large numbers. In northern regions, look for it in late August or September and examine your puffball finds carefully; the young *Boletus parasiticus* emerges from the base of the *Scleroderma* and is often concealed by its bulk. Separate the boletes from their hosts and clean them well in the field—hemlock needles often stick tightly to the caps.

In the Kitchen: (John David Moore) Clean your finds under running water with a brush to remove the needles that you may have failed to remove in the field. Remove the tubes from older individuals. As with most boletes, they may be slimy when cooked. You may be disappointed by the weak flavor of this bolete. Quite frankly, it's not one of the best for culinary purposes. It does, however, have a mild taste of carrot and a chewy texture. Its carroty quality possibly recommends membership in a stew featuring root vegetables and other, more flavorful mushrooms. Feel free to experiment.

13 The Black Trumpet: *Craterellus cornucopioides*

Edibility Rating: Great.

Distinguishing Features: Black trumpets are funnel-shaped, terrestrial mushrooms that lack gills, false gills, pores, or teeth. They are small or medium in size (usually between 2 and 7 cm tall), and they are grayish or black. The inside surface is smooth or sometimes a little scaly. The outer surface is smooth or very slightly wrinkled. It is blackish until maturity, when the maturing spores can create a whitish, yellowish, or pale salmon dusting. The upper edge is often curled over when the mushroom is young. The flesh is very thin and brittle, and the mushroom is completely hollow. The spore print is white, yellowish, or pinkish yellow.

Ecology: Black trumpets are officially mycorrhizal partners with trees, but it would not surprise me if mycologists were to discover they are saprobes—additionally, or exclusively. Their relationship with moss is worthy of mycological investigation in my humble amateur's opinion. I challenge you to find an in-situ photo of *Craterellus cornucopioides* on the Internet or in a book that does not have moss or sphagnum in it.

Regardless of their precise ecological role, however, black trumpets grow on the ground, often in mossy areas. In eastern North America, black trumpets tend to grow gregariously or in small clusters of two or three mushrooms. On the West Coast, dense clusters are the rule. They appear under hardwoods or (more rarely) conifers in summer and fall in most areas of the continent and in winter in California.

Poisonous Look-Alikes: None.

Comments: Although black trumpets are fairly unmistakable, they are occasionally confused with the devil's urn (edible; p. 94), which appears in clusters on hardwood sticks in early spring and has a gobletlike, rather than vaselike or funnel-like, shape. Eastern North America's *Craterellus foetidus* (edible; p. 101) is very similar, but it has a somewhat veined undersurface and a stronger sweet odor; it tends to grow in clusters of three or more mushrooms. Several tiny species of *Craterellus* are more or less identical, except for their size; they are too small to consider for the table. Recent DNA evidence has led to the elimination of several former black trumpet species that had been delineated primarily on the basis of their spore print colors (*Craterellus fallax* and *Craterellus konradii*); these are now included in the broad species *Craterellus cornucopioides*. A yellow form of the black trumpet is (rarely) found on the West Coast, and whitish forms appear (again, rarely) across the continent.

In the Woods: (John David Moore) If they are not growing on rich, green moss, black trumpets are a challenge to spot, even in the open, on a trail, or in a spot clear of leaf litter. I have trampled them many a time to my dismay. The best strategy upon locating a cluster is to stop moving, get down on the ground, and examine the terrain with care. Harvesting the tasty clusters should be done carefully, with a knife, so as not to pull up the dirty substratum. Since they are small and fragile, cleaning can wait till you get them home.

In the Kitchen: (John David Moore) Wash your collection under running water to remove the grit that can accumulate in the black trumpet's wavy folds. Drain them thoroughly before sautéing a few to savor their excellent nutty flavor and somewhat chewy texture. Black trumpets gain flavor through drying, and fresh or dried they make an excellent addition to a rice dish.

Recommended Recipes: Beef Stroganoff with Wild Mushrooms (p. 303); Portuguese Steak with Mushrooms (p. 309).

14 *Craterellus foetidus*

Edibility Rating: Great.

Distinguishing Features: *Craterellus foetidus* is very similar to the black trumpet (*Craterellus cornucopioides*, p. 99), so I will refer you to the distinguishing features of that mushroom and highlight only the differences here. Unlike the black trumpet, *Craterellus foetidus* develops a veined and wrinkled undersurface, primarily along the upper edge. It also has a stronger, sweeter odor—which is best detected when several specimens are placed together in your bag or basket—though the odor can be weak or absent in dry weather. On average, it is a little bit (*just a little bit*) stockier and fleshier than the average *Craterellus cornucopioides* specimen, and in age it can become quite pale.

Ecology: See my comments under "Ecology" for the black trumpet. *Craterellus foetidus* tends to grow in clusters of three or more mushrooms. It takes a surprisingly long time to grow to maturity; I have tracked the development of fruiting bodies for over two weeks.

Poisonous Look-Alikes: None.

Comments: Compare *Craterellus foetidus* to the black trumpet (edible; p. 99) and the devil's urn (edible; p. 94). A few other blackish to grayish species of *Craterellus* with veined undersurfaces are occasionally encountered, but these have a more solid stem. They are not toxic, but they taste awful.

In the Woods: Like the black trumpet, *Craterellus foetidus* is very hard to find, even in seasons when it fruits in large numbers. In my area (central Illinois) it can be found with diligent searching on mossy ridgetops in oak-hickory woods in early summer. Once you have found a spot, return to it in subsequent years since *Craterellus foetidus* will keep appearing. Trim off the bases, which are often covered with grit, before putting your mushrooms in your paper bag or basket.

In the Kitchen: *Craterellus foetidus* should be prepared just like black trumpets; its flavor is similar and just as good—or even better. Although it does well in many recipes, it is best, I think, when briefly sautéed and served over steak. *Craterellus foetidus* dries well, but it can be tough and leathery when reconstituted, especially if you try to eat the mushrooms whole. The dried mushrooms are better when crumbled into tiny pieces and used more as a spice than a main ingredient.

Hericium Species

Edibility Rating: Good.

Distinguishing Features: These distinctive mushrooms grow from the wood of hardwoods and conifers across the continent. They lack caps, and feature long, dangling "teeth" or "spines" that are pale, fairly soft, and about 1 to 6 cm in length. One species, *Hericium erinaceus*, is pretty much a mere clump of these spines, and no stem structures or supporting branches are immediately evident. In this species the spines are fairly long, averaging about 4 cm. They are initially white but discolor yellowish or pale brownish with age. This species is usually found on standing hardwoods, well above the ground, growing from wounds in the bark. The other species of *Hericium* are usually found on fallen logs and feature spines that hang from branched structures. *Hericium coralloides* has short, whitish spines averaging about 1 cm in length; it grows

on the wood of hardwoods. *Hericium americanum,* also a hardwood lover, has longer spines that average 3 to 4 cm in length. *Hericium abietis* of the Pacific Northwest grows from the wood of conifers and has short, whitish to pinkish spines that average about 1 cm in length.

Ecology: *Hericium* species are wood-rotting saprobes, and *Hericium erinaceus,* at least, is also a parasite that attacks living trees. They tend to grow alone and usually appear in summer and fall (or in winter in warm climates). *Hericium erinaceus* and *Hericium coralloides* are widespread on the continent, while *Hericium americanum* is limited to eastern North America and *Hericium abietis* grows in the Pacific Northwest.

Poisonous Look-Alikes: None.

Comments: Most other mushrooms with spines or teeth grow from the ground and have caps and well-defined, more or less central stems (including the edible hedgehog mushrooms, p. 104). A few polypores have teeth rather than pores. *Climacodon septentrionale* (inedible; not treated in this book) is the most common of these. But, while these mushrooms grow from wood, they feature caps and are not likely to be confused with *Hericium* species.

In the Woods: (John David Moore) Unfortunately, *Hericium* species are not common. Their size (a specimen of *Hericium abietis* weighing one hundred pounds is on record), however, compensates for their rarity. Also unfortunate, particularly in the case of *Hericium erinaceus*, is their inaccessibility since they often grow high on tree trunks, well beyond the greedy grasp of ordinary mortals. Whether or not it's worth hauling an extension ladder along on your forays is up to you. When you've located an accessible *Hericium*, you will need to cut it away from its host tree or log with a knife. These mushrooms are tough, and a seriously sharp knife will be needed to trim them for suitable cooking. The stubbornly tough bases should be avoided unless you've got the time to cook them for hours. Older specimens, particularly those of *Hericium erinaceus*, should be left to their decorative forest function since they can be rather smelly and develop a sour taste.

In the Kitchen: (John David Moore) All *Hericium* species are highly watery, which makes drying them for preservation a chore. Moreover, reconstituting dried *Hericium* species in water also takes time and yields a mushroom even tougher than the fresh one. Sautéing and then freezing is probably the best method of keeping a supply on hand for awhile. I've found the branched *Hericium americanum* and *Hericium coralloides* to be the most delectable and attractive of this genus. Slow and prolonged cooking is needed to bring these tough mushrooms to a pleasant, chewy texture. This method also assures that the abundant water in the mushroom cooks off before you add butter and seasoning. It also helps to cut them small and thin, preserving some of their appealing, coral-like shape. Unseasoned and sautéed, *Hericium* species have a fruity and vaguely lemony taste that is improved by salt and pepper and perfected with the addition of lemon juice, which enhances the natural fruitiness of the flavor. Sautéed and then marinated, *Hericium* species make an attractive ingredient in shrimp dishes, including shrimp salads.

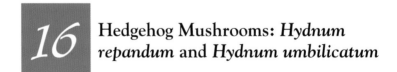

16 Hedgehog Mushrooms: *Hydnum repandum* and *Hydnum umbilicatum*

Edibility Rating: Great.

Distinguishing Features: Hedgehogs are small to medium-sized terrestrial mushrooms that feature spines (or "teeth," if you prefer) rather than gills or pores. The caps are brownish yellow to pale orangish, and have a smooth or somewhat roughened surface. The spines, which are found on the underside of the cap, are colored like the cap (or a little paler) and are less than 1 cm in length. They often bruise or discolor dark orange to yellowish brown. The stem is fleshy and whitish, but brown stains often develop on its surface in age or when it is handled. The flesh is white and fairly soft—not tough or leathery. The odor is mild, and the taste is mild or slightly peppery. The spore print is white.

Ecology: *Hydnum repandum* is widely distributed in North America and grows alone, scattered, or gregariously on the ground under hardwoods and/or conifers. *Hydnum umbilicatum* grows gregariously in conifer bogs in northern and montane North America and in the Great Lakes region. These species may be mycorrhizal and/or saprobic—or even parasitic; there is evidence that some *Hydnum* species cause heartwood rot in living trees.

Poisonous Look-Alikes: None.

Above: photo by Dianna Smith

Comments: *Hydnum repandum* has a large cap (2–17 cm wide), while *Hydnum umbilicatum* has a smaller cap (2–6 cm wide) that often features a central depression or "navel." Other spiny or toothed mushrooms with caps and more or less central stems are either extremely tough and leathery (e.g., *Hydnellum* species—inedible; not treated in this book) or feature scaly caps, unpleasant tastes, or mealy odors (*Sarcodon* species—inedible; not treated). Research has shown that the hedgehogs are fairly closely related to the chanterelles (edible; pp. 135 and 139).

In the Woods: (John David Moore) Hedgehog mushrooms have the virtue of being shunned by maggots and kindred vermin. *Hydnum* species are best cleaned in the field since dirt from caps and stems may get into the mushrooms' delicate, crumbly teeth, where even the best kitchen dentist loses patience trying to remove it. A delicate brushing of the cap, stem, and especially the fragile spines or teeth should suffice before bagging and later cooking your harvest. Before it is added to the pan, *Hydnum umbilicatum* should be halved lengthwise to check the recesses of its "navel" for dirt and vagrant insects.

Focus Point
Toothed Mushrooms

Mushrooms with spines or teeth, like all mushrooms, are spore factories. Like gills or pores, the teeth serve to increase the production area; each tooth is covered with microscopic spore-manufacturing machinery. Some toothed mushrooms, like the hedgehogs, have central stems and grow on the ground. Others grow on wood and lack stems, resembling polypores until their undersides are inspected (the same has been said of me, incidentally). Species of *Hericium* (edible; p. 102) have developed the tooth strategy so far that virtually nothing is left but the teeth. Occasionally, the pore surfaces of some polypores will develop toothlike structures, especially near the point of attachment to the wood—but while this is sometimes a useful character in identifying these polypores, they are primarily "poroid" (featuring pores), to use the Mycologese term, rather than "dentate" (featuring teeth).

In the Kitchen: (John David Moore) Sautéed slowly or lengthily, both species of *Hydnum* are delectable, yielding a tender, meaty texture and a mild flavor. Although most mushrooms are, like us, mostly water, hedgehogs tend to absorb rather than yield liquid in cooking. Hence they pick up the flavors of added ingredients.

Recommended Recipes: Pasta with Hedgehogs, Bacon, and Tomato (p. 308).

Lactarius indigo

Edibility Rating: Fair.

Distinguishing Features: There are not many blue mushrooms, and *Lactarius indigo* is very distinct. It is a medium-sized gilled mushroom that grows under hardwoods or conifers across eastern and southern North America. Its centrally depressed cap is silvery blue, with faint concentric zones of color. Green stains develop with age or when the cap is bruised. The surface is smooth or finely roughened. The edge of the cap is rolled under when the mushroom is young. The dark blue gills are attached to the stem or begin to run down it and also discolor green. When damaged with a knifepoint, they exude a dark blue juice. They are not covered by a partial veil when the mushroom is young. The stem is also silvery blue (discoloring green) and is rather short in proportion to the cap. It tapers toward the base and is usually pockmarked with little potholes. There is no ring on the upper stem and no sack around the base. The flesh is crumbly and whitish but turns immediately blue when sliced. It, too, exudes a blue juice. The spore print is white or creamy.

Ecology: *Lactarius indigo* is a mycorrhizal partner with hardwoods and conifers (see the Focus Point "Mycorrhizal Mushrooms," which follows). It grows alone, scattered, or gregariously in summer and fall. It is fairly widely distributed in eastern North America, though it appears to be more common the farther south you go. It has also been reported in Arizona.

Poisonous Look-Alikes: None.

Comments: Other blue mushrooms (some of which are poisonous) are not at all squat like *Lactarius indigo* and do not exude blue juice when damaged. *Lactarius chelidonium* (edibility unknown; not treated in this book) can have a silvery blue sheen when in the button stage, and the sliced flesh can be bluish. However, it has yellowish to pale brownish gills, yellowish or yellowish-brown juice, and soon becomes greenish, orangish, or brownish—in short, by maturity it is not at all blue.

In the Woods: (John David Moore) In the Midwest, look for this striking blue mushroom in mid- to late summer in mixed woods. It's not picky about where it appears; conifers and hardwoods suit it equally. Field cleaning may do an incomplete job if the cap of *Lactarius indigo* has become slimy due to wet conditions. It will then have some debris stuck to it that will best be removed under running water at home.

In the Kitchen: (John David Moore) Clean any remaining debris from your collection with a brush, a damp cloth, or running water, depending on how attached the stuff is to the caps. When slicing, check for larvae and dispose of any mushrooms too infested to be saved by trimming. You may need to cook this mushroom longer than three or four minutes so that the characteristic grainy texture of the genus *Lactarius* disappears.

Focus Point
Mycorrhizal Mushrooms

Mycorrhizal mushrooms are involved in symbiotic relationships with trees or woody plants. The tiny rootlets of the tree form "mycorrhizae" with the mycelium of the mushroom: the fungal cells surround the rootlets, creating a protective sheath that helps the tree absorb water and nutrients. In exchange, the fungus gets goodies it needs from the tree. Estimates vary, but it is safe to say that *nearly all* of the major natural trees in North America have evolved completely dependent on this symbiotic relationship—and the same is true, in reverse, for the fungi. In short, trees do not survive without mycorrhizal fungi, and the fungi cannot make it without the trees. Recent studies of the mycorrhizal relationship, armed with DNA technology, have been able to judge what fungal mycelia are present in studied tree communities (this was nearly impossible before DNA analysis since fungal mycelia are often virtually indistinguishable otherwise)—and the preliminary results are a bit disconcerting. In the words of one of these studies, "[T]here is a poor correspondence between species that fruit abundantly, and those that are abundant on roots" (Horton and Bruns 2001, p. 1862). In other words, though you may find *Lactarius indigo* popping up everywhere under your favorite woodland oak tree, you may have difficulty finding evidence of its mycelium in a soil sample. On the other hand, you may find all kinds of mycelia that are *not* producing mushrooms. Mycologists are still uncertain as to how to interpret this unexpected finding.

Sautéed, *Lactarius indigo* has a tender consistency and a delicate but indistinct flavor. One of its virtues is that it retains its indigo hue when cooked. This mushroom has "presentation" written all over it and should be used in dishes in which its unusual color can be displayed to advantage.

Recommended Recipes: Salted Mushroom Salad (p. 309).

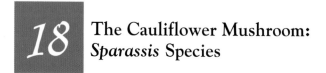

18 The Cauliflower Mushroom: *Sparassis* Species

Edibility Rating: Great.

Distinguishing Features: The cauliflower mushroom grows at the bases of trees—in eastern North America under hardwoods and under conifers in the west. It is officially a polypore, but thinking of it as such is likely to cause confusion among beginners, who expect (correctly, most of the time) polypores to be fleshier mushrooms with clearly identifiable tube layers and pore surfaces. Alexander Smith, one of the giants of North American mycology, described the cauliflower mushroom as "resembling a cluster of egg noodles," and this comparison works very well. The cluster can be quite large (up to 60 cm across), and the individual "noodles" are thin and crisp, attached to branches that arise from a massive fleshy structure. The surfaces often have a faintly greasy feel to them and are whitish to yellowish (especially with age). The large, fleshy stem structure is rooted in the ground or wood; in one western cauliflower mushroom the underground portion can be quite long. The flesh is firm and whitish. The spore print is white.

Ecology: Species of *Sparassis* are parasites on living tree roots and saprobes on deadwood, causing a yellow or brown rot. They appear next to the trunk (or stump) on the ground but are attached to the wood beneath. The western cauliflower mushroom attacks conifers, and the eastern version prefers hardwoods, though it will attack conifers in a pinch. The cauliflower mushroom appears in summer and fall or in winter in warm climates.

Below: Shannon Stevens holding a cauliflower mushroom (see Shannon's entry on pickled stinkhorn eggs, p. 198)

Poisonous Look-Alikes: None.

Comments: Although this delicious mushroom is fairly unmistakable, beginners should compare it with the hen of the woods (edible; p. 163) and especially *Polyporus umbellatus* (edible; p. 207).

In the Woods: Younger, whiter specimens are the best for the table. Slice the cauliflower mushroom near the ground, high enough that you avoid as much dirt as possible. It is worth giving your cauliflower mushroom a healthy, upside-down shake before putting it in your basket (don't watch what falls out if you're squeamish). Since the cauliflower mushroom is large and does not fare very well when preserved, you will probably only need to collect one healthy specimen.

In the Kitchen: Cleaning this mushroom is, as one might expect, a royal pain. A combination of shaking and slicing away unpalatable sections will remove some of the debris and vermin, but a good, thorough washing under running water is the best strategy. The cauliflower is not particularly absorbent, making it a mushroom that can withstand immersion in water. The massive stem structure is tougher than the "noodles," and you may want to treat the cauliflower mushroom more or less as one treats a real cauliflower or broccoli spear, using only the tender outer portions. The taste is remarkably like that of yellow morels (edible; p. 87), in my opinion, and the cauliflower mushroom works well in morel-friendly dishes—though it requires longer, slower cooking. Some authors recommend parboiling it before cooking it in recipes.

Experience Required

*T*he mushrooms in this section, in my judgment, require some experience with identification before they can be safely picked and eaten. Even though there are several fantastic edible mushrooms you have probably heard about in this section—such as the chanterelles (pp. 135 and 139) and the king bolete (p. 123)—I don't recommend that you eat them in your first season of hunting wild mushrooms. They are not *difficult*, but they are not easy to identify either.

The poisonous look-alikes now include *deadly*, not merely poisonous, species—which ought in itself to deter anyone from taking the matter too lightly. Readers familiar with the so-called Foolproof Four— four edible mushrooms that some authors believe are distinctive enough to be foolproof—may notice that I have put *three* of them under the "Experience Required" heading. Perhaps I am being too conservative, but I did not eat any of the species in this section for several years after I got excited about mushrooms and, well, I am still alive.

The Focus Points scattered throughout the section are meant, as always, to help you add to your mushroom identification repertoire.

19 The Prince: *Agaricus augustus*

Edibility Rating: Great.

Distinguishing Features: The prince is a large gilled mushroom found in western North America (but see "Comments" for *Agaricus subrufescens*, which is widely distributed). It grows on the ground, usually in disturbed-ground settings. The cap is often blocky and squarish when the mushroom is young, but expands to broadly convex or nearly flat in maturity. Its dry surface is adorned with small brownish to golden brown scales, and the center area is often darker than the rest. When rubbed repeatedly, the edge of the cap will sometimes turn yellowish. The gills are free from the stem and are covered with a tissuelike partial veil when young. They are initially pale and remain so for quite a long time before turning dark brown when the spores mature (sometimes exhibiting a pinkish stage in between). The stem is thick and substantial. Its surface is often shaggy and frequently features golden brown scales like those on the cap. In many collections the stem bruises and discolors yellowish. A prominent, skirtlike ring hangs on the upper stem. There is no sack around the stem's base. The flesh is white and thick and is *not* bright yellow in the stem base. The odor is thickly sweet and reminiscent of almonds. The spore print is chocolate brown.

Ecology: *Agaricus augustus* is a saprobe found in the woods—usually in disturbed-ground areas (along paths, in clearings, and so on) or in urban areas under trees. Its primary distribution is on the West Coast, where it appears in spring and summer. In older field guides the prince is sometimes listed as "widely distributed," but eastern collections probably represent *Agaricus subrufescens* or similar species (see "Comments").

Poisonous Look-Alikes: *Agaricus xanthodermus* and other *Agaricus* species (p. 70); species of *Amanita* (p. 43).

Comments: *Agaricus subrufescens* (which is apparently widely distributed in North America) is a robust species very similar to the prince. It has an even stronger almond odor. It may be the case that *Agaricus augustus* and *Agaricus subrufescens* can be definitively separated on the basis of microscopic features, but the *augustus*-like species of *Agaricus*

Above: Agaricus augustus (photo by Taylor Lockwood); *below: Agaricus subrufescens* (photo by Pam Kaminski)

are currently under investigation by mycologists and a definitive method for separating the mushrooms on the basis of field characters has yet to emerge. The cultivated *Agaricus blazei*, of Internet and junk e-mail fame, is apparently identical to *Agaricus subrufescens* according to one recent study. Fortunately, given the confused taxonomic state of affairs, no mushroom in the prince's royal entourage is known to be poisonous—but be sure to double-check the almond odor and the flesh in the stem base, which should *not* be bright yellow.

In the Woods: (Darvin DeShazer) Timing is everything for collecting this mushroom. It is loved by grazing mammals, forest snails, and the mushroomer's sworn enemies, insect larvae. You have to collect the prince shortly after it pops up or some other creature will beat you to it. In California, it can be found wherever redwood trees grow, and it often fruits when no other mushrooms are in evidence since the slightest moisture can trigger fruiting, even in the heat of summer. This majestic, golden beauty can be spotted from a distance, and many specimens are collected by means of hunting from the car—which is a dangerous yet common activity among serious fungal foragers.

In the Kitchen: (Darvin DeShazer) The ideal time to harvest the prince is when the partial veil breaks. At this point it has its maximum flavor. After this occurs the mushroom's chemistry changes and the biochemical pathways concentrate on spore maturation, which often causes a change in taste. It's still edible, but it declines in sweetness. All parts of this mushroom are good to eat, and nothing should be wasted. Sliced thin and added raw to a turkey and cheese sandwich is my favorite way to eat it, but small amounts in a chef's salad also get rave reviews. Cooked caps with caramelized onions is a marvelous flavor combination and can be used with rice, polenta, or noodles. The prince can be added to almost any dish because of its strong, rich flavor—but be forewarned: a little goes a long way. Sautéing the prince and adding it to an omelet, for example, will often overpower the eggs.

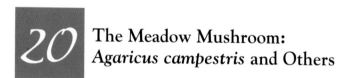

20 The Meadow Mushroom: *Agaricus campestris* and Others

Edibility Rating: Good.

Distinguishing Features: The meadow mushroom is a squat, medium-sized gilled mushroom that grows in grassy areas across North America. Its convex to nearly flat cap is whitish or pale brownish, with a smooth or finely scaly surface (the scales, when present, are usually small and brownish). The edge of the cap, when rubbed repeatedly, may turn slightly pinkish (never yellowish). In wet weather the cap surface may be somewhat watery pink. The gills are free from the stem and are covered by a white partial veil when the mushroom is young. They are deep pink but become dark brown as the spores mature. The stem is fairly

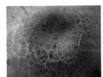  

Lower left: a brown-capped form; *lower right:* a fairy ring (see p. 285)

short and tapers to the base. It occasionally features a fragile ring, but more often the ring disappears. The stem surface is whitish (or pinkish in wet weather or when bruised). There is no sack around the stem's base. The flesh is thick and white and rather hard in the stem. It may turn slightly pink when sliced, but never turns yellowish (the flesh in the extreme base of the stem is *not* bright yellow). The odor is pleasant and mild. The spore print is chocolate brown.

Ecology: *Agaricus campestris* is a saprobe that grows in grassy areas (lawns, meadows, and so on). It grows alone, scattered, or gregariously in late summer and fall (or in winter in warm climates). It is widely distributed in North America.

Poisonous Look-Alikes: *Agaricus xanthodermus* and other *Agaricus* species (p. 70).

Comments: Several similar species, including *Agaricus andrewii* and *Agaricus solidipes*, are virtually indistinguishable without a microscope.

These species, however, are equally edible and delicious, so the point is moot if you are collecting for the table. Forms of the meadow mushroom with pale brownish fibers on the cap are frequently encountered—often growing alongside their whiter, more common counterparts—but sorting out the fine distinctions in the meadow mushroom complex is a task best left to specialists. Compare the meadow mushroom with *Agaricus bisporus* (edible; p. 239), which grows in compost piles (and grocery stores), has a more prominent ring, and bruises pink with more gusto.

In the Field: (John David Moore) In most areas, you can find the meadow mushroom in late summer and through the fall, sometimes up to the first frosts. It often can be spotted from the road on lawns and playing fields, though sometimes it can be hidden in high grass. Keep your eyes scanning the ground about a yard in front of you and take care not to step on young ones couched in the grass. Since the meadow mushroom loves fertilized areas, you may want to avoid gathering grounds that have obviously been treated with chemicals (see p. 20). Use your judgment and be sure to wash your harvest carefully in the kitchen. In the field, check that the gills are pink or, in older specimens, brown. Dig up the base of a few young buttons with a knife to be certain there is no sack around the stem. Discard any individuals that show yellow staining. Once you're sure of what you have, trim the dirty stem bases and brush or wipe clean before bagging. Meadow mushrooms can be dirty. They pick up a lot of grass debris (especially in damp conditions), so you should plan on further cleaning in the kitchen. Gather mature, large individuals as well as young buttons; although they have a much stronger taste, the large, dark-gilled mushrooms are good for stuffing or drying.

In the Kitchen: (John David Moore) Clean your harvest carefully under running water and drain well on dishcloths or paper towels. Sliced and then sautéed, or stewed in their own water, young meadow mushrooms have a rich grassy flavor that ranges from delicate to strong—especially strong if older mushrooms are included. I find that a little goes quite a ways in most cases. The meadow mushroom makes an excellent soup, combines well with other mushrooms, and provides caps that can be effectively stuffed and broiled with seasoned breadcrumbs and a hard grating cheese. They also dry and rehydrate with body and flavor. Fresh ones, if well cleaned, will keep for two or three days in the refrigerator.

Recommended Recipes: Jaeger Sauce for Schnitzel or Steak (p. 306); Stuffed Mushrooms (p. 311).

21 *Albatrellus* Species

Edibility Rating: Good.

Distinguishing Features: Species of *Albatrellus* are terrestrial poly-pores that grow from the ground rather than wood. The caps are often irregularly shaped, and the mushrooms are frequently fused together in small clusters. They have pores on the underside of the cap, but the tube layer runs down the stem and is *not* easily separated (as a layer) as it is in boletes. The stems are frequently off center and lack rings. The flesh is somewhat stringy and leathery. The spore print (which may be difficult to obtain) is white. Western North America's *Albatrellus flettii* and its eastern counterpart, *Albatrellus caeruleoporus*, are the easiest to identify since when fresh and young they are blue or bluish gray (the former is blue on the cap and sometimes the stem but has a white pore surface; the latter is blue overall). Several brownish capped species with green-staining caps, pore surfaces, and/or flesh are com-monly encountered—including *Albatrellus ellisii*, which is found under conifers in west-ern North America, and *Albatrellus cristatus*, which is found under hardwoods (and occa-sionally conifers) in the East. *Albatrellus ovi-nus*, sometimes called the sheep polypore (for reasons I can't imagine) has very tiny pores and a pale cap that becomes yellowish to pinkish brown (or purplish in one form); it grows pri-marily under conifers and is widely distributed—though it is more common in the spruce-fir elevations of the Rocky Mountains than else-where. *Albatrellus confluens* is a widely distrib-uted conifer-loving species that is best separated from *Albatrellus ovinus* with the use of a micro-scope. There are look-alikes for most species of *Albatrellus* (even the blue ones; see "Com-ments"), but none is known to be toxic.

Above: Albatrellus confluens; below: Albatrellus cristatus

Ecology: Species in the genus *Albatrellus* are mycorrhizal partners with trees, which means they are truly terrestrial in their growth (some species of *Polyporus*— e.g., the long-rooted *Polyporus radicatus*—can appear terrestrial but actually arise from underground wood). Most *Albatrellus* species fruit gregariously, often in small clusters.

Poisonous Look-Alikes: None.

Comments: Look-alikes for species of *Albatrellus* include members of the genus *Boletopsis* and some faux-terrestrial mushrooms in the genus *Polyporus*. Most of these impostors can be eliminated by making sure your mushroom has *none* of the following features: a long "root" that extends the stem deep into the ground; a bitter taste; a pore surface that develops purplish-red stains in age or when bruised; a pore surface or flesh that turns blackish when potassium hydroxide is applied; or warted, angular, or cylindrical spores. Chemical reactions and microscopic features are, of course, undeterminable for most amateurs—but, since no species of *Boletopsis* or *Polyporus* is known to be poisonous, confusion with these genera would not constitute a tragic mistake. Species of *Albatrellus*, like most polypores, can cause minor gastric distress to some people, so be sure to follow the precautions on p. 24 when trying them for the first time.

In the Woods: (John David Moore) In early fall in eastern North America, you may find *Albatrellus cristatus* in open woods and grassy glades, often over roots. It is well worth gathering if not old and discolored. It is usually free of larval pests; after it has been cut near the stem base, it requires only some quick brushing in the field before further cleaning in the kitchen. *Albatrellus caeruleoporus* is largely a northern species best hunted in moist areas near streams under a mix of hemlocks and hardwoods. The striking indigo color of this polypore is hard to miss, and it will fruit each fall for several years in the same spot. Avoid older specimens, which are characterized by fading to gray or orange brown. They will be tougher and sometimes invaded by larvae. Check the cut stems of younger individuals for maggots and brush them clean before bagging.

In the Kitchen: (John David Moore) Rinse *Albatrellus cristatus* in water and drain before slicing it across the grain. Cook it slowly for three to five minutes, and you will find it has a robust, nutty flavor and a texture like eggplant but firmer. Slow stewing for longer periods will make it more tender. It recommends itself to treatment like eggplant in a casserole, but its use will depend on how much you are able to gather. Freezing after sautéing or stewing is the best method of preservation since dried specimens tend to be leathery even after long cooking. *Albatrellus caeruleoporus* has a more earthy flavor than *Albatrellus cristatus*—but regrettably, if you like blue foods, it does not retain its color in the pan.

Recommended Recipes: Chicken of the Woods with Lemon Cream (p. 305), substituting *Albatrellus* species for the chicken of the woods; Pasta with Hedgehogs, Bacon, and Tomato (p. 308), substituting *Albatrellus* species for the hedgehogs.

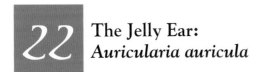

22 The Jelly Ear: *Auricularia auricula*

Edibility Rating: Fair.

Distinguishing Features: Let's put it this way: when you find the jelly ear in the woods, you're not likely to think, "There's my dinner." *Auricularia auricula* appears on sticks, logs, and the wood of living trees as a gelatinous, semitranslucent, brownish thing that usually approximates the shape of an ear or a rubbery cup. This is one mushroom for which careful comparison with a photo goes a long way toward identification, despite my insistent warnings against this strategy. The surface of the jelly ear is often veined, and the flesh is—well, jellylike. Other brownish jelly fungi tend to be more amorphous, resembling shapeless brown

blobs or, in the case of *Tremella foliacea* (edible; not treated in this book), a tightly packed cluster of gelatinous leaves.

Ecology: The jelly ear is a saprobe found on the decaying wood of hardwoods and conifers across North America. It can appear year-round, providing conditions are right. Cooler temperatures appear to be optimal; it is often found by morel hunters in the spring and by honey mushroom enthusiasts in the fall. It can even appear in winter during warm spells or in areas with mild climates. But I have also seen prolific fruitings after heavy rains in the middle of a hot midwestern summer, so the jelly ear should be expected whenever it wants to appear.

Poisonous Look-Alikes: Various brown cup fungi; see "Comments."

Comments: If the flesh of your putative jelly ear is brittle and breakable rather than gelatinous and rubbery (try folding it in half), you have switched mushroom channels to the BBC (boring brown cups) network, and you might as well turn off the TV. The *Peziza repanda Show,* for example, is a very dull crime drama about a brown, inedible cup fungus with a whitish underside. Spin-offs from this show (*Peziza: Miami* among them) are equally boring and inedible, as are the many not so funny sitcoms about life in the wacky *Gyromitra* (née *Discina*) family.

In the Woods: (John David Moore) The bizarre, rubbery jelly ear can be found on dead and decaying wood from spring to fall, and even during winter warm spells. If the right weather prevails, it can be gathered in the same spot repeatedly. Its earlike shape is more apparent in larger, mature specimens. Don't select material that is more mushy than rubbery or that has started to dry and stiffen. The fresh mushroom is best removed from the wood with a knife, and you may have to trim it some around the attached area to remove the rotting wood debris to which it clings tightly. Brush it as clean as possible, bag it, and you'll then have a harvest of the North American counterpart to the black wood ear often sold dried in Asian markets.

In the Kitchen: (John David Moore) A quick rinse in water should clean your jelly ears enough for drying or immediate consumption. Sautéed or stewed for a couple of minutes, they can best be described as chewy Jell-O, lacking any flavor except for the taste of whatever butter or oil you've used. Their sole culinary raison d'être is texture, so add them to clear soups and stir-fried dishes in combination with more flavorful mushrooms. Small jelly ears can be used whole; large ones can be

Focus Point

Jelly Fungi

There are many "jelly fungi" in the world of mycology. Although mycologists define these mushrooms and separate the species primarily on microscopic terms, mushroom hunters can recognize the jelly fungi by their amorphous shapes and gelatinous consistency. The jelly ear is just about the most distinctive and easy to recognize jelly fungus; most of the rest are boring blobs. The question of edibility is not likely to come up once you have seen the jellies (and, according to reports from those who have—unaccountably, in my opinion—tried them, they turn into watery juice in the pan), but you may be interested in trying to identify them—in which case you will need a microscope and a trip to the library for technical literature (my personal favorite treatise is "Jelly Fungi: Then and Now!"). Most jellies grow on wood, though some grow on plants or even on other mushrooms. Some slime molds (particularly *Fuligo septica*, the so-called dog vomit slime, which can appear in gardens and compost piles) might be mistaken for jelly fungi, but these are *so* amorphous that they lack any definable shape at all, refusing to form recognizable, coherent fruiting bodies. Aside from the jelly ear, the jelly fungus most often included in field guides is *Tremella mesenterica*, often called witch's butter, but it has many look-alikes. They are best separated by means of microscopic analysis, so the inclusion of *Tremella mesenterica* in guides should be seen more as a wide portal into Jellystone Mycological Park than a narrow doorway leading to an easily identified species.

sliced in thin strips. Dried ones return to their original rubbery quality when reconstituted. Freezing them is not advised since they become very watery when thawed.

23 *Boletellus russellii*

Edibility Rating: Fair.

Distinguishing Features: This striking bolete grows under conifers or hardwoods in eastern North America. Its brown to reddish-brown cap is smooth at first, but it begins, like many of us, to crack up in middle age, resulting in a mosaiclike appearance. The nonbruising pore surface is yellow or greenish yellow. It is not covered by a partial veil when young. The stem of *Boletellus russellii* is its showpiece: it is quite long in proportion to the cap and deeply pocketed and ridged. It lacks a ring. The flesh, which is soft in the cap but tough in the stem, is pale yellow and does not change color when sliced. The cap surface turns red when

Photo by Pam Kaminski

a drop of ammonia is applied. The spore print is olive brown.

Ecology: *Boletellus russellii* is a mycorrhizal partner with oaks and other hardwoods—and occasionally with conifers. It grows alone or scattered in summer and fall in eastern North America and perhaps in riparian southwestern forests (primarily in Arizona) whose ecosystems mimic those of the East.

Poisonous Look-Alikes: Poisonous boletes (p. 53).

Comments: The edible *Boletellus betula* (not treated in this book) of southeastern North America has a similar shaggy (but yellow) stem; its cap, however, is slimy and yellow. Eastern North America's *Boletus frostii* (not treated) also has a similar stem, but its pore surface is red and it bruises blue. It is apparently edible for some people but affects others negatively; like all red-pored, blue-bruising boletes, it should be avoided. Other boletes with deeply pocketed and ridged stems include *Boletus ornatipes* (edible; p. 126) and *Boletus griseus* (edible; p. 126), which are fairly easily separated on the basis of their colors and proportions. The small genus *Boletellus* is separated from other bolete genera on the basis of microscopic characters.

In the Woods: (John David Moore) This unusual, slightly grotesque bolete is easily recognized by its stem. Look for it in mixed hardwood forests in late summer, where in some years it can be quite common. Minimal cleaning in the field is required. Although older individuals do not have the sponginess of many other boletes, it's best to go after the young ones so that you don't feel obliged to remove the tubes before cooking. *Boletellus russellii* attracts its fair share of larval varmints—another reason to collect young specimens.

In the Kitchen: (John David Moore) After slicing the mushrooms lengthwise to inspect the varmint population, you may prefer to remove the tubes in more mature mushrooms. The woody quality of the stems shouldn't deter you from including them in the pan. Thinly sliced, the stems are pleasantly chewy rather than tough. Sautéed for about three minutes, *Boletellus russellii* unfortunately offers no notable flavor to match its pleasingly substantial texture. It does, however, improve with the company it keeps, absorbing other flavors and mixing well with mushrooms of less substantial body. Dried versions yield a mild, nutty flavor, but they also advance chewiness in the direction of toughness. Crumbling the dried mushrooms before adding them to the liquid of a sauce or stew is recommended. Fresh *Boletellus russellii* work well combined with less chewy mushrooms such as *Cortinarius caperatus* (p. 260) in the famous Polish stew, bigos.

Recommended Recipe: Bigos (Polish Stew) (p. 304).

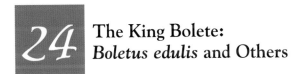

24 The King Bolete: *Boletus edulis* and Others

Edibility Rating: Great.

Distinguishing Features: The king bolete is a stately and impressive mushroom that appears in summer and fall under conifers (especially spruces). Its cap is reddish brown or brown, and has a tacky surface. The pore surface is initially whitish but becomes olive yellow at maturity; it does not change color when bruised. It is not covered by a partial veil when young. The stem, which is often quite swollen when the mushroom is young, has a fine netlike covering of tiny ridges over the upper half—and sometimes over the entire length of the stem. Its surface is whitish or pale brown, and it lacks a ring. The flesh is white and does not change color when sliced. The taste of the flesh is pleasant and not at all bitter. The cap turns orangish when a drop of ammonia is applied. The spore print is olive brown.

Ecology: Several forms of the king bolete occur in North America (see "Comments"), all of which are mycorrhizal. The reddish-capped king of the Rocky Mountains seems to prefer spruces, especially Engelmann spruce. It appears in August during the monsoon season. In eastern North America the king often has a browner cap, and it appears under various conifers—as well as hardwoods—in summer and fall. In California it prefers pines and appears sporadically in the spring and summer, then in large numbers after the first fall rains.

Top row: photos by Pam Kaminski

Poisonous Look-Alikes: Poisonous boletes (p. 53).

Comments: See also the entry for porcini on page 32. There are a number of North American mushrooms that loosely fit the description of the official king bolete, *Boletus edulis,* which was originally described from Europe. Whether any of our kings actually match the "true" king bolete genetically has not to my knowledge been determined. On physical features alone, the reddish-capped form found in the Rocky Mountains is closest to European specimens I have collected. Kings collected under hardwoods east of the Rocky Mountains, in my experience, are browner than their conifer-loving western counterparts and have drier caps. How the problem of the "*edulis* complex" will be resolved, mycologically speaking, is unknown at the moment. DNA analysis may reveal many of these seemingly different mushrooms to be genetically identical—or it may reveal the opposite; a rigorous study of many mushrooms in the complex from across the continent is required. Poisonous look-alikes have red pore surfaces and/or bruise blue. *Tylopilus felleus* (inedible; not treated in this book) is often mistaken for the king bolete—

Focus Point
Reticulation

The king is an excellent representative of the often confused feature known as "reticulation" on the stem. The netlike pattern of raised ridges on the upper stem (see the photo) should be compared with "scabers" (p. 184) and "glandular dots" (p. 220). A great deal is made of reticulation in bolete identification, despite the fact that it can be variable. While a coarsely and prominently reticulate species such as *Boletus ornatipes* (edible; p. 126) is not going to possess a smooth stem, things are not always so black and white, and the "gray area" (in which bolete stems can be "finely reticulate near the apex, or not at all" or "reticulate, at least over the upper half") is larger and grayer than many keys and descriptions would lead one to believe. Outside of the realm of bolete stems, *reticulation* simply refers to a crisscrossed, netted pattern—found, for example, on the spore surfaces of many species of *Lactarius* and *Russula*.

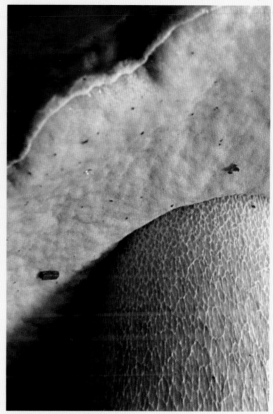

Photo by Pam Kaminski

until it is tasted. Though not poisonous, it has an incredibly bitter taste. Fortunately, the mature pore surface will usually distinguish *Tylopilus felleus* from the king bolete in the field, since it is pink rather than olive. *Xanthoconium separans* (edible; p. 232) has a yellow pore surface and spore print, a stem that is flushed with lilac brown, and surfaces that turn bright green with ammonia. Many other named species of *Boletus* in North America are so close to the king that only a boletologist would care to separate them. They include *Boletus aereus*, *Boletus atkinsonii*, *Boletus barrowsii*, *Boletus nobilissimus*, *Boletus pinophilus*, and *Boletus variipes*.

In the Woods: Despite the fact that I am inclined to agree with mycologist Nicholas Money when he says that picking mushrooms in huge quantities may endanger their survival, I can't help myself when it comes to the king, and the only limits I see have to do with the amount of mushroom dryer space available in my mother's garage. I pick the king during monsoon season in the Rocky Mountains, where my mother has retired, and her entire subdivision smells like boletes by the time I have loaded up my drying trays. When collecting, keep as much of each mushroom as you can since the stems are as good as the caps. Specimens in the button stage are best—but the king's "button stage" can include mushrooms with stems the size of a soup can! Avoid large, splatty specimens unless you are collecting where the king is a rare find and you are desperate for porcini. Brush them clean and bag them or place them in your basket.

In the Kitchen: Clean your mushrooms with a soft-bristled brush or damp cloth; I do not recommend washing the king unless you absolutely have to. Slice thinly and don't hesitate to include the stem. Sautéed for a few minutes the king has a pleasant flavor, but its texture is a bit slug-like when eaten fresh. Drying the king is infinitely preferable. Place the thin slices on your trays with plenty of breathing space and remove them from the dehydrator when they are crisp. See "In the Kitchen" for porcini (p. 33) for cooking tips and recommended recipes.

25 *Boletus griseus* and *Boletus ornatipes*

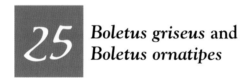

Edibility Rating: Good.

Distinguishing Features: These boletes are found under hardwoods in eastern North America. *Boletus griseus* has a slightly velvety, gray to grayish-brown cap. Its pore surface is whitish to dirty gray and often bruises brownish in age or when handled. It is not covered by a partial veil when young. The stem is covered with a prominent net of raised, crisscrossed ridges, which are whitish or yellowish at first but become brown with age or when handled. The base of the stem develops bright yellow stains—and as the mushroom matures the yellow spreads upward. There is no ring on the stem. The flesh is primarily white but usually bright yellow in the very base of the stem. *Boletus ornatipes* is very similar—as though evolution merely twisted the yellow knob from "medium" to "high." The cap is yellowish to yellow-brown; the pore surface, stem, and flesh are all yellow. Other features parallel those of *Boletus griseus*, including the yellowing—which in *Boletus ornatipes* is best described as "yellower-ing." Neither species bruises blue, and both feature olive brown spore prints and caps that are pale brown or unchanged when ammonia is applied.

Ecology: *Boletus griseus* and *Boletus ornatipes* are mycorrhizal associates with hardwood trees —primarily oaks—in eastern North America. They grow alone, scattered, or gregariously in summer and fall. In my experience, both species are partial to mossy ridgetops.

Poisonous Look-Alikes: Poisonous boletes (p. 53).

Comments: In their "pure" forms these species are fairly easily distinguished from each other— but I have found plenty of "intergrading" specimens so mixed in their features that I gave up trying to decide which species I had collected.

In the Woods: (John David Moore) As an edible, *Boletus griseus* does not get much favorable press, but it's well worth trying. Look for it in mid- to late summer in the central Mid-

Above: Boletus griseus; below: Boletus ornatipes

west and in late August into September farther north. You may find it in open woods where there is a preponderance of oak. The challenge is to find specimens unpopulated by hungry larvae. Together with its rather dull and dirty appearance, the popularity of *Boletus griseus* as a twenty-four-hour larval diner has long kept me from sampling it. The larvae move quickly through this bolete, so field inspection and cleaning/trimming are essential. It's wise to slice the mushrooms in half to check pest progress in specimens that may externally appear young and fresh. Look for *Boletus ornatipes*, the more attractive relative of *Boletus griseus*, along hardwood forest edges and along roads or trails. Although less attractive to varmints than *Boletus griseus*, this golden-hued fungus is best treated in the field with the same cautionary cleaning. In my experience it has the virtue of appearing in both central and northern regions of the Midwest, whereas my collections of *Boletus griseus* have been limited to regions south of the Great Lakes. *Boletus ornatipes* has the vice of occasional bitterness in flavor, perhaps depending on where it's found. It may help to keep your collections separated by fruiting spots when gathering it, so each can be taste tested later.

In the Kitchen: (John David Moore) If you're solidly committed to keeping a supply of *Boletus griseus* on hand, mildly infested mushrooms can be trimmed, washed, drained, and sliced before putting them in a dehydrator. If luck has granted you some pest-free individuals for ready consumption, you may well be pleased with their delicate flavor when they are sautéed for a couple of minutes. They are slightly sweet, with a fruity aftertaste, and the texture is pleasingly firm. Dried and reconstituted in water, however, *Boletus griseus* has a stronger, nuttier flavor. Treat *Boletus ornatipes* as you would *Boletus griseus*, but you may find that a sautéed sample yields a similar flavor with an unfortunate added bitterness. If you've gathered *Boletus ornatipes* in more than one spot and kept the collections separate, you can test each with a small sautéed sample, hoping for an absence of bitterness among some of them. On the other hand, it may not be worth the bother. There are, after all, other mushrooms.

26 *Boletus illudens*

Edibility Rating: Good.

Distinguishing Features: This small to medium-sized bolete grows under oaks in eastern North America. The cap, like the caps of many eastern boletes, is reddish brown and smooth. The pore surface is yellow at first, but develops olive tones in maturity. It does not bruise blue and is not covered with a partial veil when young. The pores are usually fairly large and angular. The stem is tough, frequently short in proportion to the cap, and tapered to the base. It features a very wide-meshed net of raised ridges, usually over the upper third (but sometimes covering nearly the whole stem). It lacks a ring. The flesh is whitish or pale yellow and does not turn blue when sliced. The spore print is olive brown. The most distinctive feature of *Boletus illudens* is the cap's reaction to ammonia: a bright, blue-green flash of color that resolves to gray.

Ecology: *Boletus illudens* is a mycorrhizal partner with oak trees in eastern North America. It grows alone, scattered, or gregariously in summer and fall and is especially fond of disturbed-ground settings such as paths and ditches.

Poisonous Look-Alikes: Poisonous boletes (p. 53).

Comments: Be sure to bruise the pore surface since several poisonous boletes in Group Two (p. 54) look very similar but bruise blue. The cap's reaction to ammonia will also help eliminate confusion with these mushrooms. Confusion with several edible species is also possible, and perhaps inevitable, since *Boletus tenax* and *Boletus spadiceus* are very close in their physical features and also flash green with ammonia. In fact, the distinctions among these three species are tentative at best, and I wouldn't bet the house that they will last once some enterprising young mycologist with a DNA sequencer gets hold of them. Other nonbruising (edible) look-alikes are typically much larger when mature, feature more substantial (more "normal") stems, or lack the blue-green flash created by ammonia.

In the Woods: (John David Moore) *Boletus illudens* tends to be fairly free of parasites, but you should inspect your harvest in the field by removing the stems, which are, in any case, more tough than appetizing. This bolete fruits in mid- to late summer, and I often find it in the company of *Xanthoconium separans* (edible; p. 232) and *Leccinum rugosiceps* (edible; p. 186).

In the Kitchen: (John David Moore) Remove the stems and check for larvae if you haven't already done so in the field. Brush or wipe clean, slice thinly, and sauté slowly for up to ten minutes. These boletes, both young and older specimens, tend to be tough if undercooked. *Boletus illudens* is not spoken well of in some guidebooks, but with sufficient cooking I have found its texture to be pleasingly chewy and its flavor mild and nutty.

 Boletus pallidus

Edibility Rating: Great.

Distinguishing Features: This nondescript, medium-sized, eastern bolete grows under hardwoods. It features a very pale brownish cap with a smooth or very finely suedelike surface. The pore surface is initially whitish but soon becomes yellowish and eventually olive yellow. It is not covered by a partial veil when young. Frustratingly, the pores bruise bluish in some collections, bruise brownish in others, and sometimes do not bruise at all. The stem is smooth and whitish and lacks a netlike covering. In some collections the stem develops brownish stains (especially near the base) and/or pinkish streaks *and/or* yellow hues near the apex. It lacks a ring. The flesh is whitish or pale yellow and sometimes turns slightly sky blue when sliced, especially in the area just over the tubes. However, the flesh is just as likely to remain whitish (or yellowish) or turn slightly pinkish. The cap turns pale orange or demonstrates no reaction when ammonia is applied. The spore print is olive brown.

Ecology: *Boletus pallidus* is a mycorrhizal partner with oak trees in eastern North America. It grows alone, scattered, or gregariously (often in clusters of two or three mushrooms) in summer and fall.

Poisonous Look-Alikes: Poisonous boletes (p. 53).

Comments: As you can tell from the description, *Boletus pallidus* can't make up its mind on several of the features that usually help distinguish boletes. Don't mushrooms read field guides so they know what they're supposed to look like? The stable features of *Boletus pallidus* are its pale cap, smooth stem, and white then yellow then olive pore surface. When it bruises blue (which is about two-thirds of the time in my experience) it does so faintly—which helps to separate it from two of its closest look-alikes, which bruise with more gusto, more of the time. One of these species, *Boletus inedulis* (edibility unknown; not treated in this book), also grows under oaks but typically develops darker red colors on its stem. The other, *Boletus huronensis* (edible; not treated in this book), grows only under hemlock, has a swollen stem base, and has a cap that flashes green with a drop of ammonia.

In the Woods: (John David Moore) This is an especially common mushroom in northern hardwood forests, where it can be found singly or sometimes in close clusters from late July to early September, weather permitting. Look for it especially in forests featuring oak. Although it rivals the king bolete (p. 123) in flavor, it is considerably less robust and soon becomes spongy. Thus the youngest and firmest individuals are best for consuming fresh. Gather older, larvae-free specimens for the dryer. Cleaning in the field may involve removing leaf litter stuck to the caps under rainy conditions.

In the Kitchen: (John David Moore) You may have to further clean your collection with water if any leaf litter can't be removed in the field. Otherwise a soft mushroom brush or a paper towel should do the job. Slice lengthwise to check for parasites and separate older, softer specimens for drying. You may prefer to remove the tubes from the older and larger mushrooms before drying. Fresh *Boletus pallidus* sautéed for two minutes tastes slightly nutty and woody, with a soft texture in the caps and more chewiness in the stems. A bit of salt enhances the nutty quality, which also becomes more pronounced in the dried state. I have found that finely chopped, reconstituted *Boletus pallidus*, combined with Parmesan cheese and parsley, makes a successful stuffing for ravioli.

Recommended Recipes: Mushroom Quiche (p. 307); Mushroom Ravioli (p. 307).

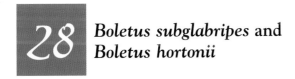

28 *Boletus subglabripes* and *Boletus hortonii*

Edibility Rating: Fair.

Above: Boletus subglabripes; below: Boletus hortonii

Distinguishing Features: *Boletus subglabripes* is a medium-sized bolete of eastern North America. Its orangish-brown to cinnamon-brown or reddish-brown cap is smooth or slightly wrinkled (*very* wrinkled in *Boletus hortonii*). Its pore surface is yellow, becoming olive yellow with maturity; in most collections it does not bruise blue, but in some it will bruise faintly blue. The pores are not covered with a partial veil when young. The stem is almost never swollen. It is whitish to pale yellow but usually features reddish streaks and colorations, often in the form of tiny fibers or dots near the apex (the apical dots can also be yellow, especially when the mushroom is young). It lacks a ring. The flesh is white or pale yellow and very soft. In some collections the flesh turns fleetingly very pale blue when sliced. The cap shows no reaction or turns slightly reddish when ammonia is applied. The spore print is olive.

Ecology: *Boletus subglabripes* is mycorrhizal and grows under hardwoods (especially birch) and conifers. It is a fairly common mushroom in many eastern North American forests, appearing in summer and fall. *Boletus hortonii* is mycorrhizal with hardwoods and also appears in summer and fall in eastern North America.

Poisonous Look-Alikes: Poisonous boletes (p. 53).

Comments: Compare *Boletus subglabripes* carefully with the potentially poisonous mushrooms in Group Two (p. 54). It is usually larger than most of these species and does not bruise blue as dramatically (if it all). The safest course is to avoid eating any blue-bruising boletes—especially those with reddish-brown caps and yellow pore surfaces—until you have complete confidence in your ability to identify species. *Boletus hortonii*, with its distinctively corrugated cap, is easier to separate from look-alikes. Even so, collections that demonstrate faint bluing should probably be avoided by beginners. *Boletus subglabripes* and *Boletus hortonii*, if they are indeed separate species, often appear to "intergrade," and collections are frequently made in which the cap is a little too wrinkled to fit *Boletus subglabripes* but not wrinkled enough to merit the *Boletus hortonii* label.

In the Woods: (John David Moore) Look for these boletes in mixed woods during the months when most boletes abound. Limit your collecting to young mushrooms since these species—especially *Boletus subglabripes*—become soft and spongy fairly quickly. They are favored by larvae, so cut through the stems in the field to check for larval tunnels. Also slice a few of your specimens from each gathering spot to check for bluing flesh—a sign that your finds are probably best left alone if you are a beginner. Brush the mushrooms clean before bagging and plan on further inspection for varmints when you get to the kitchen.

In the Kitchen: (John David Moore) Since the caps can be tacky, especially under wet conditions, you may need to do additional cleaning with a brush and damp cloth to remove attached debris. Remove the tubes from more mature specimens if you've gathered any. These may be spongy and thus best for the dryer. Keep an eye out for larval infestation when slicing them for the pan or dryer. *Boletus hortonii* has the virtue of being more free of varmints, and it is also firmer in texture. Both species, when sautéed for two to three minutes, have a tender texture and mild, nutty flavor. Neither, however, ranks among the more flavorful boletes. Drying improves the flavor somewhat, and, fresh or dried, these boletes mix well with other, more distinctive mushrooms.

Boletus zelleri

Edibility Rating: Mediocre.

Distinguishing Features: This gorgeous bolete is found on the West Coast under conifers and hardwoods. Its cap, when young, is dark brown or nearly black and often conspicuously wrinkled or corrugated. As it matures the cap sometimes becomes smoother and lighter brown. In old age it usually develops a cracked surface, and reddish flesh can be seen between the cracks. The pore surface is yellow and becomes olive with maturity. It occasionally bruises bluish, but in most collections is nonbruising. It is not covered with a partial veil when young. The smooth

Left and middle: photos by Hugh Smith

stem can be completely red, especially when young, but is often yellowish or tan with reddish granules overlaid. It lacks a ring. The flesh is whitish or pale yellow and sometimes turns bluish when sliced. The cap displays no reaction when ammonia is applied. The spore print is olive.

Ecology: *Boletus zelleri* is presumed to be mycorrhizal since it is a species of *Boletus*. It appears in fall, winter, and spring, growing alone, scattered, or gregariously on the ground under various West Coast hardwoods and conifers. But it is also reported under redwoods, sometimes growing in the very rotted wood of ancient trunks, by many authors (including this one). Since this habitat suggests a saprobic role, and no mushrooms are known to be mycorrhizal with redwoods, one wonders.

Poisonous Look-Alikes: Poisonous boletes (p. 53).

Comments: When it is being picturesque, *Boletus zelleri* is fairly unmistakable. However, it is often caught with its guard down, not ready to say "cheese," and in this state it can resemble several boring, brownish boletes, including *Boletus chrysenteron* (edible; not treated in this book), which also has a cracked cap with reddish flesh between the cracks. The latter species, however, has a paler cap when young, usually has a more slender stem, and grows only under hardwoods, especially in disturbed-ground settings. If you are not already familiar with *Boletus zelleri*, be sure to collect and identify it several times, with collections representing all stages of development, before trying it.

In the Woods: (Darvin DeShazer) This small bolete is often found at the edges of forests, along footpaths, and on the banks of road cuts. The variability of both the red stem and the saturation of colors on the cap leads to confusion with *Boletus chrysenteron*. However, both are edible and of about the same quality.

In the Kitchen: (Darvin DeShazer) *Boletus zelleri* can be used as a filler mushroom and thus add bulk to any dish. The flavor is almost non-existent, and the texture is poor because it's on the mushy side. Prime specimens are firm and have a lemony flavor, but collectors rarely find enough of the excellent young fruiting bodies to make a dish. However, they dry well, and some claim that drying improves the flavor.

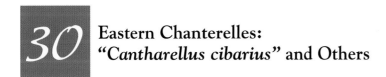

30 Eastern Chanterelles: "*Cantharellus cibarius*" and Others

Edibility Rating: Great.

Distinguishing Features: Chanterelles are medium-sized mushrooms that appear on first glance to have gills but actually have false gills (see the Focus Point "False Gills," p. 137). They grow *on the ground*—in eastern North America primarily in hardwood forests. The caps are broadly convex, flat, or shallowly vase shaped and often feature wavy or irregular edges when mature. The surface is dry and fairly smooth. The cap colors of eastern chanterelles range from egg-yolk yellow to orangish yellow, cinnabar red, or peach. The false gills are colored like the cap (or a little paler) and run down the stem. They are often forked and include many cross-veins. The stem lacks a ring and is colored more or less like the cap. There is no sack around its base. The flesh is thick and white and does not change color when sliced. Fresh chanterelles have a faint but characteristic sweet odor often described as "fruity" or "like apricots." It is best detected when you have several mushrooms together in a paper bag or basket. The spore print is white or pale yellow.

Ecology: Chanterelles are mycorrhizal partners with trees. In eastern North America they are primarily associated with hardwoods, but they don't seem to be too finicky in their choice of arboreal allies and can be found in various types of hardwood forests. They grow alone, scattered, or gregariously in summer and fall.

Poisonous Look-Alikes: *Omphalotus* species (p. 65).

Above: "Cantharellus cibarius"; below: Cantharellus cinnabarinus

Comments: There are several species of chanterelles in eastern North America, including *Cantharellus cinnabarinus*, which is fairly small and bright cinnabar red; the peach colored *Cantharellus persicinus*; and the familiar egg-yolk yellow "*Cantharellus cibarius*," which I have placed in quotation marks because chanterelle experts, now armed with DNA evidence, are beginning to doubt that our North American species matches the original European *Cantharellus cibarius* collected and named in the nineteenth century. In fact North American mycologists are discovering that many of the chanterelles that have been passing as *Cantharellus cibarius* over the years are actually quite distinct genetically and deserve new names (see "Western Chanterelles," pp. 139–40, for some

Focus Point
False Gills

Assessing the false gills of chanterelles is a tougher task than is frequently supposed, if my experience helping mushroom hunters is any indication. Over the years I have tried to create various simple tests to make the job easy for those who are unfamiliar with chanterelles, but these inevitably lead to wishful-thinking mistakes. What the uninitiated actually need, rather than a fallible, quick-fix test, is experience observing mushrooms—in this case, mushroom gills. Fortunately, mushroom gills for comparison are readily available, already identified as such for beginners, 365 days a year and probably within ten minutes of your house. The commercial button mushroom (p. 28 sold in grocery stores has true gills, and if you spend some quality time slicing, prying, poking, and picking at one, you will see that true gills are individual, platelike or bladelike things, structurally separate from one another and

Photo by Hugh Smith

the flesh of the cap and stem. The "gills" on a chanterelle, by comparison, are mere folds in the mushroom's surface, not structurally distinct units. In some chanterelles the false gills are shallow and sparse; in others they can be quite deep and gill-like. Often, the false gills of chanterelles are punctuated by cross-veins and forking—and in some specimens they are so convoluted, forked, and crisscrossed that they are not likely to be mistaken for gills at all.

of these species). To top off this taxonomic teapot tempest, mycologists are also beginning to wonder whether all the *European* chanterelles passing as *Cantharellus cibarius* actually deserve the name and whether the name can be accurately applied at all, since we now have no way of knowing which genetically distinct chanterelle the founding fungal fathers had in mind. Other chanterelles in eastern North America include *Cantharellus appalachiensis* (edible; p. 141) and the smooth chanterelle, *Cantharellus lateritius* (edible; p. 142). Tiny chanterelles such as *Cantharellus minor* and other possibly distinct, miniscule species should be avoided—not only because they are too small to eat but also because considering them for the table would lengthen the list of lackluster look-alikes unacceptably.

In the Woods: (John David Moore) Look closely for traces of yellow peeking out of the leaf cover. Chanterelles often hide beneath the leaves and fruit under the overhanging cover of logs and fallen branches. Once you've detected some visible ones, looking under the nearby leaves will often reveal other clusters. Chanterelles are relatively clean mushrooms. Brush off the caps and ridges and trim the dirty portions of the stems when picking. This should suffice to keep dirt from spreading throughout your collection and makes for less work in the kitchen. Chanterelles also remain fairly free of larvae, though older individuals may display larval tunnel openings in the cap centers. Invaded portions can sometimes be trimmed to fill out the harvest if the pickings are meager. Chanterelles will sometimes start to go bad around the edges of the caps, but if you trim these brown areas away, your mushroom will be perfectly edible. If your crop has been growing in wet followed by dry conditions, leaves and other debris may be tightly affixed to the cap surfaces and will require additional cleaning methods in the kitchen.

In the Kitchen: (John David Moore) Avoid using much water when any further cleaning of your harvest is required. Put chanterelles under the tap only if a damp cloth fails to remove affixed debris. They have a naturally high water content unless they have been sitting around in dry weather for a few days. When slicing them lengthwise for the pan or dryer, keep an eye out for larvae. Sautéed for a few minutes (or stewed in their own juices if your collection has been picked in wet conditions), chanterelles have a fruity flavor and meaty texture that is much prized. When deciding how many to cook for a meal or as an ingredient in a recipe, keep in mind that they will cook down to about a third of their original bulk. Cleaned with a brush or cloth and then arranged loosely in a bowl or tray, chanterelles will keep well for three or four days in the refrigerator. After this time you may need to do some sorting and trimming to obtain palatable specimens. Thinly sliced, dried, and sealed in jars, they will last perhaps longer than you will. Dried chanterelles can be reconstituted in water, wine, or cream. Longer drying at lower temperatures will prevent them from becoming too leathery, a drawback I find common with the dried versions. If the leathery quality is bothersome, you can use them finely chopped or powdered in a dressing, stuffing or soup. Some people find the rehydrated stems more leathery and remove them before drying. If you need to transport fresh chanterelles for a day or two, clean the mushrooms carefully and arrange them in a box or basket in loose layers between paper towels.

Recommended Recipes: Beef Stroganoff with Wild Mushrooms (p. 303); Chanterelles in Brandy Cream Sauce (p. 305); Lamb with Mint and Mushrooms (p. 306).

31 Western Chanterelles: *Cantharellus* Species

Edibility Rating: Great.

Distinguishing Features: The chanterelles of western North America are medium-sized to large mushrooms with false gills that grow on the ground in woods. The caps are broadly convex, flat, or shallowly vase shaped and often feature wavy or irregular edges when mature. The surface is dry and fairly smooth. The cap colors of western chanterelles range from egg-yolk yellow to orangish yellow to white. The false gills are colored like the cap (or a little paler) and run down the stem. They are often forked and include many cross-veins. The stem lacks a ring and is colored more or less like the cap. There is no sack around its base. The flesh is thick and white and does not change color when sliced. Fresh chanterelles have a faint but characteristic sweet odor, often described as "fruity" or "like apricots." It is best detected when you have several mushrooms together in a paper bag or basket. The spore print is white or pale yellow.

Left: Cantharellus subalbidus (photo by Taylor Lockwood); *top right: Cantharellus formosus; bottom right:* "mud puppies"

Ecology: Chanterelles are mycorrhizal partners with trees. In western North America they can be found under hardwoods or conifers—and this information can be helpful in separating the species (see "Comments"). They grow alone, scattered, or gregariously, appearing from fall through spring on the West Coast (or sometimes in summer as a result of fog drip in coastal ecosystems) or during the fall monsoons in the Rocky Mountains.

Poisonous Look-Alikes: *Omphalotus* species (p. 65).

Comments: The chanterelles of western North America are currently being studied by mycologists, and as a result several "new" species recently have been named (more are likely to come). The white chanterelle, *Cantharellus subalbidus*, is very clearly distinct on the basis of its color and was named in 1947. It grows in California and the Pacific Northwest under pines, Douglas-fir, and madrone. Other western chanterelles have passed as "*Cantharellus cibarius*" (a European species; see "Comments" under "Eastern Chanterelles," p. 135), including *Cantharellus formosus*, which grows under Sitka spruce and other conifers, primarily in Oregon, and features tiny brownish scales on its cap, as well as pinkish false gills and a frequently long and tapered stem; *Cantharellus cascadensis*, which grows under conifers in the Cascades and has a more substantial stem; and the San Francisco area's "mud puppy," an unnamed, putative species that grows primarily under live oak and can attain very large sizes.

In the Woods: See "In the Woods" under "Eastern Chanterelles," p. 137.

In the Kitchen: (Darvin DeShazer) Dry buttons with inrolled cap edges are a culinary delight, but beware of the waterlogged, floppy giants. The buttons remain firm when sautéed and retain both their crunchiness and their flavor, both of which are lacking in the large, insipid "mud puppies" found later in the season in northern California. After heavy rains, these soggy chanterelles lose part of their culinary appeal. They are an undescribed species from the California oak woodlands and always fruit after the bulk of the winter rains. Even though the white chanterelle lacks the apricot odor found in the other chanterelles, it is still an excellent edible.

Recommended Recipes: Beef Stroganoff with Wild Mushrooms (p. 303); Chanterelles in Brandy Cream Sauce (p. 305); Lamb with Mint and Mushrooms (p. 306).

32 *Cantharellus appalachiensis*

Edibility Rating: Great.

Distinguishing Features: *Cantharellus appalachiensis* is a small to medium-sized mushroom with false gills that grows from the ground in eastern North America's hardwood forests. Its cap measures about 1–5 cm—slightly smaller than many eastern chanterelles (edible; p. 135). The dry surface is nearly completely brown when the mushroom is young, but as it matures the egg-yolk yellow shades familiar to eastern chanterelle collectors begin to dominate so that only the center of the cap

is brownish. The edge of the cap is usually wavy and irregular. The underside of the cap features yellow false gills that run down the stem. The stem is brownish or yellowish and lacks a ring. There is no sack around the stem's base. The flesh is whitish or very pale brownish and does not change color when sliced. The odor is faintly fruity. The spore print is whitish or pale yellow.

Ecology: *Cantharellus appalachiensis* is a mycorrhizal partner with hardwoods. It grows alone or gregariously in summer and fall. As its name suggests, it was originally collected in the Appalachian Mountains—but its recognized range has since been extended to roughly the Mississippi River.

Poisonous Look-Alikes: *Omphalotus* species (p. 65).

Comments: Mature specimens that have lost their brown color can easily be confused with "*Cantharellus cibarius*" (edible; see p. 135), which is sometimes found growing nearby. In this case a chemical test will separate the two mushrooms; *Cantharellus appalachiensis* is the only chanterelle known to turn reddish when iron salts are applied to the flesh. Fortunately, since this test is unavailable to most mushroomers, mistaking *Cantharellus appalachiensis* for other chanterelles is no tragedy; it is as delightfully delicious as its better-known brethren.

In the Woods: Sadly, *Cantharellus appalachiensis* is adored by critters, which enter the mushroom from the ground and proceed up the stem, eventually making their way into the cap. When collecting this species for the table, I slice the stem about halfway up and examine it for critter tunnels; if the flesh is solid, it goes into my basket.

In the Kitchen: *Cantharellus appalachiensis* is best when it is fresh and should be prepared like other chanterelles (see "In the Kitchen" under eastern chanterelles, p. 138). Its taste is indistinguishable from that of the classic "*Cantharellus cibarius*."

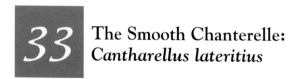

33 The Smooth Chanterelle: *Cantharellus lateritius*

Edibility Rating: Great.

Photo by Pam Kaminski

Distinguishing Features: The smooth chanterelle, like other chanterelles in eastern North America, grows on the ground in hardwood forests. Its cap is shallowly vase shaped at maturity and has a wavy or convoluted edge. The surface is smooth and yellow or orangish yellow. The underside of the cap is similarly colored, and the surface is smooth or composed of a few shallow wrinkles or folds—though some specimens develop deeper wrinkles and veins near the cap margin in age. The stem is also smooth and colored like the cap or paler. It lacks a ring, and there is no sack around its base. The flesh is thick and white and does not change color when sliced. Most collections demonstrate the apricotlike fruity odor familiar to chanterelle collectors—in fact, many think the odor is *stronger* in the smooth chanterelle. The spore print is creamy or pale yellow.

Ecology: *Cantharellus lateritius* is a mycorrhizal partner with hardwoods. It is common in oak forests in summer and fall, where it often appears in disturbed-ground areas: on paths, in ditches, in clearings, and so on. If my experience is any indicator, the smooth chanterelle is usually found growing in clumps or loose clusters of several mushrooms, though solitary and scattered specimens are also common.

Poisonous Look-Alikes: None.

Comments: The smooth underside of *Cantharellus lateritius* makes it less of an identification challenge than the "true" eastern chanterelles (edible; p. 135)—but be sure to compare it with *Clavariadelphus truncatus* (edible; p. 146) and similar club mushrooms. A southeastern species, *Craterellus odoratus* (probably edible; not treated in this book), is somewhat similar but less substantial and more vase shaped; additionally, it grows in densely packed clusters in which the stem bases are typically fused together.

In the Woods: Like many eastern chanterelles, the smooth chanterelle has often been dined on by others before you find it in the woods. Slice the stem to examine the interior for worm channels and discard specimens that have been raided. *Cantharellus lateritius* is the primary species of chanterelle in western Pennsylvania, where I lived for several years. In one particularly dry year, my mushrooming buddy and I were so desperate to find *Cantharellus lateritius* in our usual spots that we hauled bucket after bucket of water out to the woods, watering our chanterelle patches. Sadly, nothing happened. We decided the problem was that we had used tap water and vowed to use rainwater the next year. Fortunately, there was plenty of rain the next year and we didn't have to embarrass ourselves further.

In the Kitchen: The smooth chanterelle is indistinguishable from other chanterelles in taste and consistency; it should be prepared like other eastern chanterelles (p. 138).

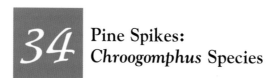

34 Pine Spikes: *Chroogomphus* Species

Edibility Rating: Fair.

Distinguishing Features: Members of the genus *Chroogomphus*, sometimes called the pine spikes, grow under conifers. The small to medium-sized caps are convex (broadly so in age), and the surface is often slimy—though it dries quickly, usually creating a shiny, polished appearance. The color varies between species but often involves purplish, reddish, orangish, brownish, or nearly black shades. The gills are attached to the stem, and usually run down it for some length. They are pale—usually orangish or yellowish—before they begin to mature and then

Upper left: photo by Tim Zurowski; *lower left and lower middle:* photos by Hugh Smith; *middle right:* cystidium and spores; *lower right:* cells in Melzer's Reagent

turn blackish. They are not covered with a partial veil when young. The stems are often tapered to the base and have fairly smooth surfaces. They lack rings and are not enclosed at their bases by sacks. The flesh demonstrates orangish, yellowish, reddish, or purplish colors, especially in the cap. The spore print is blackish or olive black.

Ecology: Pine spikes are mycorrhizal partners with conifers, fruiting alone, scattered, or gregariously from the ground beneath them. Like many conifer associates, they seem to prefer cool weather and typically appear in late summer or fall. On the West Coast they are particularly common, appearing in fall, winter, and spring. Elsewhere, pine spikes are locally common in northern and montane regions with natural conifer populations and along the Gulf Coast in association with two- and three-needle pines.

Poisonous Look-Alikes: None.

Comments: There are about a dozen recognized species of *Chroogomphus* in North America. Identifying the individual species ranges from fairly easy to fairly difficult. Since all are edible, the point is moot from a culinary perspective. The pine spikes, as a group, can be difficult to separate from species of *Gomphidius* (edible; p. 159)—another genus of conifer-loving, black-spored slimeballs. Although the official, definitive feature separating *Chroogomphus* from *Gomphidius* requires a microscope to observe (the cells in the caps of the former turn purple when mounted in Melzer's Reagent), this arcane character can usually be bypassed since *Gomphidius* species tend to be slimier and softer, have white flesh, and often develop bright yellow stains on their stems at maturity.

In the Woods: (Darvin DeShazer) Pine spikes grow predominantly with pines, and they often fruit with species of *Suillus* (edible; see the Glossary and Index), so look for both together. Hemlock and larch are also good trees to search under. Maggots tend to avoid them, so they transport well and store for days.

In the Kitchen: (Darvin DeShazer) Since *Chroogomphus* species stand tall and clean above a bed of pine needles, they rarely need extra cleaning—so with a minimum amount of effort they can quickly land in the cooking pot. They dry very well and can be stored for the off-season, but either fresh or dried they lack appeal for most collectors, partly because of their burgundy-colored flesh and their lack of flavor.

 Clavariadelphus **Species**

Edibility Rating: Good.

Distinguishing Features: The members of the genus *Clavariadelphus* worth considering for the table are medium-sized, club-shaped mushrooms characterized by their smooth or slightly wrinkled surfaces, their white and stringy interiors, and their terrestrial growth. The fruiting bodies are unbranched or, occasionally, forked. The colors range from pinkish to pale orange, yellowish, or very pale brown. The spore print is white or pale yellowish. Smaller club-shaped fungi are numerous, so be sure your mushroom is at least medium sized.

Ecology: The species of *Clavariadelphus* treated here grow from the ground and are mycorrhizal partners with conifers and/or hardwoods

Upper left: photo by Hugh Smith; *upper right:* photo by Dianna Smith

across North America. They tend to prefer cool weather, fruiting in late summer or fall (and winter in warm climates). Although they occasionally fruit in small clusters, they are more apt to appear alone, scattered, or gregariously.

Poisonous Look-Alikes: None.

Comments: The genus *Clavariadelphus* is divided into two major groups: the larger, mycorrhizal species such as the ones treated here; and the smaller, litter-decomposing saprobes that typically arise from a matted mass of whitish mycelium that binds leaves, needles, or even woody debris together. Members of the second group (officially the subgenus *Ligulus*) should not be considered for the table. Although they are not likely to be poisonous, edibility is not reliably documented for most of them and they are easily confused with a host of other mushrooms. *Clavariadelphus truncatus* is the most widely distributed and common of the edible species; it is a conifer lover characterized by its flattened top, which is sometimes so well developed that it approaches the appearance of a cap. The most commonly collected hardwood-loving species is eastern North America's *Clavariadelphus pistillaris*, which has a long, sometimes forked, brown-bruising fruiting body. It is primarily associated with beech. *Clavariadelphus occidentalis*, a West Coast species, is primarily associated with conifers and is similar to *Clavariadelphus pistillaris*.

In the Woods: (Darvin DeShazer) These mushrooms rise majestically above the forest floor and are easy to spot. They are often ignored by collectors, as their shape is far removed from the shapes of "normal" mushrooms.

In the Kitchen: (Darvin DeShazer) Both raw and cooked, the clubs should have a mild to sweetish taste—with the flat-topped species decidedly sweeter than the round-topped species. The texture is firm for only a short period and quickly becomes pithy and unappetizing as it ages. Select young, firm clubs for the table. Slice them into round disks and gently sauté before using them in your favorite recipe.

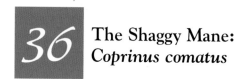

36 The Shaggy Mane: *Coprinus comatus*

Edibility Rating: Great.

Distinguishing Features: Shaggy manes are medium-sized to large gilled mushrooms that grow in grass or disturbed ground (on paths, in ditches, along road banks, and so on), often in troops. Young specimens have a very distinctive shape—rather like a shaggy egg that someone has begun to stretch by pulling on the top. The cap is whitish and covered with soft scales, but it has a brownish "skullcap" in the center. At maturity, the edge of the cap begins to roll itself upward, and the gills dissolve into a jet black "ink" from the margin inward. In this stage the shaggy mane looks like a bell-shaped hat with a gooey, blackening, tattered brim stuck atop a high white pole. The gills are white and crowded when very young, but you will only see them in this stage if you slice

open a button. Later they turn gray, and finally black, before dissolving. They are covered with a tissuelike partial veil when young. The stem features a ring, but it often breaks or falls away. There is no sack around its base. The surface is whitish and fairly smooth. The flesh is white and does not change color when sliced. The spore print is black—if you can manage to obtain one; you are more likely to wind up with slimy black ooze on your paper.

Ecology: Shaggy manes are terrestrial saprobes. They are occasionally found in woods (especially along paths or in clearings) but are more commonly encountered in disturbed-ground settings: lawns, gardens, ditches, roadsides, in the middle of remote dirt roads, and so on (be sure to consider the possibility of toxins from pollution; see p. 20). They almost always fruit in the company of other shaggy manes, either loosely scattered or in impressive lines or clusters. They are widely distributed in North America, appearing in summer and fall (or fall and winter in warm climates).

Poisonous Look-Alikes: Species of *Amanita* (p. 43); *Chlorophyllum molybdites* (p. 50).

Comments: Rare negative reactions to shaggy manes have been reported in cases in which the consumption of alcohol was involved. Since shaggy manes are related to inky caps (*Corpinus atramentarius*; not treated in this book), which combine negatively with alcohol (they contain the chemical used in the drug Antabuse), avoid alcohol when eating them. Many mushroom guides place the shaggy mane in the "easy" category, but I have decided not to recommend it to beginners because its most distinctive feature (the fact that the gills turn into black ink) appears *after* the mushroom looks appetizing. Beginning mushroom hunters should therefore collect it in all stages of development and identify it—more than once—before experimenting. About once a year I am consulted on, or receive news of, a poisoning case in which someone has eaten *Chlorophyllum molybdites* thinking it was a shaggy mane. Most states do not allow someone to buy a gun without some kind of a delay between wanting to buy the lethal weapon and actually receiving it. Mushroom hunters should enact similar "waiting period" laws for themselves and avoid eating any mushroom, no matter how scrumptious looking, until they have collected it several times. If you follow my advice, however, you will be sitting at home with uneaten shaggy manes and you will need entertainment; the following three Focus Points may help you in your quest for fungal fun.

Focus Point
Crowded Gills

When mycologists and mushroom guides describe the spacing of gills as crowded, they mean *crowded*. The shaggy mane's gills—best observed by slicing open a button—are a good example. Perhaps because I am an English teacher, I feel obligated to point out that the oft-used phrase "close to crowded" is an attempt by mushroom authors to represent a *range* of possibilities in gill spacing; they mean "close or crowded" and have ignored the ambiguity created by the phrase "close to."

Focus Point
Dissolving Gills

Many mushrooms in the genus *Coprinus*, like the shaggy mane, have evolved an amazing technique for dispersing spores into air currents. The spores begin to mature, on each gill, in the area nearest the edge of the cap. After these spores have been released, this area of the gills "deliquesces," dissolving and turning into black goo. The flesh in the cap is so thin that the result is a peeling back of the cap's edge—exposing the next area of the gills for the process. Thus, the spore-manufacturing machinery is protected from the elements by the tightly closed, egglike shape of the cap until it is time to fire up each stage of the assembly line, and the whole operation is timed accordingly.

Focus Point
Gravity and Mushrooms

Try carefully removing the cap from a shaggy mane and pinning the headless stem to a wall, sideways, so that it is parallel to the floor (exactly perpendicular to its natural state). Be sure to pin it at the *base*, rather than in the middle or at the apex. Now mow the lawn, wash the dishes, watch a baseball game, whatever. When you return, you are likely to find that your headless shaggy mane stem knows which way is up and has curved itself upward in a pathetic attempt to arrange its now missing cap for proper spore dispersal. Now *that's* entertainment! See how much fun mushrooms can be? If you're ready for more proof that mushrooms sense gravity and adapt to it, pick an *Amanita* (p. 43) with a long stem and set it down on your counter. Since it might be deadly, be sure your children and pets can't gain access. Now wait a few hours: *voila!* Amanitas are notorious for continuing to grow after they have been picked and for bending themselves in order to drop spores. Still bored? Don your walking shoes and head for the woods, where you will search for a perennial polypore (one that remains for years, developing a new marginal growth layer each season—see p. 81) that has been handed a midlife crisis when its host tree fell to the ground. Rather than buying a motorcycle or flirting with the pizza delivery guy, however, your polypore has probably simply plodded ahead, adapting to the ninety-degree change in gravity by altering the direction of its pore surface. If you are still not satisfied, see "The Enoki," (p. 35) for further experimental fun with mushrooms and gravity—but you may need to take out a second mortgage to continue, since you'll be hiring a space shuttle.

In the Woods: (John David Moore) Actually, if you're "in the woods" you may be in the wrong place. This familiar fungus is quite fond of human-altered environments such as lawns, playing fields, margins of trails, roads, and highways and has been known to erupt through asphalt on tennis courts and in similar locations. When gathering shaggy manes for the table, avoid those with blackening cap edges. They're starting the rapid process of deliquescence and thus may not make the trip back to the kitchen. Deliquescing specimens, while not toxic, are undesirable in both appearance and watery texture (the black liquid resulting from the dissolving gills is, however, said to make a passable writing ink when a bit of water is added). Some cleaning in the field before bagging or "basketing" your finds is advisable since the mushroom's rapid eruption, usually under damp conditions, causes it to pick up dirt and debris. Based on gut-level experience, a caution about gathering this species is in order here. The shaggy mane's habit of loitering along roadsides and its ability to absorb airborne pollution can sometimes lead to a less than satisfactory postprandial condition. Unless you regard carbon monoxide or other auto emissions as a tasty food additive, avoid shaggy manes found along roadsides with even moderate traffic.

In the Kitchen: (John David Moore) A collection of *Coprinus comatus* should be hustled to the kitchen and prepared for eating or storage immediately. The shaggy mane's freshness is ephemeral, and some will start deliquescing in a matter of an hour. They can be cleaned with light brushing or wiped with a damp cloth. They can also be cleaned directly in water if you're using them in soups or stews, where picking up extra liquid won't matter. Cutting the mushrooms into rings, sautéing, and freezing is the preferred preservation method. Drying, while possible, can require a delicate process of temperature adjustment and can sometimes end in an inky mess. Frozen, the mushrooms keep well and hold their flavor for several months. Although they are excellent dipped in egg and bread crumbs and fried (some people have never eaten a mushroom any other way), the shaggy mane's flavor is most suitable for a rich soup.

Recommended Recipes: Asparagus Garnish with Mushrooms (p. 303); Shaggy Mane Soup (p. 310).

37 *Craterellus tubaeformis*

Edibility Rating: Great.

Distinguishing Features: *Craterellus tubaeformis* is almost always found in conifer woods, growing densely and gregariously in moss (on the ground or on well-decayed, mossy logs). Its cap is brown and has a characteristic waxy texture when fresh. The edge of the cap is usually wavy and irregular, and the center typically becomes perforated by ma-

turity. The underside of the cap features a grayish, veined surface that can *almost* approximate gills; see "Eastern Chanterelles" (p. 137) for help determining whether you are looking at true or false gills. The stem is hollow, smooth, and yellow (often brightly so) or yellowish brown. It lacks a ring, and its base is not enclosed in a sack. The flesh is insubstantial. The spore print is white or pale yellow.

Ecology: *Craterellus tubaeformis* is officially a mycorrhizal species—but I suspect this is because of its association with chanterelles (which are proven to be mycorrhizal) in now outdated taxonomic schemes rather than its association with the rootlets of trees. *Craterellus tubaeformis* is pretty clearly a saprobe, at least much of the time, as it appears on mossy logs. When it grows terrestrially, it is almost always found in the presence of moss or needle debris in conifer bogs. It is a cool weather mushroom, appearing in the fall (and in winter in coastal California). Its distribution is primarily northern, but it (or a similar, as yet unnamed species) also appears in California, where collectors call it the yellow foot.

Poisonous Look-Alikes: None.

Comments: There are several similar species with yellow or orange, rather than brown, caps, including *Cantharellus ignicolor* and *Cantharellus xanthopus* (both of which will likely be transferred to the genus *Craterellus* once they are DNA tested). Probably all of these species are edible, but edibility is not officially recorded for a few of them. Tiny mushrooms that are superficially similar should be avoided; not only are they too small to eat, but they are also much more difficult to identify with certainty and could potentially be confused with several poisonous mushrooms.

In the Woods: Slice these mushrooms well above the stem base, since moss and conifer duff are usually present. I have found it is worth paying extra attention when bagging *Craterellus tubaeformis*, since it is a fragile and often moist mushroom. The trick is to let them breathe, either by spacing them well in your basket or by placing only a handful in each individual paper bag (do not close or fold over the top of the bag). Collect specimens in all stages, if you can; the ones that are too old to eat usually tear apart or disintegrate when you attempt to pick them.

In the Kitchen: Despite your efforts in the woods, the wrinkled undersurfaces and perforated caps are likely to contain forest debris when you get home. *Craterellus tubaeformis* withstands washing well, since its flesh is not porous, so rinse your collection under running water and pat it dry with paper towels. It can be treated like chanterelles (pp. 135 and 139), though its texture is not as meaty. The taste is similar, however, and equally delicious. The best cream of mushroom soups I have ever eaten were in Finland, where *Craterellus tubaeformis* is a popular mushroom (often piled high in open-air markets) commonly used as a soup base.

Recommended Recipes: Chanterelles in Brandy Cream Sauce (p. 305); Shaggy Mane Soup (p. 310), substituting *Craterellus tubaeformis* for shaggy manes.

38 *Fistulina hepatica*

Edibility Rating: Fair.

Distinguishing Features: *Fistulina hepatica* is a soft, fleshy polypore that looks like a slab of beef stuck to the side of a tree. The fruiting body is fairly large (up to 30 cm across) and shaped more or less like a large kidney or tongue. The upper surface is reddish or liver colored, and the pore surface beneath it is whitish or pale pinkish—bruising reddish brown with age or when handled. The tubes that make up the pore surface are very distinctive: they are individually discrete so that you can see each individual tube (with your unaided eyes or, if your vision is as bad as

Photos by Hugh Smith

mine, with the help of a magnifying glass). The flesh is whitish, watery, and streaked with reddish areas. When squeezed hard, *Fistulina hepatica* exudes a reddish juice. The spore print is pinkish to pinkish brown.

Ecology: Like other polypores, *Fistulina hepatica* is a wood-rotting saprobe. It is also sometimes parasitic, attacking living trees. It grows on hardwoods and tends to appear near the base of the tree, a few feet above ground, alone or in small groups. It causes a brown rot of the heartwood. It is occasional on oaks in eastern North America in summer and fall and is apparently found in Texas. In California it is fairly rare, appearing on chinquapin oaks in fall and winter.

Poisonous Look-Alikes: None.

Comments: Although several authors recommend eating this mushroom raw, I do not. Uncooked wild mushrooms, even when edible, affect many people adversely—as do polypores in general. Follow the precautions on page 21 and try only a small amount—cooked—the first time. Although there are no poisonous look-alikes, there is at least one southern, oak-loving polypore of unknown edibility that is very similar to *Fistulina hepatica*, which I have collected and tentatively identified as *Inonotus quercustris* (not treated in this book). This mushroom lacks the individual, discrete tubes of *Fistulina hepatica* but shares many of its other features, including the streaked, watery flesh.

In the Woods: (Darvin DeShazer) In my area (northern California), *Fistulina hepatica* favors aging or dying hardwoods with an extra supply of water nearby. When hunting this species be sure to look under tree limbs that overhang a pond or creek. A common fruiting location on the Pacific bayberry (*Myrica californica*) occurs between several limbs in the crotch of the tree. Often you have to stand on tiptoe even to see it, so it goes undiscovered by many collectors.

In the Kitchen: (Darvin DeShazer) One slice of the knife and you will know that *Fistulina hepatica* is a unique mushroom. The interior resembles a thick juicy steak but tastes bitter and has an acidic aftertaste. One solution is to not eat it! The thick gooey slime on top of the mushroom has enzymes that tenderize meat. If you lay the fungus upside-down on a steak for several hours before barbecuing, the meat becomes tender— and some people then discard the mushroom. If you want to consume it, use it in a dish that requires lemon juice and it will blend in well. Vegetarian pizza is a favorite in our house, and for this *Fistulina hepatica* is often combined with other fresh mushrooms.

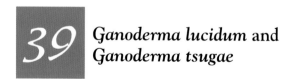

39 *Ganoderma lucidum* and *Ganoderma tsugae*

Edibility Rating: Inedible; used for teas.

Lower right: photo by Hugh Smith

Distinguishing Features: These varnished-looking polypores, when fresh, are gorgeous. They grow on decaying logs and from living trees and can attain sizes of 20 to 30 cm. The fresh cap surface is liver red to reddish brown and distinctively glossy, as though it has been shellacked. The surface is arranged in lumpy-looking "zones," which may be white or yellow near the edge of the cap when the mushroom is young. The undersurface is white at first and becomes brownish with age; it usually bruises slowly brownish when scratched with a knife. The pores comprising the undersurface are so small that they are almost invisible to the naked eye. The stem is sometimes absent, but more often it is present as a lateral extension. Its surface has the same lacquered appearance as the cap surface. Very young specimens, especially those growing on the tops of logs, occasionally have long stems and angled caps, reminding one of a tiny periscope the mycelium has sent out from its log submarine. The mushrooms are fairly tough; under the lacquered outer shell, the white or brownish flesh is tough and corky. The spore print, if you are able to obtain one, is brown.

Ecology: *Ganoderma lucidum* and *Ganoderma tsugae* are wood-rotting saprobes that cause a whitish, brown, or straw-colored rot. They fruit annually, appearing alone or in groups on stumps, logs, and living trees. *Ganoderma lucidum* is found on the wood of hardwoods, and *Ganoderma tsugae* grows on conifer wood (especially hemlock). Both species appear from spring through fall throughout North America, but since the mushrooms are so tough they are often found (as lackluster shells of their former selves) well after they have matured—in the winter or even the next year.

Poisonous Look-Alikes: None.

Comments: The traditional distinction is that *Ganoderma lucidum* grows on hardwoods and *Ganoderma tsugae* on conifers. Recent DNA studies, however, suggest that these may not be "good species" and other species lines may need to be drawn. *Ganoderma oregonense* is a similar species found on conifer wood in the Pacific Northwest and New Mexico, while *Ganoderma curtisii* is a southern species found on hardwoods. While *Ganoderma* species are decidedly too tough to eat, they can be used to prepare "teas" and brews. Avoid specimens found on the wood of locust trees (see p. 20).

In the Woods: (Ken Gilberg) Although you may find this woody mushroom any time of year, the best specimens for making tea are found in late summer and fall. To collect it, you may find it easier to break the mushroom off the tree than to try to cut it off.

In the Kitchen: (Ken Gilberg) The active ingredients of the reishi or ling chih (the Japanese and Chinese names for *Ganoderma*, respectively) remain after drying. In Asian apothecaries, it is sold whole or in capsules and prescribed for any number of ailments. It is considered one of the greatest of traditional Chinese medicinals, ranked up there with ginseng. It is traditionally steeped in hot water and used as a tea. A decade ago Gerry Miller, a guide to shamanic adventures, demonstrated to me how Amazon jungle people soak bark, roots, and berries in rum to extract their essences. I started making my "Elixir of Spiritual Potency" with *Ganoderma*. I cannot attest to any particular health benefit, but how can one argue with thousands of years of reverence for this mushroom? The French would call my elixir a *ratafia*—a cordial of fruits, flowers, and/or herbs steeped in alcohol. To make a *ratafia* from *Gano-derma*, slice the hard fungus into quarter-inch pieces. It is probably best, and certainly easier, to slice this tough mushroom when it has been recently picked. You still may need a cleaver to cut it—use caution. Put the slices in a widemouthed glass jar or stuff them through a thin-necked bottle. You need not fill the entire bottle. Cover the contents with rum. A cheap rum is fine—don't ruin the flavor of a good rum with the overpowering taste of *Ganoderma*. The mushroom will flavor the rum in a day, but it will keep a long time preserved in the alcohol. No need for refrigeration. My five-year-old stock is quite mellow. Inspired by the 120 herbs that go into the famous cordial Chartreuse, I have adapted my elixir to include a host of herbs gathered in the fall, soak-ing all of the following ingredients in the rum: *Ganoderma lucidum*, *Ganoderma curtisii*, *Trametes versicolor* (otherwise inedible; not treated in this book), *Schizophyllum commune* (otherwise inedible; not treated), red cedar berries, spicebush berries and leaves, hawthorn berries, stag-horn sumac berries, rue, tansy, lemon verbena, bay, hyssop, mint—and, to top it off, cinnamon, clove, and star anise. A simpler version, and quite tasty, is to soak just the *Ganoderma* and spicebush berries in rum. Sometimes I add maple sugar for sweetening—but no matter what you add, the Elixir of Spiritual Potency is a bitter concoction best sipped from a small cordial glass like grappa.

Gomphidius Species

Edibility Rating: Mediocre.

Distinguishing Features: These slimy, small or medium-sized gilled mushrooms grow under conifers, primarily in northern North America and montane regions. Their caps are convex and smooth, and are often pinkish or purplish. When fresh the surface is slimy. The gills run far down the stem and sometimes have a somewhat waxy texture. They are initially pale, but turn dark gray or black as the spores mature. In a few species they are covered with a tissuelike partial veil when young, but other species feature a "slime veil," which looks pretty much like it sounds, protecting the immature gills and later pulling away to sheathe the stem. The stem is often tapered downward. It features a fragile ring or "ring zone" in some species, but other species lack a persistent ring

Top left: photo by Dianna Smith; *right and lower left:* photos by Tim Zurowski

or have stems sheathed in slime. The stem surface is usually whitish, but in most species it develops bright yellow stains from the base up. The stem base is not enclosed in a sack. The flesh is white to pale gray, but it often stains and discolors yellow, especially in the stem. The spore print is dark gray or black.

Ecology: The mushrooms in *Gomphidius* are mycorrhizal partners with conifers—although they are less fond of pines than they are of spruces, firs, hemlocks, and (especially) Douglas-firs. They fruit alone, scattered, or gregariously in late summer or fall and are distributed wherever the host trees are found.

Poisonous Look-Alikes: None.

Comments: *Gomphidius* species might easily be referred to as "gilled *Suillus*," since they seem to resemble a gilled equivalent of *Suillus* species (see the various species listed in the Glossary and Index). The dozen or so species of *Gomphidius* in North America (all apparently edible) are fairly similar and can be separated from species of *Chroogomphus* by their softer, slimier consistency, their mycorrhizal hosts, their white flesh, the yellow stains on the stems of most species, and their microscopic features (the cells in the caps of *Gomphidius* species do not turn purplish in Melzer's Reagent). Identifying *Gomphidius* species with precision is usually a matter of careful observation of fresh specimens; microscopic differences can often be bypassed with reference to geographic area.

In the Kitchen: (Darvin DeShazer) The slimy "skin" of the cap should be peeled and discarded, as should the covering of a dirty stem. Both can be slimy in wet weather, and the adhering dirt may be difficult to remove. The flesh is soft when old and often swollen with water. Use young, prime mushrooms or skip the genus *Gomphidius* altogether.

41 *Gomphus clavatus*

Edibility Rating: Good.

Distinguishing Features: This odd, medium-sized mushroom, sometimes called pig's ears, grows in lumpy, clumpy clusters under conifers—primarily in the Pacific Northwest but also in northern and montane conifer forests across the continent. The "individual" mushrooms are often hard to pin down since *Gomphus clavatus* usually develops several fairly distinct fruiting bodies that share a stem structure. The caps are often fused and irregular, but they are more or less vase shaped at maturity. The cap edge is irregular and wavy and often more developed on one side than the other. The upper surface is pale purple at first but soon becomes yellowish brown or dirty buff. It is smooth or finely roughened and often develops fine scaly areas in the center. The undersurface is shallowly and broadly wrinkled or veined and lacks gills or pores. It is purplish at first but begins to fade to dull brownish or dirty buff from the cap edge downward. The stem is usually short and stubby and often serves to support several caps. It is whitish and smooth or finely fuzzy. The flesh is whitish or pinkish and does not change color when sliced. The spore print is brownish yellow to dirty olive.

Left: Photo by Mike Wood

Ecology: *Gomphus clavatus* is a mycorrhizal partner with conifers and grows in dense clusters on the ground beneath them. The clusters are often gregarious, forming impressive troops or arcs. It is most common in the Pacific Northwest, but its range extends across northern and montane North America. In the higher elevations of the Appalachian Mountains, it is found under hemlock. It fruits in late summer and fall in most locations, though it will sometimes appear in winter on the West Coast from the Bay Area northward.

Poisonous Look-Alikes: None.

Comments: Specimens of *Gomphus clavatus* in the button stage look like flat-topped clubs and should be compared with *Clavariadelphus truncatus* (edible; p. 146). Other species of *Gomphus* (probably nontoxic but often unpalatable and causing "allergic" reactions in some; not treated in this book) are somewhat similar but do not typically grow in fused clusters and lack purplish colors. Compare *Gomphus clavatus* with the chanterelles (edible; pp. 135 and 139), which have false gills and lack purplish colors. *Gomphus clavatus* is notorious for affecting some people adversely, so be sure to follow the precautions on page 24 when you try it for the first time.

In the Woods: (John David Moore) Known by the less than appetizing but comfortably folksy moniker pig's ears, *Gomphus clavatus* is an especially common inhabitant of hill- and mountainsides in the Olympic and western Cascade ranges of the Pacific Northwest. Look for it especially in old-growth Douglas-fir forests in late summer and fall when hunting the more popular chanterelles (p. 139). Despite its size, *Gomphus clavatus* can be easily missed since its brown to tan color with dull purple shadings blends well with needle duff on the forest floor. If you find one cluster, look carefully for more in the area; it often appears in arcs or circles. Its habit of growing in fused clusters causes it to pick up a fair amount of dirt and needle litter. Field clean carefully and slice off the dirty stem bases. Older specimens will often be lighter in color and loosely leathery around the edges. They should be avoided since they will be on the tough side and possibly inhabited by larvae.

In the Kitchen: (John David Moore) It is best to break up the clusters of *Gomphus clavatus* to more easily reach any dirt and debris not removed in the field. Brush or wipe them clean with a damp cloth before slicing—the thinner the better to avoid the rubbery toughness characteristic of this fungus. Four to five minutes of slow cooking are recommended to get a sense of this mushroom's qualities. Sample only a small amount the first time since some people experience gastric upsets. *Gomphus clavatus* has a meaty texture and mildly earthy flavor that goes well with red meat dishes. Dried and rehydrated, it tends to be a bit tougher but is still flavorful. Some people even prefer fresh pig's ears to the yellow chanterelles that so often grow on the same wooded slopes and usually take precedence with collectors.

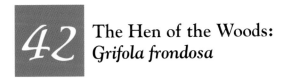

42 The Hen of the Woods: *Grifola frondosa*

Edibility Rating: Good.

Distinguishing Features: The hen of the woods is a soft, fleshy polypore found primarily (but not exclusively) on hardwoods in eastern North America. It grows in dense clusters so that the entire "hen" is quite large (up to 60 cm or more across). The individual caps are fan shaped and grayish to smoky brown, often with a somewhat velvety surface. They are usually 2 to 10 cm across. The pore surface on the underside of the

Above: photo by Pam Kaminski

cap is whitish or lavender gray at first but becomes whitish or pale yellowish with maturity. The caps are attached to lateral, rudimentary stems. The flesh is soft, white, and somewhat stringy. It does not change color when sliced. The mushrooms do not blacken with age or when bruised. The spore print is white.

Ecology: The hen of the woods is a parasite that attacks living trees and causes a white butt rot in the wood. It is also probably a saprobe, continuing to rot the wood after the death of the tree and even, perhaps, assisting in the decomposition of dead trees it did not kill. It appears in summer and fall primarily on hardwoods (especially oaks) in eastern North America—but it is also reported, rarely, from western North America. There are also occasional reports of the hen of the woods on the wood of conifers. It almost always appears near the base of the tree.

Poisonous Look-Alikes: None.

Comments: Two similar polypores, both edible, can be easily confused with the hen of the woods. *Meripilus giganteus* (edible; not treated in this book) differs in having slightly larger caps and surfaces that discolor black with age or when bruised. *Polyporus umbellatus* (edible; p. 207) features smaller, rounder caps, a pore surface that is white in all stages of development, and stems that branch from one or more larger stem structures. Collectors who have not tried the hen of the woods should eat only a bite or two the first time; it is notorious for affecting some people adversely. I am one of those people, and I can tell you that the experience, while not traumatic in the grand scheme of things, is not pleasant. Always follow the precautions on page 24 when trying new wild mushrooms.

In the Woods: (John David Moore) Once you find a hen, it's worth returning to the spot for future harvests. Like many other polypores, it will appear perennially and sometimes more than once in a season. There is no reason to yank the whole thing up and drag it home with you unless you want to pose the family around it for a photo opportunity. The cap clusters are the only part worth eating, since the rest is rather tough. Trim off the number of caps you think you can use, keeping in mind that if this is going to be your first culinary encounter with the hen you'll want to sample only a small quantity to see how your digestive system handles it. Make sure your hen is fresh—not drying out, becoming crumbly, or turning mushy in any of its parts. Brush off what you cut before bagging it. It's usually free of pests, but it's worth checking the interior flesh as you cut the caps away.

In the Kitchen: (John David Moore) Washing the hen is recommended, since you never can be sure about what sort of animal activity transpires around tree trunks. Slice it thinly to achieve maximum tenderness. Sautéed for four to five minutes, its texture holds its own with the best of the edible polypores, but I have found its flavor to be a bit strong and it leaves a less than pleasing "chalky" coating in the mouth. Drying intensifies these traits. Perhaps I've consumed poor quality specimens. In any case, I'm sure I'll be trying the hen again the next time it crosses my path.

Recommended Recipes: Chicken of the Woods with Lemon Cream (p. 305), substituting hens for chickens; Portuguese Steak with Mushrooms (p. 309).

43 *Gyrodon merulioides*

Edibility Rating: Bad.

Distinguishing Features: This distinctive bolete grows only under ash; if you don't see the familiar grayish bark with chiseled X's somewhere in the vicinity you are probably not looking at *Gyrodon merulioides*. The mushroom is distinctive in its appearance, beginning with its irregularly lobed and wavy cap. The surface of the cap is brown and often has a shiny, vaguely metallic luster. The underside of the cap features a yellowish pore surface that is often wrinkled and veined radially. The pores are quite large and elongated. They are not covered with a partial veil when the mushroom is young. The stem is usually a stubby affair, and it is not typically attached to the center of the cap. It lacks a ring. It is colored like the cap but usually turns very dark brown or black from the base up. The flesh is whitish or pale yellowish and rather leathery. In many collections, the pore surface and/or the flesh bruise slightly greenish or bluish— sometimes slowly. The cap turns black then slowly reddish or orangish when ammonia is applied. The spore print is olive brown.

Ecology: *Gyrodon merulioides* is a mycorrhizal partner with ash trees. It grows alone, scattered, or (more often) gregariously, often seeming to cover every available space under the tree. It fruits in summer and fall throughout the range of the host tree (eastern North America and small pockets of the Southwest).

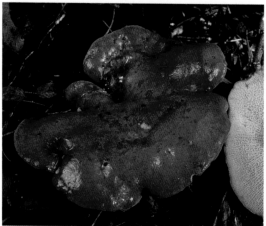

Below: photo by George Barron

Poisonous Look-Alikes: None.

Comments: Some species of *Suillus* (edible; see the Glossary and Index) can be similar in appearance, but they grow under conifers and feature one or more of the following: a slimy cap and/or stem, a partial veil that covers the young pore surface, a ring on the stem, and/or glandular dots (see p. 220) on the upper stem. *Paragyrodon sphaerosporus* (edible; not treated in this book) of the Great Lakes region grows under hardwoods and has a very similar cap. It might be confused with *Gyrodon merulioides*—but it has a partial veil that collapses against the base of the stem (appearing almost like the sack common to many species of *Amanita*), as well as a pore surface that bruises quickly and dramatically brown. Hunters of yellow morels (edible; p. 87) who encounter *Gyrodon merulioides* in the summer or fall might want to make a mental note of the location and return the next spring to search for ash-loving morels.

In the Kitchen: (Kate Klipp) The key to cooking this mushroom is sauce. Lots and lots of sauce. It is very easy to begin making excuses for this poor little fungus. "Well, it was buried in the dirt. Perhaps if I just clean it up a bit more" or "Michael Kuo said that boletes are typically better dried. I'll try that." Well, I'm afraid not, my friend. No amount of cleaning, drying, or seasoning will do anything to cover this mushroom's uncanny resemblance to a Brillo pad. On the plus side, some people love it! The spongy consistency, the dirty-metal taste of it, and even the odd aftertaste it leaves in your mouth. These are a very special few, but more power to them.

 Gyroporus castaneus

Edibility Rating: Great.

Distinguishing Features: This small to medium-sized bolete grows under hardwoods across the continent. Its smooth to slightly velvety cap is brown or yellowish brown. The edge of the cap often splits in age. The pore surface is whitish at first but becomes yellowish as the spores mature. It does not change color when bruised and is not covered with

Photo by Pam Kaminski

a partial veil when the mushroom is young. The stem is very brittle and soon becomes hollow. Its surface is colored more or less like the cap surface and often becomes slightly wrinkled. The stem lacks a ring. The flesh is brittle and white and does not change color when sliced. A drop of ammonia on the cap surface produces a yellowish to pale orange reaction. The spore print is yellow.

Ecology: *Gyroporus castaneus* is a mycorrhizal partner with hardwoods. In eastern North America it is found in summer and fall under oak and beech; it is fairly rare in Illinois, but I have collected it in abundance in Minnesota and Pennsylvania. On the West Coast it (or an unnamed, similar, slightly more robust species) is reported under live oak and tan-oak in summer and fall.

Poisonous Look-Alikes: Poisonous boletes (p. 53).

Comments: The wine red to purplish-brown *Gyroporus purpurinus* (edible; not treated in this book) is virtually identical aside from the color of its cap and stem. *Xanthoconium separans* (edible; p. 232) is more robust, has a fleshy stem, and turns green with ammonia. *Xanthoconium affine* (edible; p. 230) is usually larger and has a fleshy stem. Other, similar boletes have olive spore prints and fleshy stems.

In the Woods: (John David Moore) This hollow, brittle-stemmed mushroom, which favors oak woods in mid- to late summer, is well worth gathering for the table. Unfortunately, however, you should prepare for disappointment since the hollow, chambered stems offer an open invitation to larvae and a disconcerting number of other critters. Moreover, *Gyroporus castaneus* tends to be small and sometimes insubstantial, fruiting in clusters of usually no more than three or four. Field inspection and cleaning/trimming is essential, and you may find yourself discarding more than you keep.

In the Kitchen: (John David Moore) Halve your finds lengthwise to expose the hollow stems for cleaning. It's best to clean the halved mushrooms in a bowl of water, remove with a straining spoon and then rinse in a colander. Strenuous cleaning will break up the brittle stems. After you've drained the mushrooms thoroughly, sauté them for a minute over medium heat to experience their delicate, nutty taste. Since it's rare to gather many *Gyroporus castaneus* in one excursion (in my area, anyway), you might prefer to dry your finds, adding to them until you have enough for cooking. Besides, there is more of the nutty quality in the dried mushrooms.

Recommended Recipes: Mushroom Quiche (p. 307); Mushroom Ravioli (p. 307); Porcini Sauce for Pork Roast (p. 309).

 ## *Gyroporus cyanescens*

Edibility Rating: Great.

Distinguishing Features: This medium-sized bolete is fond of sandy soil in eastern North America. Its straw yellow cap has a roughened surface that turns greenish or bluish when bruised. The pore surface is white to yellowish and also bruises promptly greenish or blue. It is not covered with a partial veil when the mushroom is young. The stem is very brittle and soon becomes hollow. It is colored like the cap or a little paler. It lacks a ring. Its surface is smooth or roughened like the cap surface, and it bruises greenish or blue when handled. The brittle flesh is white or pale yellow and turns greenish or blue when sliced. The mushroom's

reaction to ammonia is not recorded (and I have not tested it), but I doubt it is dramatic. The spore print is pale yellow.

Ecology: *Gyroporus cyanescens* is most frequently encountered in and near the Great Lakes region and along the eastern seaboard in sandy soil. It is occasionally reported from the Pacific Northwest. It seems to have a preference for disturbed ground, often appearing on sandy trails, along roadbeds, and so on—but it also appears in woods under hardwoods (especially beech) or conifers (especially hemlock). It fruits in summer and fall. It is presumed to be mycorrhizal.

Poisonous Look-Alikes: Poisonous boletes (p. 53).

Comments: Be sure to verify the hollow, brittle stem and the yellow spore print. The blue bruising is so pronounced that one wonders whether simply blowing hard on its surfaces would produce the reaction.

In the Woods: (John David Moore) When hunting this *Gyroporus*, the type of woodland is of less importance than the type of soil. This incredibly blue-staining mushroom favors sandy soil and open areas in forests or on forest edges. It makes a notable find, if only for the fun of watching it turn deep blue when field cleaning it. Indeed, its preference for sandy soil necessitates some meticulous brushing in the field. However, it has the virtue of being pretty much free of larvae even when mature.

Focus Point
Chemical Reactions

The way a mushroom's surfaces react to chemicals is occasionally an important feature in its identification. The principal chemicals used are ammonia, potassium hydroxide, and iron salts—though the latter two chemicals are admittedly difficult to obtain. Scientific suppliers used to accept online orders, but things are more difficult in the post-9/11 climate and you may need to make friends in your local school's chemistry or biology department. For ammonia, the common household ammonia sold in grocery stores will work perfectly (be sure to buy the clear, undyed kind). I have heard that a mixture of Drāno and water can take the place of potassium hydroxide, but I do not know the details and I haven't tried it myself. The potassium hydroxide and iron salts are occasionally used to provoke color reactions in gilled mushrooms and/or polypores—but all three chemicals come into play with bolete identification. The cap surfaces and the flesh of boletes will often demonstrate color changes when the chemicals are applied. Since ammonia is readily available, I have listed the reaction of the cap surface, when it is documented or I have checked it, for the boletes in this book. Frustratingly, the bolete literature is full of gaps when it comes to documenting reactions to chemicals, and the mushroom at hand, *Gyroporus cyanescens*, is a species for which the color changes are undocumented—probably because the species is easy enough to identify without this information. So here, dear reader, is your chance for mycological fame and glory: does the cap surface change color with ammonia?

In the Kitchen: (John David Moore) Getting the sand out of your collection is best managed by washing the mushrooms in a bowl of water so the sand sinks to the bottom of the bowl. Drain *Gyroporus cyanescens* thoroughly before slicing for the pan or dryer. By this time your collection will probably be completely blue due to handling, but most of the color disappears when the mushroom is sautéed for about two minutes. The mushrooms offer a mild, nutty flavor and meaty texture. The nutty flavor is more pronounced if you fry them nearly to crispness. Dried specimens also are stronger in taste and retain some of the blueness in the tubes.

Recommended Recipes: Asparagus Garnish with Mushrooms (p. 303); Mushroom Quiche (p. 307); Mushroom Ravioli (p. 307); Porcini Sauce for Pork Roast (p. 309).

 Ischnoderma resinosum

Edibility Rating: Good.

Distinguishing Features: This medium-sized to large polypore is found in cool weather on the deadwood of hardwoods and conifers across North America. Its fleshy cap is shaped more or less like a large kidney (up to 15 cm or more across) and has a thick, wavy edge. The upper surface is brown and finely velvety, but the margin is white. The pore surface is white and soft when the mushroom is young and often extends down and around the wood so far that the cap seems to have been an after-thought. The pores are very tiny, and the pore surface bruises promptly brown. As it matures, the cap of *Ischnoderma resinosum* becomes dark brown, all the way to the margin, and the pore surface becomes brownish. The flesh is white and soft when young but becomes brownish and tough with age. The spore print is white. When a drop of potassium hydroxide is applied, the surfaces and flesh of *Ischnoderma resinosum* turn black.

Ecology: *Ischnoderma resinosum* is a wood-rotting saprobe that helps to decay fallen hardwood and conifer logs. It appears annually on recently fallen wood or wood that has been dead for several years—but not on well-decayed logs. Its mycelium causes a whitish to yellowish rot that separates the annual rings of the trees and sometimes smells of anise. The fruiting bodies often seem to begin their development on the un-derside of the log, where they consist merely of a white, brown-bruising pore surface. The caps develop when the pore surface has spread up the side of the log and requires a supporting structure in order to align the pores properly for spore dispersal. *Ischnoderma resinosum* grows alone occasionally, but is more often found in overlapping clusters. It appears in the fall throughout northern temperate North America.

Poisonous Look-Alikes: None.

Comments: *Ganoderma applanatum* (inedible; not treated in this book) is similar on casual inspection, but it is so tough and woody in all stages of development that eating it would be out of the question. It is perennial, rather than annual, and its hard cap surface develops a new zone each year. Most other potential look-alikes in the polypore world are also too tough and woody to cause confusion. The edibility of *Ischnoderma resinosum* is listed as "unknown" in most field guides, but John David Moore and I have eaten it with no ill effects (we definitely followed the safety precautions on page 24!) and were surprised by its quality. Be sure to try only a bite or so the first time, especially since it is a polypore—one that few people have eaten, which means there is no established record documenting "allergic reactions" and the like.

In the Woods: Collect only young specimens with fat, fleshy cap margins since older specimens are too tough to be appetizing. I use a knife to trim away roughly the outer half of the mushroom. Since *Ischnoderma resinosum* is fat and fleshy and has a high water content, don't pile it too high in your paper bag or basket; you are likely to find a mushy mess at the bottom otherwise.

In the Kitchen: Like most polypores, *Ischnoderma resinosum* requires slow, lengthy cooking. Its taste is comparable to the taste of the chicken of the woods (p. 79), but its texture is not quite as firm. It could be prepared successfully with any method or recipe that works for the chicken of the woods. My culinary imagination can't come up with a plausibly delicious way to combine *Ischnoderma resinosum* with beef, rather than poultry or vegetables, but this may be my limitation rather than the mushroom's.

Recommended Recipes: Chicken of the Woods with Lemon Cream (p. 305), substituting *Ischnoderma resinosum* for the chickens.

 ## *Lactarius deliciosus*

Edibility Rating: Fair.

Distinguishing Features: *Lactarius deliciosus* is a medium-sized gilled mushroom that grows from the ground under conifers in northern and montane areas. Its cap is flat or shallowly vase shaped, and usually somewhat sticky when fresh. The surface is carrot orange or pale orange but develops green areas and discolorations with maturity. The gills begin to run down the stem and are orange or pale yellow. When damaged with the point of a knife, they exude an orange juice—at least in fresh, young specimens. There is no covering over the young gills. Like the cap, the gills also discolor green with age. The stem is fairly short in proportion to the cap, and it lacks a ring. Its surface is colored like the cap (or a little paler), and it may feature little potholes. It, too, stains green with age. There is no sack around the base of the stem. The flesh is pale yellow or orange; it also exudes an orange juice when sliced. The spore print is creamy or very pale yellow.

Ecology: *Lactarius deliciosus* is a mycorrhizal partner with conifers. It grows alone, scattered, or gregariously on the ground in northern and montane areas of the continent, appearing in summer and fall (or in winter in warm climates).

Poisonous Look-Alikes: Species of *Russula* in Group Two (p. 69).

Comments: *Russula subfoetens*, an orangish species in Group Two (p. 69), does not exude juice, does not develop green stains, and smells like bad maraschino cherries. *Lactarius thyinos* (edible; p. 178), also a conifer lover, is very similar to *Lactarius deliciosus* but does not develop green stains. There are several varieties of *Lactarius deliciosus*, some of which are considered by (some) mycologists to be separate species. Microscopic features separate these mushrooms, as well as choice of mycorrhizal host, distribution, and minor differences in some of the physical features listed here. All of these varieties—or species, if you prefer—are edible.

In the Woods: (John David Moore) In late summer and early fall, especially in northern regions, hunt this green-staining orange mushroom

Focus Point
Potholes on the Stem

One of the more curious features of some *Lactarius* species is the presence of small potholes on the stems. These species are said to be "scrobiculate" in Mycologese, and the potholes are called "scrobiculi." The potholes represent areas where the cells on the stem surface have become gelatinized. Under the microscope, a layer of gelatin-like material can be seen over the potholes. Since identifying species of *Lactarius* sometimes hinges on whether or not the stem and/or cap are slimy, and since weather conditions can easily dry out mushrooms, the presence or absence of potholes can serve as a secondary indicator of the stem's "slime factor." Sadly, this does not transfer to other mushroom genera where the sliminess of the stem is taxonomically important (e.g., *Hygrocybe* or *Cortinarius*) since mushrooms in those genera do not develop potholes.

in bog lands featuring cedar and pine. You can also spot it in the open in moist, clear areas and lawns under white pine. In denser boggy spots in northern North America, it may fruit with its more appetizing and cleaner-looking cousin, *Lactarius thyinos* (edible; p. 178). If so, collect both mushrooms to see which you prefer. *Lactarius deliciosus* has an unfortunate problem with pests. It's very hard to locate even the preferred young specimens without an active larval population. Field checking is absolutely necessary unless you want to end up tossing most of your collection by the time you get home. Brushing the mushrooms free of debris is also necessary—but difficult because of the often slimy caps. The green staining is not attractive either, but it has no effect on edibility.

In the Kitchen: (John David Moore) Unless your collection comes from a debris-free, open area, you will probably have to run your mushrooms under water to remove tightly stuck needles, dirt, and leaves. Drain or wipe them dry before slicing for the pan or dryer. Whether you're working with a fresh or dried collection, slow cooking is needed to overcome the grainy texture and occasional bitterness. Mushroom author Charles McIlvaine suggests no less than forty minutes of stewing or baking, which seems extreme. Other authorities recommend rapid frying with little butter or oil. I find that frying it in olive oil with a garlic clove for about ten minutes over low heat works well, as long as you later add some white wine, herbs, and lemon juice and reduce the liquid to a thick sauce. Without these additions, *Lactarius deliciosus* clearly fails to be very delicious. It's flavor is so mild as to be nondescript. If you like orange mushrooms, *Lactarius thyinos* is a far better bet.

Recommended Recipe: Salted Mushroom Salad (p. 309).

48 Lactarius rubidus

Edibility Rating: Good.

Distinguishing Features: This medium-sized gilled mushroom appears on the ground under oaks and tanoaks on the West Coast. Its cap is convex at first but usually becomes shallowly vase shaped with age. The dry to slightly sticky surface is somewhat roughened. It is reddish brown or orange brown and does not feature concentric zones of color or texture. The gills are attached to the stem or begin to run down it and are not covered with a partial veil when young. They are very pale orange but develop cinnamon stains at maturity. When fresh or young gills are damaged, a thin, watery juice is exuded. The stem is colored like the cap, or a little paler, and has a smooth surface. It lacks a ring, and its base is not enclosed in a sack. The flesh is very pale orange and does not change color when sliced. It, too, exudes a watery juice when fresh specimens are sliced. The odor is distinctive and reminiscent of burned sugar, maple syrup, or curry. It is best detected in mature specimens. The spore print is white or pale yellow.

Ecology: *Lactarius rubidus* is a mycorrhizal partner with hardwoods—primarily coast live oak and tanoak. It grows alone, scattered, or gregariously on the ground in fall and winter on the West Coast.

Poisonous Look-Alikes: *Lactarius xanthogalactus* (see "Comments").

Comments: This mushroom is a popular edible on the West Coast, where it is sometimes called the candy cap owing to its distinctive odor and taste. It should be compared with *Lactarius deliciosus* (edible; p. 173), which grows under conifers, stains green, and lacks the distinctive odor. Most field guides use the older name *Lactarius fragilis* for *Lactarius rubidus* and cite its range as "widely distributed"—but there are *several* small species of *Lactarius* in eastern North America that have a burned sugar or currylike odor and pale cinnamon to orangish caps, most of which have gone under the name *Lactarius fragilis* at one time or another. I do not recommend this eastern "*fragilis*" group for the table since the mushrooms have been insufficiently studied and species identification, when possible, often hinges on microscopic examination. Additionally,

the eastern versions are smaller and less appetizing. For the time being, the safest course is for eastern collectors to leave the candy caps to the folks on the West Coast, who have a larger, more easily recognized, clearly distinct species. The potentially poisonous *Lactarius xanthogalactus* is also mycorrhizal with coastal live oak and tanoak on the West Coast—but it lacks the distinctive odor and features copious white milk that turns yellow when exposed to air.

In the Woods: (Darvin DeShazer) It's a delight to stumble on hundreds of candy caps, and such a patch can be quickly snatched. Use two fingers under the cap and pluck so that the cap snaps cleanly from the stem. Next, use your thumb to confirm identification by gently rubbing the top of the cap and feeling for the bumpy to corrugated texture. However, when only a single mushroom is found don't pass it up because more will likely be around the bend.

In the Kitchen: (Darvin DeShazer) Unless you are an experienced collector, the candy cap should always be dried for confirmation and positive identification: remove each cap from the dryer and pass it under your nose to confirm the smell of maple syrup. Beginners should reject any cap that does not have the right odor. Cooking with candy caps is a rare treat since they compliment breads, pastries, cakes, cookies, and almost any type of dessert from strawberry tarts to candied apples!

To use them, simply powder the dried caps and add to any recipe. Their strong flavor will blend into any dish—and don't forget to try candy cap waffles!

Recommended Recipes: Candy Cap or Matsutake Waffles (p. 304).

49 *Lactarius thyinos*

Edibility Rating: Great.

Distinguishing Features: *Lactarius thyinos* is a gorgeous, medium-sized gilled mushroom that fruits under cedars in northeastern North America. Its cap is convex at first, but flat or shallowly depressed at maturity. The surface is finely roughened and features vague, concentric zones of carrot orange and pale orange. It does not discolor green with age. The orange gills are attached to the stem or begin to run down it, and they exude an orange juice when damaged with a knifepoint. They are not covered with a partial veil when young. In age they may discolor slightly brownish, but they do not turn green. The stem is fairly short, and its

surface features tiny potholes. It is also orange and does not turn green with age. There is no ring on the upper stem, and the base is not enclosed in a sack. The flesh is whitish and crumbly, but it exudes a dark orange juice when sliced. The spore print is whitish or pale yellow.

Ecology: *Lactarius thyinos* is a mycorrhizal partner with conifers—primarily northern white cedar. It grows alone, scattered, or gregariously on the ground in late summer and fall in northeastern North America and in the Great Lakes region.

Poisonous Look-Alikes: Species of *Russula* in Group Two (p. 69).

Comments: *Russula subfoetens*, an orangish *Russula* species in Group Two, does not exude juice and smells like bad maraschino cherries. Also compare *Lactarius thyinos* with *Lactarius deliciosus* (edible; p. 173), which stains green. Small, orangish species of *Lactarius* in the *fragilis* complex (see "Comments," for *Lactarius rubidus*, p. 176) smell like burned sugar, maple syrup, or curry and should be avoided.

In the Woods: (John David Moore) Although this brilliant, carrot-colored mushroom dulls somewhat with age, it remains free of the green staining that serves to make *Lactarius deliciosus* (edible; p. 173) somewhat off-putting when considered for the table. The color of *Lactarius thyinos* makes for easy detection on the dark forest floor of its native bogs and in the damp grassy areas of bog edges. Because of its slimy, sticky surface it may readily pick up dirt and debris and is thus best cleaned in the field before tossing it into a bag or basket. *Lactarius thyinos* has a further advantage in being one of the least desirable real estate properties for larval settlements. Maggots move in with reluctance, if at all, and by the time they take up their rare residence you probably wouldn't let the mushroom into your kitchen anyway.

In the Kitchen: (John David Moore) *Lactarius thyinos* retains much of its cadmium orange color in cooking. Tasted raw, its bright orange latex is soapy and slightly bitter, but when sautéed its flavor is far superior to that of the perhaps inaptly named *Lactarius deliciosus*. Its texture, if not overcooked, is firm but not rubbery, and its flavor is fruity. Salt and pepper enhance its flavor, as does a squeeze of lemon juice.

Recommended Recipes: Lamb with Mint and Mushrooms (p. 306); Salted Mushroom Salad (p. 309).

50 *Lactarius volemus*

Edibility Rating: Fair.

Distinguishing Features: This medium-sized gilled mushroom grows on the ground in eastern North America's hardwood forests. Its cap is convex at first but becomes flat or shallowly depressed with age. The brownish-orange surface is fairly smooth and does not feature concentric zones of color or texture. The gills are attached to the stem or begin to run down it. They are neither distantly spaced nor crowded tightly together. They are whitish or creamy, but in age they are often discolored brownish; when damaged with a knifepoint they exude a copious white "milk" that stains them brown. There is no covering over the young gills. The stem is straight and smooth and colored like the cap. It lacks a ring, and its surface does not feature tiny potholes. The base of the stem is not enclosed in a sack. The flesh is brittle and white, but since it also exudes milk it stains brown over time. The milk is likely to stain your fingers brown as well (good luck washing it off). The odor, which is usually quite strong if you have collected several mature specimens, is reminiscent of dead fish—probably *Dorosoma cepedianum*, the gizzard shad, which is among the most malodorous members of the underwater world. The spore print is white or pale yellow.

Ecology: *Lactarius volemus* is a mycorrhizal partner with hardwoods, though it is occasionally reported under conifers. It grows alone, scattered, or gregariously in summer and fall in eastern North America.

Poisonous Look-Alikes: Species of *Russula* in Group Two (p. 69).

Comments: Two similar species, both edible, are also common in eastern hardwood forests. *Lactarius corrugis* features a cap that is reddish brown and distinctively wrinkled. Its milk also stains tissues brown, but it usually lacks the fishy odor. *Lactarius hygrophoroides* has a cap like *Lactarius volemus*, but its gills are very well spaced, it lacks the fishy odor, and its milk does not stain tissues brown. Whitish and yellowish varieties exist for *Lactarius volemus* and *Lactarius hygrophoroides*. *Russula subfoetens*, an orangish *Russula* species in Group Two (p. 69), does not exude juice and smells like bad maraschino cherries.

In the Woods: (John David Moore) If you are deliberately setting out to gather *Lactarius volemus*, you might want to take along some gardening gloves to guard against stained and smelly paws. The smell is indeed a lingering one and even seems to enter the room when I type this mushroom's name. Field cleaning is best done with a disposable paper towel or rag so the odor doesn't permeate your brush. If all this puts you "off your feed," you may want to search out *Lactarius corrugis* and/or *Lactarius hygrophoroides* with their pleasant absence of dead seafood aromas.

In the Kitchen: (John David Moore) If you've brought home some *Lactarius volemus*, put on some rubber gloves before wiping your harvest clean with a damp paper towel. Unless your specimens are especially dirty, washing should not be necessary, and it certainly won't get rid of the odor. *Lactarius volemus* has the virtue of usually being free of varmints, especially if you've selected fresh, young individuals, but keep an eye out for them anyway when slicing your mushrooms for the pan or dryer. Slow cooking for at least six to eight minutes is best, especially if you don't like the granular texture common to *Lactarius* species. The hard, granular texture becomes more of a pleasing crispiness when this mushroom is cooked sufficiently, preferably in a good amount of butter. I find the flavor mildly nutty but with a slightly bitter aftertaste. At least the flavor has no connection with the fishy odor, which thankfully disappears during cooking. Rehydrated dried specimens require even more cooking to eliminate graininess, though the nutty taste is more pronounced.

Recommended Recipe: Salted Mushroom Salad (p. 309).

51 Brown *Leccinum* Species

Edibility Rating: Good.

Distinguishing Features: Species of *Leccinum* are boletes that feature little tufts of fibers on their stems known as "scabers." See the Focus Point "Scabers" (p. 184) for help recognizing this distinctive feature. There are at least a dozen *Leccinum* species with brownish caps in North America. Beyond being boletes with brown caps and scabers on their stems, they of course differ fairly widely in other features (texture of the cap, color of the pore surface, bruising and staining, and so on). All are edible, so distinguishing between them is unnecessary unless you are interested in *Leccinum* identification (though you may lose your interest after reading the "Comments"). The important safety points are: (1) the presence of scabers on the stem of your bolete, (2) a pore surface that is not red or orange, and (3) a cap that is brown and lacks the slightest hint of orange or red.

Ecology: Species of *Leccinum* are mycorrhizal partners with trees. Although one or two species can be found in nearly every part of North

Photo by Dianna Smith

America, the genus flourishes in ecosystems that contain quaking aspen and birch. Thus, the species diversity is much higher in northern and montane areas. Most species appear in summer and fall and grow alone, scattered, or gregariously.

Poisonous Look-Alikes: Poisonous boletes in Group Three (p. 55).

Comments: There are many frustrating, and frankly ridiculous, characters used in *Leccinum* identification. Topping the list is the discoloration (or lack thereof) of the sliced flesh. Entire subgenera are arranged on the basis of whether the flesh—particularly the flesh in the apex of the stem, near the juncture with the cap—remains whitish when sliced, turns pinkish, turns grayish, or turns pinkish *then* grayish (all of this over the course of as much as an hour) under the assumption that you have collected very fresh mushrooms and have not waited too long before skipping your favorite TV show in order to slice boletes and stare at their flesh. Other characters used in *Leccinum* identification include colors, whether the pore surface bruises or not, the presence or absence of skin flaps along the cap edge (a result of the cap surface extending beyond the edge of the cap), and microscopic features. However, what I suspect will eventually turn out to be one of the most informative and taxonomically useful characters in *Leccinum* identification—namely, their mycorrhizal affiliations and other ecological preferences—are often virtually ignored in *Leccinum* literature.

In the Woods: (John David Moore) Species of *Leccinum*, unlike many other boletes, have the virtue of remaining varmint free until they are somewhat mature, at which time they are rather unappetizing anyway due to their watery sponginess. When gathering these mushrooms, go after young, firm specimens. Trim and brush them clean in the field.

In the Kitchen: (John David Moore) Most fresh, cooked species of *Leccinum* have at best a mild, nutty taste but a bland and watery quality. Many species blacken when dried or cooked. Thus, for reasons of taste and appearance they are best mixed with other mushrooms in soups and stews. Drying concentrates the flavor, however, and I highly recommend this approach. Slicing lengthwise into thin strips before drying moderates the chewy, fibrous nature of the stems. Some people also prefer removing the tubes from the caps, especially in more mature specimens.

Recommended Recipes: Mushroom Quiche (p. 307).

Focus Point
Scabers

The presence of "scabers" on a bolete's stem, indicating the genus *Leccinum*, is a feature that often confuses beginners. A great deal of bolete identification hinges on whether the stem is smooth or adorned with scabers, "reticulation," or "glandular dots." Despite my vociferous warnings against using photographs to identify mushrooms, the best way to distinguish between scabers, reticulation, and glandular dots is probably to study the stems in photos or (preferably) mushrooms identified by experts. The photo on the right displays scabers found in *Leccinum*, the photo on page 125 demonstrates reticulation on *Boletus edulis*, and the photo on page 220 shows the glandular dots of *Suillus granulatus*. The scabers in *Leccinum* are composed of tiny fibers tufted together. In some species they are dark brown or black from the beginning, contrasting nicely with the whitish stem surface; in other species the scabers are initially pale but darken with age or handling. In a few species the scabers remain pale throughout the mushroom's development.

52 **White *Leccinum* Species:**
Leccinum holopus and Others

Edibility Rating: Good.

Distinguishing Features: The white-capped species of *Leccinum*, like all members of this genus, are boletes that feature scabers on their stems. The caps are smooth or very finely velvety and are whitish—or such a pale version of tan that they look white from a distance. With age, the caps may develop grayish, pinkish, olive, or pale brownish colors, especially near the center. The pore surface is whitish, pale gray, or pale brown and may bruise brown when damaged, depending on the species.

There is no partial veil covering the young pore surface. The stems of the white-capped species of *Leccinum* are typically fairly long in proportion to the caps, and the scabers on the surface darken with maturity. In at least one white *Leccinum*, pale blue or blue-green stains are frequently found on the stem near the base. The flesh is white when initially sliced but may turn to pinkish and/or grayish (often very slowly) after being exposed to the air. The flesh in the base of the stem may be somewhat bluish. None of the white-capped *Leccinum* species is known to react to ammonia with a color change worth noting. The spore print is brownish, pinkish brown, or yellowish brown.

Ecology: Most of the species treated here are eastern in distribution and are mycorrhizal partners with various trees—especially birch and aspen. They grow alone, scattered, or gregariously in summer and fall.

Poisonous Look-Alikes: Poisonous boletes (p. 53).

Comments: See "Comments" under the "Brown *Leccinum* Species" (p. 183). The white-capped species are separated by mycologists on the same ridiculous set of characters used for their brown counterparts. The two species most commonly treated in field guides are *Leccinum albellum* and *Leccinum holopus*. The former has a very skinny stem and flesh that does not change color when sliced (after at least a fifteen-minute interval); it grows under oaks. The latter species has several "varieties," one of which (*Leccinum holopus* var. *americanum*) has reddening flesh and one of which (var. *holopus*) doesn't; both varieties are partial to birch, aspen, and the edges of woods near conifer bogs.

In the Woods: (John David Moore) Look for *Leccinum holopus* in mossy bog areas where birch is in the vicinity. It is quite common in late August and early September in northern regions. Gather firm, white specimens to avoid the typical sponginess of most aging boletes. Like most *Leccinum* species, it is unadulterated by larvae in its young state. Older individuals can be distinguished by their dull gray-green color, and if free from larvae they can be collected for drying (though why bother with them if you've got the choice between age and youth?). Minimal field cleaning is required; trimming of the stems and a quick brushing will suffice.

In the Kitchen: (John David Moore) *Leccinum holopus* has a mild, slightly sweet flavor, especially when it is sautéed for two to three minutes. The addition of fresh herbs, such as marjoram, improves the sweet, fruity quality. If you've field cleaned your finds, kitchen cleaning should be restricted to wiping the mushrooms with a damp cloth. Tubes should be removed from more mature specimens. Although the stems are fibrous, they needn't be discarded, since they add a pleasant chewy texture to the meal. As with other *Leccinum* species, dried versions yield more flavor, though in the case of *Leccinum holopus* the hint of sweetness found in fresh specimens dissipates with drying.

Recommended Recipes: Mushroom Quiche (p. 307).

 ## *Leccinum rugosiceps*

Edibility Rating: Great.

Distinguishing Features: Like other species of *Leccinum*, *Leccinum rugosiceps* is a bolete with prominent scabers on its stem (see the Focus Point "Scabers," p. 184); it is an oak-loving species of eastern North America. When very young its cap can be brown or yellow, but with age it is usually tan or yellowish brown. The surface of the cap is distinctively wrinkled when the cap is young, and its "skin" projects over the

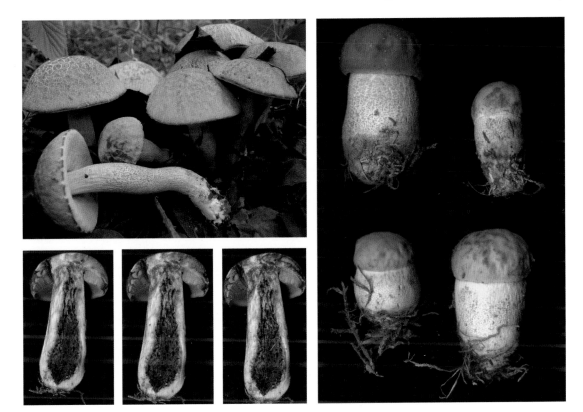

edge, creating little flaps. In older specimens the cap surface is prominently cracked and rugged. The pore surface is yellowish, becoming
dingy yellow with age; it does not change color appreciably when bruised.
There is no partial veil covering the young pore surface. The stem is
whitish beneath the pale to dark brown (or even yellowish) scabers, but
it may develop reddish colors, particularly in wet weather. The flesh is
firm—firmer, in fact, than it is in most species of *Leccinum*. It is white
but turns slowly reddish when sliced, especially in the area where the
stem meets the cap. Over a period of an hour or more, the reddish discoloration may become gray, fade back to white, or remain. The spore
print is brown or olive brown.

Ecology: *Leccinum rugosiceps* is a mycorrhizal partner with oaks and perhaps other hardwoods. It is a frequently flourishing fungal find in the
oak-hickory forests of eastern North America, appearing in summer and
fall. It grows alone occasionally but is more often scattered or densely
gregarious.

Poisonous Look-Alikes: Poisonous boletes, especially those in Group
Three (p. 55).

Focus Point
Color Changes
through Development

Throughout this book I have stressed the need to collect multiple specimens, representing all stages of development, in order to identify mushrooms successfully. *Leccinum rugosiceps* is a perfect example of why this is essential: its cap goes from fairly bright yellow to dark brown and finally pale tan. Imagine trying to identify a yellow button of this species by comparing it to a photo of mature, tan specimens. Boletes and species of *Russula* are notorious for appearing in the woods as "lone soldiers," but *all* mushrooms can be solitary on occasion—even those, such as the honey mushrooms (edible; p. 244), that typically grow in dense clusters but have gone AWOL. Mushroom authors—this one included—are under serious pressure from their publishers to limit the number of illustrations they include, and this is perfectly understandable given the enormous cost of reproducing the illustrations. The result, however, is that many mushroom authors are forced to pick *one* photo to represent a mushroom. Add to this equation the author's desire to include attractive and picturesque illustrations and you can see why the lone soldier you picked in the woods may not look much like the field guide photo. Now bring back the fact that the mushrooms themselves often refuse to cooperate and maintain stable colors (to say nothing of textures, shapes, and other key characters). . . . Well, you get the idea. Other mushrooms in this book that regularly feature dramatic color changes include *Boletus zelleri* (edible; p. 133), which has a stem that can transform itself from bright red to nearly white, and the Blewit (edible; p. 255), which is purplish in the button stage but can lose all traces of purple within a few hours of growth.

Comments: Some experts separate *Leccinum crocipodium* (formerly *Leccinum nigrescens*) from *Leccinum rugosiceps* on the basis of its darker cap, paler scabers, and slightly wider spores. However, either the two "species" grow together consistently under the same trees year after year (along with others that have kind of darker caps, sort of paler scabers, and just barely wider spores) or these characters are unreliable taxonomic indicators. Since these mushrooms are equally delicious and virtually indistinguishable, we will leave the matter to Leccinumologists.

In the Woods: (John David Moore) This *Leccinum* species is relatively easy to identify. It is more flavorful cooked fresh than other *Leccinum* species I've eaten—and it is the only *Leccinum* that often fruits plentifully in the hardwood forests of the central Midwest. In central Illinois it can be found in August in mixed woods of maple, oak, and hickory. The yellow to brownish, wrinkled caps blend well with leaf litter, so an attentive eye is required. Generally, the lighter yellow the cap color, the younger the mushroom. Older individuals are not necessarily larger but do tend to have darker, brown caps and, inevitably, a population of mainly stem-dwelling larvae. Cleaning specimens in the field will usually eliminate any need to clean them in the kitchen.

In the Kitchen: (John David Moore) Check for unwanted larvae in the stems when slicing. Sautéed for a couple minutes, thinly sliced *Leccinum rugosiceps* yields a delicate, nutty taste and a pleasingly firm texture. Older specimens have the flavor but tend to lack the firm texture of the young mushrooms. As with other *Leccinum* species, dried collections have a stronger taste.

Recommended Recipes: Mushroom Quiche (p. 307); Mushroom Ravioli (p. 307); Porcini Sauce for Pork Roast (p. 309).

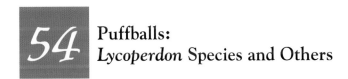

54 Puffballs:
Lycoperdon Species and Others

Edibility Rating: Good.

Distinguishing Features: For this "mushroom" I have lumped together dozens and dozens of species from several different genera, all of which share the features listed here. Cross-checking your mushroom against the listed features, to be honest, will result in the elimination of many edible mushrooms that could conceivably be called puffballs (a term with little or no scientific meaning and debatable vernacular stability)— but the process will also eliminate the poisonous, inedible, or merely unpalatable contenders.

- Your puffball should be somewhere between the size of a large cotton ball and a softball. If it is larger, see the "Giant Puffballs" (p. 91). If it is smaller, it may be a puffball (by anyone's definition) but it is not worth your culinary time, and the look-alikes list becomes unmanageable.
- The overall shape should be more or less round or roughly like an inverted pear. In other words, the *ball* part of your puffball should be all there is to it, with the exception of a slightly tapering bottom half in some species. The ball does not sit atop a high, clearly distinct stem, and there are no tentacle-like or petal-like structures surrounding it.
- Your puffball should be growing on top of the ground (not

submerged in the soil) and not on wood (with the exception
of the wood-loving *Morganella pyriformis*).

- The interior, when your puffball is sliced, should be pure
  white and softly fleshy. At maturity the inside of a puffball
  turns to dust, and you do not want to eat it at this stage. On
  the way to maturity, the white flesh may begin to turn yellowish, olive, brownish, and so on—but only puffballs with pure
  white interiors should be eaten.

- The composition of the flesh should be fairly even, with, at
  most, a textural difference between the fat, upper portion and
  the more slender, lower portion in puffballs that are shaped
  like inverted pears. The flesh should be neither hard and
  crunchy nor gelatinous. Be absolutely sure you *cannot* see
  the outlines of a "mushroom to be" within the interior
  (see the illustration on p. 42)!

- The color of your puffball's exterior should be in the white-gray-brownish range and not pink, orange, red, green, or otherwise brightly colored.

Ecology: The puffballs not eliminated using this list are mostly saprobes that grow terrestrially in the woods or, quite often, grassy areas. The various species range the continent and appear primarily in summer and fall or in winter in warm climates.

Poisonous Look-Alikes: Poisonous puffballs (see "Comments") and buttons of some *Amanita* species (p. 43).

Comments: I have in mind primarily the genera *Lycoperdon*, *Vascellum*, *Morganella*, and the smaller (rather than giant) species of *Calvatia*. A few of the species in this group have unpleasant tastes, but they are few and far between. Figuring out which species of puffball you have picked can be fairly difficult, but it is always a good idea to practice your identification skills, even if—in this group, anyway—specific identification is not necessary for safety reasons. If your puffballs were growing in an urban area, be sure to consider the possibility of toxic pollutants. Also follow the safety precautions on page 24 and eat only a bite or so the first time you try a new puffball since even the "safe" ones are occasionally reported as having laxative effects on some individuals. *Poisonous* puffballs in the genus *Scleroderma* have a hard, blackish or purplish-black interior throughout most of their development. One species,

Focus Point
Puffballs

As spore factories, puffballs have listened to different efficiency consultants than the factory-floor-minded consultants heeded by gilled mushrooms, polypores, boletes, and morels. All of the latter mushrooms have evolved to increase the surface area of their spore-producing machinery, but the puffballs prefer to run sweatshops where all the machines are crammed into one giant workroom. As spore production finishes, the product is not even conveyed away from the machinery. Instead, the walls of the sweatshop begin to crumble and decay. In some puffballs, a single perforation develops on the top of the ball, in some the ball's outer rind begins to peel back in sections or rays, and in some the walls come toppling down willy-nilly. The spores are thus exposed to air currents—though the puffballs with a hole at the top appear to rely on raindrops or small, food-sniffing mammals to tap their surfaces and force jets of spore dust through the perforation and into the air (a process one can mimic with a fingertip or garden hose for hours of fungal entertainment).

Scleroderma citrinum, is the parasitized host for the edible bolete *Boletus parasiticus* (p. 96).

In the Woods: (John David Moore) Small puffballs can be gathered on stumps and rotting logs, on forest floors, and in open fields and pastures. They can simply be plucked or cut away from the ground or log with a knife. Trim the base to remove dirt and debris. Brush them off a bit and bag them, selecting only the firm individuals. You may want to slice some specimens open to test for white interiors. Further checking for freshness can be done when slicing in the kitchen.

In the Kitchen: (John David Moore) Small puffballs can be halved, sautéed in butter and seasoning, or tossed into soups as a sort of fungal dumpling. If you're sure that your collection has fresh white interiors, you can use them whole with only the bases trimmed. Their flavor is pretty much indistinguishable from that of the giant puffballs (edible; p. 91) and can best be described as mild but rich, especially if they have soaked up a lot of butter when being sautéed.

Recommended Recipe: Asparagus Garnish with Mushrooms (p. 303).

55 Half-Free Morels: *Morchella* Species

Edibility Rating: Good.

Distinguishing Features: Half-free morels grow from the ground in woods in the spring. They are distributed fairly widely across the continent but are apparently much more common in eastern North America. Their caps are completely hollow and usually fairly small. By maturity the tip of the cap is usually somewhat pointed. Its surface features pits and ridges. Although the ridges may be pale initially, they darken as the mushroom matures and are eventually dark brown or black. The pits are pale yellowish brown. The cap is "half free" from the stem, meaning that it is attached about halfway up, leaving a substantial overhanging flap. It is not, however, *completely* free from the stem and does not hang on the stem's apex like a thimble atop a pencil eraser. The stem is usually quite long, proportionally, when the mushroom is mature. It can be very fragile, and its surface is grainy and whitish. The interior of the

Above and right: photos by Mark Davis; *bottom middle:* photo by Neil Selbicky

stem is completely hollow and does not feature little wisps of fiber that resemble cotton candy. The spore print is whitish, yellowish, or pale orange.

Ecology: Half-free morels are presumably like yellow morels (edible; p. 87) and black morels (edible; p. 84), which are mycorrhizal partners with trees until the death of the host, at which point they become saprobes. They are found under hardwoods and occasionally under conifers—but, unlike the yellow and black morels, they do not seem to be particularly fond of any specific type of tree. They appear in spring, bridging the black and yellow morel "seasons." For some reason, half-free morels are prolific in some years and rare or absent in others. There does not appear to be any regular cycle involved, however, and mycologists are currently at a loss for an explanation. The various species are primarily distributed in eastern North America, but at least one half-free morel occurs in the Pacific Northwest.

Poisonous Look-Alikes: False morels (p. 55).

Comments: Compare half-free morels carefully with species of *Verpa* (treated with the false morels on p. 57), which have completely free, rather than half-free, caps and usually have cottony fibers inside their stems. Also compare them with the edible yellow morels (p. 87) and black morels (p. 84). There are at least two or three North American species of half-free morels, according to ongoing DNA studies, and they are apparently indistinguishable on the basis of their physical features. One species appears to be widespread east of the Rocky Mountains; another has been collected, to date, only in Oregon. Whether any of our half-free morels is a genetic match to the European species *Morchella semilibera* has yet to be decided. Thus, the common name half-free morel is the most scientifically accurate label currently available for the North American species and we will have to wait for mycologists to come up with Latin species names.

Focus Point
Asci

The morels and false morels belong to the phylum Ascomycota, in which the spore-producing machinery consists of sausage-shaped structures, called "asci," that hold the microscopic spores. When the spores are mature, the end of the ascus opens and they are forcefully ejected into air currents. In the morels, the asci line the surface of the pits on the cap (the ridges are "sterile") and they are even angled so that they point outward, away from the mushroom. Most of the mushrooms in the Ascomycota collected by mushroom hunters have asci that contain eight spores, like the morels. Viewing asci with a microscope is much easier than viewing the basidia found in the Basidiomycota (see the Focus Point "Basidia," p. 241)—but it is admittedly unnecessary for beginning and intermediate mushroom identification. Of the 100 edible mushrooms in this book, only the morels, the devil's urn (p. 94), and the lobster mushroom (p. 267) have asci; the rest have basidia (the *poisonous* members of the Ascomy-cota treated in this book include only the false morels [p. 55]). But, necessary or not, viewing the microscopic machinery of these mushrooms is fun and can even be accomplished with a cheesy, garage-sale microscope and a tap-water mount—especially since the asci and spores of morels are very large compared to the stuff one looks at with most mushrooms. With a very sharp razor blade, simply slice a tiny, paper-thin section of tissue off the surface of one of the pits (stay away from the ridges) on the cap and transfer it to a slide. Add a drop of tap water and a coverslip. Use a pencil eraser to gently crush the mushroom section, flattening it out under the coverslip. View the slide with the highest magnification your microscope can produce, and, when they are brought into focus, the asci should be visible. There may or may not be spores present in the asci, however (*now* he tells me), since immature morels will not yet have manufactured spores and morels past maturity will already have ejected their spores from the asci. But if you are willing to play around with some middle-aged specimens you'll get results eventually.

In the Woods: (John David Moore) In years when these fragile, elongated morels are fruiting, you'll run across them while hunting black morels (p. 84) and sometimes during later hunts for yellow morels (p. 87). Composed more of cap than of stem in its youth, the half-free morel will often be hidden under the leaves. When the stem grows, however, it will become much easier to spot. Clean your finds with care in the field since this is a delicate mushroom—especially when it has matured to its long-stemmed state.

In the Kitchen: (John David Moore) If you have to wash your finds, do so with care in a colander if you want them to remain whole. Otherwise wipe them lightly clean with a fine, damp cloth. If you sauté or stew them, do so only for a couple of minutes. Overcooked, this morel becomes watery and even more insubstantial. The taste is similar to that of black morels, but the texture clearly lacks appeal. Unless you are hard up for any sort of morel, the half-free morel is best dried and then powdered to use as a seasoning.

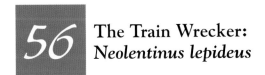

56 The Train Wrecker: *Neolentinus lepideus*

Edibility Rating: Mediocre.

Distinguishing Features: This medium-sized to large gilled mushroom grows on deadwood—in the forest or on fence posts, old railroad ties, and the like. The cap is convex or nearly flat, and its surface is whitish or pale tan underneath brownish-tipped scales. The gills are attached to the stem (sometimes by a notch) or begin to run down it. Their edges are distinctively jagged or serrated when the mushroom is mature. They are whitish to yellowish and sometimes discolor or bruise slowly brownish. When young they are covered with a whitish partial veil. The stem is central to the cap or somewhat off center. It is quite tough and hard and usually features a fragile whitish ring—though the ring may disappear. Its surface is whitish, but brown to reddish-brown scales often develop below the ring and in age it may discolor brownish. The base of the stem is not enclosed in a sack. The white flesh is very hard and may discolor yellowish in old age or when sliced. The odor is fragrant and spicy, vaguely reminiscent of anise. The spore print is white.

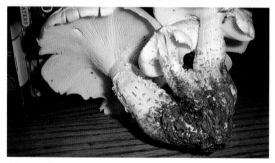

Above: photo by Irene Andersson; *middle and bottom:* photos by David Lewis

Ecology: The train wrecker is a wood-rotting saprobe that grows primarily on the wood of conifers, where it causes a brown rot. It is also reported on oak, causing a whitish rot. Look for it on stumps and logs in the woods—but also on fence posts, old railroad ties, and lumber. It grows alone, scattered, or in small clusters across North America, appearing from spring through fall or in winter in warm climates.

Poisonous Look-Alikes: None.

Comments: The rot caused by *Neolentinus lepideus* is reported to have decayed railroad ties so much that trains have derailed—though it should be pointed out that other organisms, both fungal and bacterial, may have been at work on the ties. Be sure that your putative train wrecker is medium-sized or large since a number of smaller, jagged-gilled wood lovers are inedible or unpalatable. Edible look-alikes include the matsutake (p. 297) and *Catathelasma* species (p. 251)—both of which grow on the ground rather than wood and have straight gill edges under normal conditions—and *Neolentinus ponderosus* (not treated in this book) which shares the jagged gills but lacks a partial veil and is *very* large (up to 50 cm across!). The latter species is found only in western North America and grows on the (woodland) wood of conifers or from dead conifer roots, appearing terrestrial.

In the Woods: (Darvin DeShazer) The train wrecker is a stunning find and can be located in the strangest locations—from downed timber or silver mine struts to telephone poles, fence posts, foundations of homes, and, of course, railroad ties. Avoid collecting for the table specimens growing from treated wood or polluted sites; healthy mushrooms from the forest are your safest bet.

In the Kitchen: (Darvin DeShazer) This large mushroom is very tough and even after long cooking remains very chewy. The taste is average, and the texture is tough, begging the question often posed by Robert Mackler: "If it's not at least as good as a portobello, why eat it?"

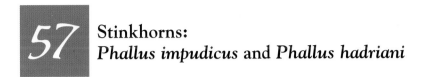

57 Stinkhorns: *Phallus impudicus* and *Phallus hadriani*

Edibility Rating: Good.

Distinguishing Features: Stinkhorns are medium-sized mushrooms that pop up in lawns, gardens, wood-chip beds, and other cultivated areas. When young they look like partially submerged "eggs" up to about 6 cm across with a whitish to yellowish or purplish surface. Sliced, the eggs reveal the "stinkhorn to be" encased in a gelatinous brown substance. Soon the stinkhorn ruptures the egg and soars skyward, often in a matter of hours. At maturity it has a hollow cap with a pitted and ridged surface somewhat reminiscent of that of morels (pp. 84 and 87)—but, unlike the morels, the surface is thickly coated with a brown to olive-brown, foul-smelling slime. Insects or weather conditions eventually clean the slime away, and the surface underneath is revealed to be whitish or yellowish. The stem is hollow, and its whitish to pinkish surface is finely dotted or grainy. The base of the stem is enclosed in a whitish, yellowish, or purplish sack.

Ecology: Stinkhorns are saprobes that grow alone or gregariously in cultivated areas. They appear in summer in most areas but can come up in winter in warm climates. Their technique for dispersing spores is fascinating, if a little disgusting: the foul-smelling slime is saturated with microscopic spores, and greedy insects gobble it up, covering their wings and legs with the stuff. Then they fly to other locations—say, your picnic—where they crawl around on the hamburger buns, spreading stinkhorn spores like micromayonnaise.

Poisonous Look-Alikes: *Amanita* buttons (see p. 43).

Comments: There are many stinkhorns in North America—including some truly bizarre orange ones with tentacles—but here I am describing and, um, recommending *Phallus impudicus* and *Phallus hadriani*, which are virtually identical except that the latter has purplish rather than

Lower left: photo by Mark Davis; *lower right:* photo by Konnie Robertson, sent to me in an e-mail in which she explained that *Phallus hadriani* was growing "in my wind-break" and that the mushrooms "gave me a chuckle upon discovering them." Note the unruptured "eggs" and the, um, sack around the base of the mature specimen.

whitish or yellowish eggs and a purplish sack around the stem base. Although I have received e-mails from folks who ate mature stinkhorns thinking they were morels, I do not recommend you try it. People who eat stinkhorns, like Shannon Stevens (below), eat the eggs.

In the Woods: (Shannon Stevens) Well *I* wasn't in the woods when I found these critters, but technically *they* were. There is a very small patch of landscaping at the entrance to my workplace, and that's where they were, under a pine tree (the "woods") in the mulch. I smelled the buggers before I saw them—something I seem to have a talent for. Most people, of course, can smell the malodorous mature fruiting body of a stinkhorn, but how many people actually know what it is they are smelling? I pride myself on my ability to track them down once I smell them. My personal best is about thirty yards. The first time I ran across these things, back in 1988, I was walking by a convent, well defended by iron fencing, when I got a whiff of something god-awful. Peering through the bars, I could see a patch of weird-looking things in some landscaping. I just had to get closer. Not wanting to trespass and incite the ire of the nuns, I rang the bell and asked permission to explore the grounds. They really didn't believe I wanted to check out their mushrooms, so they escorted me to my quarry, which I harvested for later identification. The nuns invited me to hunt their grounds anytime, as long as I asked first, but I've never gone back. Anyway, back to the ones at my workplace. I crawled through some bushes, and there they were, magnificent stinkhorn specimens. What really got my attention, though, were the dozens of ovate eggs the size of ping-pong balls all over the place. Man. I don't know where that mulch came from, but it was just bustin' with stinkhorns. I hadn't read up on the edibility of stinkhorn eggs, but if these things were edible I was going to eat well! I made a few calls that night and did a bit of research and came to the conclusion that I'd try pickling them.

In the Kitchen: (Shannon Stevens) After harvesting the stinkhorns I brought them home and cleaned them up. I cut a few open to check out the development of the stinkhorn inside and to get an idea of which ones were too far along; you want them as fresh and young as possible, before the critter inside has a chance to think about becoming a fully grown stinkhorn. I just love pickles, and I always have big jars of pickle juice left over when the pickles are gone. A while back I stopped wasting this good stuff and started using it to pickle other stuff: eggs, peppers, tomatoes, whatever tickles my fancy. That's what I used for my stinkhorn eggs; I believe it was a combination of juice from bread and butter slices and kosher dills. I stuffed the jar full and let 'em sit in the fridge for about two months. There was an outer, skin-type layer that came off when I took them out. The taste was not all that bad, and what came to mind was hazelnuts. I decided to share my wealth at our annual winter luncheon for the Missouri Mycological Society. Everybody brings unusual dishes, so I figured, why not? I tended the bar that year and set up shop there with cutting board, knife, and little toasts on which to put the pieces of stinkhorn egg. Nobody had tried this culinary curiosity before, but by the time the luncheon was over the eggs were gone. There is definitely a sense of pride when you eat stinkhorn eggs and join a very select group of mycophagists who have tried this delicacy. My recommendation is to try them at least once. I'm looking forward to my next batch!

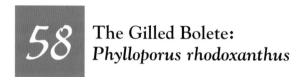

58 The Gilled Bolete: *Phylloporus rhodoxanthus*

Edibility Rating: Good.

Distinguishing Features: *Phylloporus rhodoxanthus* is a medium-sized mushroom that grows from the ground in woods. Its stature, colors, and texture suggest that it is a bolete—but it has gills rather than tubes. The cap is convex or flat (never vase shaped), and its surface is dry and very finely velvety. The color is quite variable, ranging from brown to yellow brown to reddish brown. In age the cap surface often becomes cracked. The gills are very thick and are well spaced. They are yellow, and they run down the stem. They are not covered with a partial veil when young. The stem is slender and smooth and lacks a ring. It is very pale yellow but is often flushed with the cap color. There is no sack around its base. The flesh is white or yellow and does not change color when sliced. The cap surface turns bluish when a drop of ammonia is applied. The spore print is yellowish.

Ecology: The gilled bolete, like the "true" boletes, is a mycorrhizal partner with trees. It grows alone, scattered, or gregariously under hardwoods (especially oaks and beech) in summer and fall. It is widespread on the continent but is apparently rare or absent in some areas.

Poisonous Look-Alikes: Species of *Paxillus* (see "Comments").

Comments: One form of the gilled bolete, also edible, has gills that bruise blue. A small, sand-loving gilled bolete occurs on the West Coast. It has gills that are attached to the stem but do not begin to run down it. It is presumably edible. Poisonous species of *Paxillus* either have fuzzy stems and grow on wood or have shallowly vase-shaped caps with strongly rolled-under edges. Additionally, the gills in *Paxillus* species can be fairly

Photo by George Barron

easily separated from the cap *as a layer,* just as the tubes of most boletes can be peeled from the cap.

In the Woods: (John David Moore) Mid- to late summer bolete hunting in many areas will eventually result in an encounter with the gilled bolete. Viewed from above, a *Phylloporus* specimen will lead you to expect tubes under the cap. Once you've recovered from nature's little prank of putting gills there instead, brush the mushrooms clean, trim them, and run a maggot check before bagging them for the kitchen. They are usually relatively free of pests, but it's always best to go after young mushrooms, if only for their firmer quality.

In the Kitchen: (John David Moore) If you've field cleaned your harvest carefully, further cleaning should only require wiping with a damp cloth. Slice the mushrooms, stems and all, and sauté for two to three minutes over medium heat. You'll find this an attractive mushroom in

Focus Point

Convergent Evolution

DNA testing has revealed that the gilled bolete is exactly what its common name implies: a bolete with gills. This means that its gills evolved *independently*, on the bolete branch of the evolutionary tree, far away from the "gilled mushrooms." Although this seems like an astounding coincidence, scientists call it "convergent evolution" and believe that two factors come into play: (1) a distant ancestor of both organisms had the genetic potential to develop the feature (gills in this case), and all its descendants retained the potential whether they "switched it on" or not; and (2) the physical limitations of life on our planet (gravity, for example) limit the number of viable evolutionary possibilities so that there is a relatively small set of plausibly successful physical forms. If the independent, convergent evolution of gills on separate branches of the evolutionary tree amazes you, consider this: zoologists now believe that "eyes," depending on how you define them, evolved independently in the animal world forty to sixty times!

its cooked state since it retains its bright yellow flesh color as well as the deep red of the young caps. I find that it tastes as good as it looks—tender and nutty. The dried mushroom loses some of its attractive colors but offers an enhanced nutty flavor. It recommends itself for inclusion in a wild berry sauce for duck or a stuffing for pork with raisins, apples, or cranberries. Fresh and on its own, it makes a very colorful garnish. Its taste on the West Coast has been described as slimy and bland, but this may either be a matter of individual palates or an actual difference in species. In any case, the midwestern specimens I've encountered rank high on my gastronomical list.

Recommended Recipes: Glazed Duck with Cranberry and Mushroom Stuffing (p. 306).

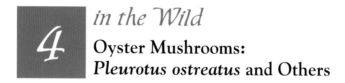

in the Wild

4 Oyster Mushrooms: *Pleurotus ostreatus* and Others

Edibility Rating: Great.

Distinguishing Features: Oyster mushrooms are medium-sized to large gilled mushrooms that grow on wood, often in overlapping shelves or clusters. The cap usually comprises most of the mushroom and is shaped

like a fan or kidney. It has a smooth, greasy surface, and its color ranges from white to brown.
The gills are soft and white or grayish and run
deeply down the stem (or stem stub). They are
not covered with a partial veil when young.
The stem is a stubby, lateral affair when the
mushrooms are growing on the side of the
wood, though it can become more developed
and more central when the mushrooms are
growing on top of a log. It lacks a ring, and
there is no sack around its base. The flesh is
white and a bit flabby and thin in the cap. The
spore print is lilac, grayish, or white.

Ecology: Oyster mushrooms are wood-rotting
saprobes that cause a white rot in deadwood.
They appear primarily on the wood of hardwoods but can also be found on conifer wood.
The various species and forms of the oyster
mushroom are found across North America in
summer and fall (or in winter in warm climates).

Photos by Mark Davis

Poisonous Look-Alikes: None.

Comments: In my experience, oyster mushrooms are often home to
hordes of black beetles, which can be found in the gills. "Mating studies"
and DNA analysis have recently provided a clearer picture of the various species in the oyster mushroom complex. *Pleurotus pulmonarius* is
white and appears on the wood of various hardwoods in the summer.
Pleurotus populinus grows on the wood of aspens and is also white; its
spore print is always white (never lilac). *Pleurotus ostreatus* appears in
the fall, or even in winter, and has a brown cap; its spore print is lilac.
The closest commonly encountered look-alike for oyster mushrooms
is *Hypsizygus ulmarius* (edible; not treated in this book), which has a
rounder, more convex cap, has a well developed stem, and grows in vertical clusters of two to four mushrooms, primarily on standing elms and
box elders. Species of *Crepidotus* (unpalatable or edibility unknown; not
treated) sometimes resemble oysters but are usually smaller and have
brown spore prints. One or two funky, large, yellow-staining species of
Pleurotus that feature partial veils and rings (edibility unknown) are not
treated here. See the parallel entry on page 36 for information on the
cultivated oyster mushrooms sold in grocery stores.

In the Woods: (John David Moore) In the Midwest, you can gather this mushroom from spring through fall. I have also found it during warm, wet spells in the winter months in Illinois. In northern Michigan it has the virtue of often appearing in large numbers on aspen after the morels are gone and before other edibles appear. Look up and down for it—on fallen logs and, often, high on dead trees. You may need your walking stick to knock down specimens that are out of reach. When field cleaning them, trim off the tough bases, which are often permeated with bits of rotting wood. Small, young individuals are preferable since they will be more tender and less populated with bugs. Give your mushrooms a good shake before bagging them in order to get rid of the beetles that may be competing with you for dining privileges. Although I've had no luck with this, it should be noted that if you find a transportable oyster-bearing log, you may be able to keep it watered in your yard to produce fruitings throughout the season.

In the Kitchen: (John David Moore) Oyster mushrooms should be thoroughly cleaned immediately, before any remaining beetles or larvae can wreak further damage. Wiping your collection clean with a damp cloth should suffice for the cap surfaces. Since bugs are adept at hiding out in the gills, the critters are best removed when slicing your oysters. If you really feel obliged to wash your collection under the tap, drain the mushrooms and dry them thoroughly afterward; otherwise, there will be a lot of water to cook off when sautéing them. Cooked for three or four minutes, oyster mushrooms have a chewy texture and delicate flavor. I find they are best in preparations wherein they are not lost amid other flavors. They work well simply sautéed in butter and olive oil with a bit of garlic and parsley and served over pasta. I have heard that larger specimens can be tenderized by pounding them like a steak or cutlet, although I've never tried this procedure. Slicing and drying does no harm to oysters, and their flavor is enhanced when they are reconstituted in the liquid of your choice.

Recommended Recipes: Artichoke Shiitake Pizza (p. 303), substituting oysters for shiitakes.

 Polyporus squamosus

Edibility Rating: Mediocre.

Distinguishing Features: This large polypore appears on the wood of hardwoods in eastern North America, primarily in spring. Its distinctive cap is fan shaped or vaguely funnel shaped and measures up to 30 cm across. The surface is pale tan or creamy yellowish underneath a layer of large brownish scales that are arranged in vaguely concentric arcs and zones. The pore surface is white or creamy and does not change color when bruised. The individual pores are fairly large and are angular. The stem is tough and lateral, and when mature it features a fuzzy brown or nearly black covering over at least its bottom half. The flesh is white and does not change color when sliced. Its consistency is soft when the mushroom is in the button stage but is soon very tough, especially in or near the stem. The odor is strong and mealy (see the Focus Point "Odors," p. 206). The spore print is white.

Ecology: *Polyporus squamosus* is a parasite and/or saprobe on the wood of hardwoods, causing a white rot of the heartwood. It is annual and grows alone or in clusters of two to three mushrooms on fallen logs and standing trees. It prefers cooler temperatures and is usually found in spring (often by morel hunters), though it occasionally makes an appearance in late summer or fall. It occurs throughout eastern North America.

Poisonous Look-Alikes: None.

Comments: Sometimes called the dryad's saddle, this mushroom is fairly easily recognized when mature, but younger specimens can be confused

Focus Point

Odors

I have not emphasized odors in this book because my experience leads me to believe that assessing an odor can be anything but objective. That said, there are a few consistent and distinctive odors in the mushroom world, and *Polyporus squamosus* is an excellent representative for the one mycologists usually call "farinaceous." The smell has been compared to that of cucumbers or watermelon rind, but I think "mealy" is its best nonscientific translation. Picture yourself in a damp mill, watching the huge stone wheel crush piles of grain. . . . Now take a big whiff. Regardless of what the odor smells like to you, however, *Polyporus squamosus* always has it—which means you have a stable point of olfactory comparison for the many other farinaceous species in the mushroom world. Detecting this odor can be important in identifying species of *Tricholoma, Entoloma, Inocybe,* and *Mycena*—among many others. Other odors that are frequently referred to in mushroom descriptions include the slightly foul maraschino cherry odor of some *Russula* species (p. 69); the fishy odor of *Lactarius volemus* (edible; p. 180); the shrimpy odor of *Russula xerampelina* (edible; p. 295); the sweet and sometimes aniselike odor of some species of *Clitocybe* (p. 58); the burned-sugar or currylike odor of the candy cap (edible; p. 176); the fragrant and spicy odor of the matsutake (edible; p. 297); and the "phenolic," unpleasant odor of the crushed flesh of some species of *Agaricus* (p. 70), which I cannot detect at all, even when others are gagging. If you are having trouble detecting an odor that "should" be present, your sniffer may simply be unable to register that part of the nasal spectrum—or the mushroom may be failing to match up to what mycologists require of it as a result of weather conditions, substrate composition, or what have you. Anyway, if your olfactory sensitivity is anything like mine, you are *never* going to smell things as finely as some mycologists do—as you can see from this mycological description.

> [O]dor very characteristic, not strong, but very penetrating, spermatic for an instant when the context is first exposed, but immediately becoming quite complex, predominantly a mixture of raphanoid and resinous with a trace of acetic acid, having a very decided pungency which quickly produces a tingling sensation in the back of the throat.

If you're wondering what mushroom is being described, trust me that you don't care. Just pray that you never find a mushroom whose odor matches everything in the description *except* the "trace of acetic acid" because then you'll be completely lost.

with other polypores, so be sure to collect big mushrooms until you are very familiar with the species.

In the Woods: (John David Moore) If your spring morel hunting is not going well and you yearn for mushrooms of some sort for the table, you might want to pay attention to hardwood logs, stumps, and tree bases in your morel spots. Your attention may be rewarded with the so-called dryad's saddle. Best removed from its host wood with a sharp knife, *Poly-*

porus squamosus is easily field cleaned with a brush and has the virtue of usually being free of varmints. It is, however, about as tough as a steel-belted radial tire, especially in maturity. Small, young specimens are therefore preferable, although older ones can yield more tender flesh around the outer edges.

In the Kitchen: (John David Moore) Unless the pores of your specimens are particularly dirty, washing in water should not be necessary. Wipe your finds clean with a damp cloth and then slice as thinly as possible, discarding the toughest parts near the stem. Sautéed slowly for four to five minutes, thinly sliced *Polyporus squamosus* can be pleasantly chewy, with a vaguely sweet flavor, but it always runs the risk of being as tough as a leather saddle, dryad's or otherwise, and the farinaceous taste does not altogether disappear in cooking. Drying is not recommended, as it only adds to the toughness. Longer stewing (half an hour) with other, more tender mushrooms (added later) is preferable, though the fact remains that this is not a mushroom to everyone's taste.

 ## *Polyporus umbellatus*

Edibility Rating: Great.

Distinguishing Features: This many-capped polypore is found growing in large clumps at the bases of hardwoods in eastern North America. The clump can contain dozens of caps and measure 20 to 50 cm across. The individual caps are roughly circular and fairly small (1 to 4 cm across). The surface of each cap is pale smoky brown or whitish and may have a somewhat streaked appearance. The caps are dry, and do not feel greasy when rubbed. The edge of the cap does not blacken with maturity. The pore surface is white, and does not change color when bruised. The individual stems are more or less central to the caps but might best be described as "branches" since they are fused at their bases into one or several large, fleshy structures. The flesh is firm and white. The spore print is white.

Ecology: *Polyporus umbellatus* is a parasite and/or saprobe on the roots and wood of hardwoods. It causes a white rot of the wood. It appears in summer or fall at the bases of trees or grows from buried roots. It is

annual, but in my experience it is consistent and long-lived; one cluster I am familiar with has appeared every summer at the base of an ash tree for over ten years. The distribution of *Polyporus umbellatus* is primarily northeastern, extending to Tennessee and Kansas.

Poisonous Look-Alikes: None.

Comments: Compare this mushroom with the hen of the woods (edible; p. 163) and *Meripilus giganteus* (edible; discussed with the hen of the woods), which are similar. The individual caps of these species are larger and less circular, however, and the "stems" are lateral rather than central. Also compare it with the cauliflower mushroom (edible; p. 108).

In the Woods: (John David Moore) This excellent and sometimes enormous mushroom can be found both in the fall and in the spring. Look for it at the bases of stumps and hardwoods, as well as on buried wood. Like many polypores, it can come back year after year. Don't harvest the whole thing, since it's the caps that are most tender and delectable. Harvest it like broccoli flowerets, taking just the caps and a bit of the branching stems. Field cleaning will be minimal since it is usually quite dry, with no adhering debris.

In the Kitchen: (John David Moore) Considering what dogs think of when they see trees and stumps, with or without attached mushrooms, it's best to give your collection of *Polyporus umbellatus* a good rinsing and draining before slicing it for the pan or dryer. Sautéed for two to three minutes over medium heat, it is among the best of mushrooms—tender but chewy like a good steak, nutty with a trace of sweetness. Dried it rates lower in tenderness but retains its flavor and is best chopped and added to soups and sauces.

Recommended Recipes: Chicken of the Woods with Lemon Cream (p. 305), substituting *Polyporus umbellatus* for the chickens; Spinach Mushroom Ricotta Pie (p. 310).

61 *Russula flavida*

Edibility Rating: Good.

Distinguishing Features: This gorgeous, yellow, gilled mushroom is a medium-sized, terrestrial inhabitant of hardwood forests in eastern North America. Its bright yellow cap is convex, flat, or shallowly depressed and has a fairly smooth surface. It is dry in all stages of development and is often fragile, breaking apart easily. The edge of the cap is not lined or is only very faintly lined in maturity. The gills are attached to the stem and are rather brittle. They are white when young but may develop yellowish hues with age. They do not bruise or discolor when damaged and do not exude a "juice" or "milk." There is no partial veil covering the young gills. The stem is colored like the cap (or a little paler), and its surface is more or less smooth. It lacks a ring and does not bruise when handled. There is no sack around the stem's base. The flesh is white and crumbly and does not change color when sliced, even after ten minutes. The odor and taste are mild. The spore print is white or yellow.

Ecology: *Russula flavida* is a mycorrhizal partner with oaks and other hardwoods, though it is occasionally reported under conifers. It grows alone, scattered, or gregariously on the ground in summer and fall east of the Rocky Mountains but is most frequently encountered in the Southeast.

Poisonous Look-Alikes: *Russula* species in Group Two (p. 69).

Photo by Pam Kaminski

Comments: Identifying yellow species of *Russula* with certainty is a task surpassed in tediousness only by attempting to identify *red* species of *Russula*. In the description here I have neglected some of the more arcane features used by russulologists to identify species (microscopic spore morphology and reactions to chemicals not found in grocery stores, for example), and I have omitted features that are frankly pretty ridiculous (like exactly how far you can peel the "skin" off the cap). The result of my impatience, however, is that I had better put "*Russula flavida*" in quotation marks if I want to avoid having my house stormed by rabid *Russula* specialists. The mushroom described here —a dry, yellow-capped, yellow-stemmed, mild-tasting *Russula* with flesh that does not turn ashy gray, found under eastern hardwoods— may represent one or several "true" species, and we will leave the precise labels to the experts. No *Russula* meeting the admittedly broad description is known to be poisonous (and no North American *Russula*, correctly identified as such, is going to *kill* you), but be sure to follow the precautions on page 24 if you experiment. Gray-bruising, yellow species of *Russula* found under conifers or northern and montane hardwoods such as birch and aspen are treated under *Russula claroflava* (edible; p. 291). Bright yellow *Russula* species with a strong, acrid taste are inedible.

In the Woods: (John David Moore) Look for this often bright, nearly totally yellow mushroom in late summer and early fall in hardwood forests. Like *Russula claroflava*, it never seems to appear in profusion but is well worth gathering if only to accumulate a dried collection for future use. Like many species of *Russula*, *Russula flavida* is favored by squirrels and slugs, but some judicious trimming in the field can retrieve specimens from minor gnawing and sliming. Trim the stem to check for pests, brush the mushroom clean, and place it in your bag gills down.

In the Kitchen: (John David Moore) Prepare this *Russula* as you would *Russula claroflava* (p. 293). It is not as tasty as its gray-staining relative—

it's less sweet and more mildly nutty—but it absorbs flavors well and has a slightly firm texture. It also crisps well if fried longer in butter or olive oil. Drying is recommended if you want more flavor from this mushroom.

Recommended Recipe: Salted Mushroom Salad (p. 309).

 ## *Russula virescens*

Edibility Rating: Good.

Distinguishing Features: *Russula virescens* is a beautiful, medium-sized, gilled mushroom that grows from the ground in eastern North America's hardwood forests. Its distinctive green cap is convex, becoming flat with age, and features a mosaic of small, crusty patches. The white gills are attached to the stem or nearly free from it and are not covered with a partial veil when the mushroom is young. The stem is straight, brittle, and white. It lacks a ring. Its surface is smooth and does not change color when bruised. There is no sack around the base of the stem. The

flesh is crumbly and white and does not change color when sliced. The odor and taste are mild. The spore print is white.

Ecology: *Russula virescens* is a mycorrhizal partner with hardwoods in eastern North America—though it has been reported from the Southwest and Montana. It grows alone or scattered in summer.

Poisonous Look-Alikes: Poisonous *Russula* species (p. 67).

Comments: The crusty-quilted green cap easily separates *Russula virescens* from other *Russula* species—with the exception of *Russula crustosa* (edible; not treated in this book), which is virtually identical in macroscopic features but has a brownish to yellowish-brown cap and a yellowish spore print. Since brownish versions of *Russula virescens* and greenish versions of *Russula crustosa* are not uncommon, however, the spore print color can be the only means of separating the two species without a microscope. If you are bound and determined to separate these two species, I suppose that now is not a good time to tell you I have real doubts about the stability of spore print color within *Russula* and *Lactarius*, and that you may need to get out your microscope. At any rate, confusing *Russula virescens* and *Russula crustosa* is harmless, from an edibility standpoint, so the matter is best left to mycologists.

In the Woods: (John David Moore) Hunt this attractive mushroom during summer and fall and be prepared to compete with squirrels, grubs, and other pests, which have a fondness for most *Russula* species. Its attractiveness to pests and its tendency to fruit alone make a young, untainted, and unchewed specimen quite a prize. Although young ones are perhaps best tasting, it's advisable to collect whatever you can rescue from hungry fauna. Brush and trim your finds carefully in the field; it's a brittle mushroom and breaks easily.

In the Kitchen: (John David Moore) Wipe your finds clean with a damp cloth and keep a lookout for vermin while slicing for pan or dryer. Sautéed for a couple of minutes, mature *Russula virescens* has a mild and nutty flavor; young samples, however, have a potato taste that goes well with diced shallots. Dried, *Russula virescens* has an enhanced nutty taste. Fresh or dried, this mushroom has a pleasant, firm texture. The green color is lost upon cooking.

Recommended Recipes: Polish Pork Chops with Russulas (p. 308); Salted Mushroom Salad (p. 309).

63 *Stropharia rugosoannulata*

Edibility Rating: Good.

Distinguishing Features: This beautiful, medium-sized to large (or very large) gilled mushroom grows in wood chips, gardens, compost piles, and disturbed soil across North America. When young and fresh, the cap is convex and wine red or reddish brown. It soon fades to tan (or paler), however, and flattens out. The surface is smooth and has a sticky feel when fresh. The edge of the cap often features hanging remnants of a partial veil, which covers the young gills. The gills are attached to the stem. They are pale at first but turn gray and eventually purplish black as the spores mature. The stem is whitish and may discolor yellowish or brownish with age. It features a large, distinctive ring that is finely grooved on its upper surface (and often blackened by spores) and radially split on its underside. Thin, white threads are attached to the base of the stem, and there is no sack. The flesh is thick and white and does not change color when sliced. The spore print is purplish gray to nearly black.

Ecology: *Stropharia rugosoannulata* is a saprobe that decomposes woody debris in brush piles, compost areas, gardens, wood chips, disturbed-

ground sites, and so on. The white threads on the base of its stem extend into the substrate and represent the mushroom's mycelium. It appears from spring through fall (or in winter in warm climates) across North America.

Poisonous Look-Alikes: Species of *Amanita* (p. 43), *Cortinarius* (p. 62), and members of the *Lepiota* group (p. 51).

Comments: Although this mushroom is very distinctive, be sure to match *all* the characters—and do not assume that similar, smaller mushrooms necessarily represent small *Stropharia rugosoannulata* specimens. One day in Pennsylvania I was searching rather fruitlessly for morels when a woman out for a walk on the wood chip trail that borders my morel spot asked what I was looking for. When I said "mushrooms," she replied, "What's wrong with these over here?" *Stropharia rugosoannulata* wasn't exactly what I had in mind that day, but the large clusters were, I had to admit, impressive. Moments later a troop of Girl Scouts came marching down the trail (I'm not making this up), shepherded by a very stern woman who lectured them about how fragile the forest ecosystem was, and how they should never stray from the trail or tromp on things. There were many disapproving looks in my direction, though I tried to slip behind a large tulip tree. As the troop faded away in a haze of wood-chip-directed backpacks, cell phones, and giggles, I was left to wonder whether my mushroom collecting could be as invasive as plowing up miles of trails through the woods and covering them with nonnative wood chips (and all their attendant fungal mycelia and microbes).

In the Woods: Since this mushroom is often found in wood chips and urban areas, be sure to consider the possibility of introduced toxins. Buttons and specimens with young, unexpanded caps are best. Slice *Stropharia rugosoannulata* about halfway up the stem and brush off adhering debris before bagging it. Be sure to return to your spot later since *Stropharia rugosoannulata* can fruit several times each season.

In the Kitchen: It has been many years since I last ate this mushroom, but I remember that it was good. I sampled buttons that had been sliced and fried in butter: both flavor and texture were pleasant. Mushroom authors who are more familiar with the culinary aspects of this species—including Paul Stamets, who cultivates it in his backyard—say that its quality diminishes as it matures and becomes thin fleshed. I recommend it as a good "all purpose" mushroom, adaptable to many recipes.

64 *Suillus americanus*

Edibility Rating: Mediocre.

Distinguishing Features: This bolete is found on the ground under white pines in eastern North America. Its cap is bright to dirty yellow with reddish spots and discolorations developing in maturity. The surface is slimy or sticky, and the edge of the cap features hanging remnants of a partial veil (which covers the pore surface in buttons). The pore surface is composed of large, angular pores that are arranged in vague radial lines. Its color is yellow, or nearly brownish with age, and it turns reddish brown when bruised. The stem is yellowish and often tough. It often sports a fragile ring or a zone of partial veil remnants, but this feature frequently disappears. The sticky surface is covered with cinnamon brown to reddish glandular dots. The flesh is yellowish and stains purplish brown when sliced. The cap surface flashes pinkish or reddish, then changes quickly to black, when a drop of ammonia is applied. The spore print is brown.

Ecology: *Suillus americanus* is a mycorrhizal partner with the eastern white pine (*Pinus strobus*) and is found throughout the range of its host. It grows alone occasionally but is more frequently found growing

scattered or densely gregariously. I have found specimens growing sixty-five feet from the nearest white pine—an indication of just how far a tree's rootlets can extend and how far away from the tree a mycorrhizal mushroom can appear. *Suillus americanus* appears in late summer and fall in eastern North America.

Poisonous Look-Alikes: None.

Comments: In eastern North America's white pine plantations, *Suillus americanus* can appear in amazing numbers following fall rains. In fact it is likely to appear wherever a white pine is growing; I have seen it fruit beneath a lost and lonely two-foot-high white pine sapling in a riverine ecosystem with no other white pines in sight. If you have not handled this species before, be careful; it is known to produce skin irritation in some people. It is also known to produce gastrointestinal irritation in some individuals, so follow the safety precautions on page 24 if you haven't tried it before.

In the Woods: (John David Moore) Any area, urban or wild, that features eastern white pine is a good place to gather this common and often prolific species of *Suillus*—if you decide it's worth the trouble. Don't bother to field clean them beyond cutting off the tough stems. The slimy cap skin that picks up all the dirt and debris is best removed in the comfort of the kitchen. If you're committed to making an all *americanus* meal, you'll need to gather a fair number, since there will not be much to this mushroom once the stem, tubes, and cap skin are removed. If you begin to develop skin irritation while handling your collection in the field, it's probably not worth pursuing this mushroom all the way to the platter.

In the Kitchen: (John David Moore) Peel the slimy skin of the cap with the help of running water. Slice the caps in half and remove the tubes, working from the inside to the edge. Check for larval tunnels in the flesh and discard any caps that are infested. This is not a very fleshy mushroom, so there won't be much left to slice. Thin slices sautéed three to four minutes yield a sluglike and insipid substance that you may decide is best left to be appreciated by its mycorrhizal buddies, the pine trees. Like other more substantial but equally slimy species of *Suillus*, this mushroom can be made more palatable by frying it in butter or oil until crisp. Whether slimy or crisp suits your fancy with this mushroom, try only a small amount at first since gastric problems with it are on record. It can be dried, but it's hardly worth the trouble when there's a world of finer mushrooms out there.

65 *Suillus cavipes*

Edibility Rating: Good.

Distinguishing Features: This gorgeous bolete is found on the ground under eastern tamarack and western larch wherever the host trees occur. Its beautiful cap is chocolate brown. Its surface is dry and densely hairy with brown and white fibers, and the edge of the cap often features hanging remnants of a white partial veil (which covers the young gills). The pore surface is yellow or greenish yellow and does not bruise. The pores are large, angular, and radially arranged. The stem is smooth and yellow toward the apex but hairy and brown below. It often features a ring. The flesh is white or yellowish and does not change color when sliced. The base of the stem is consistently hollow. The cap surface turns red when a drop of ammonia is applied. The spore print is brown or olive brown.

Ecology: *Suillus cavipes* is a mycorrhizal partner with species of *Larix* (which are generally called tamarack in the east and larch in the west). Since its distribution is dependent on its hosts, its range is primarily northern. It grows alone, scattered, or gregariously in fall.

Poisonous Look-Alikes: None.

Comments: The beautifully hairy brown cap, the hollowing stem base, and the tamarack/larch habitat make this one of the easier species of *Suillus* to identify.

In the Woods: (John David Moore) You will have to hunt this mushroom in the northern states where larch (in the west) or tamarack (in the east) can be found growing in mossy bog areas. If you are unsure of what you've found, slice a stem lengthwise to check for the characteristic cavity. This is a relatively clean-growing species and is generally free of larval invaders. It's also a dry species, like *Suillus pictus* (edible; p. 223), so the cap can easily be brushed free of moss and needles before bagging it for a trip to the kitchen.

In the Kitchen: (John David Moore) I consider *Suillus cavipes* the best of the genus in eastern North America. Like the similarly hairy *Suillus pictus*, it doesn't require removal of a slimy cap skin. But unlike *Suillus pictus* it doesn't serve up as an imitation of third-rate escargot. Some wiping with a damp cloth should suffice before slicing it thinly for the pan or dryer. Since about two minutes of sautéing leaves the mushroom with a rubbery and somewhat slimy texture, it's best to cook it longer, until it is brown and crisp at least around the edges. Rendered this way, *Suillus cavipes* has a nutty, potatolike flavor that is quite appealing. Some salt and pepper bring out the flavor effectively. Dried specimens are better suited for other preparations—soups and stews—since they lose some of the glutinous texture when reconstituted.

 Suillus granulatus

Edibility Rating: Good.

Distinguishing Features: This bolete grows on the ground under pines across North America. Its sticky to slimy cap is variable in color but typically progresses from pale tan (or nearly white) in youth to dark cinnamon brown in maturity. In age the color usually (but not always) breaks up, creating a patchwork appearance. There are no partial veil remnants clinging to the cap's edge. The pore surface is whitish at first,

Photo by Mark Davis

but soon becomes yellow. In rare collections it bruises slightly brownish. The young pores are not covered by a partial veil, but in some collections the young pore surface features milky droplets of liquid. The stem is white but develops yellow spots and areas, especially near the apex, as it matures. Its upper half is adorned with tiny, brownish, glandular dots (see the Focus Point "Glandular Dots," p. 220). There is no ring on the upper stem. The flesh is white at first but is soon pale yellow. It does not change color when sliced. A drop of ammonia on the cap surface produces a pale gray or bluish gray reaction. The spore print is cinnamon brown or brown.

Ecology: *Suillus granulatus* is a mycorrhizal partner with species of *Pinus* (the true pines, which have bundled needles). It grows alone, scattered, or gregariously in summer, fall, and early winter. In Illinois it is the first species of *Suillus* to appear, often showing up in early August in white pine plantations. It is widely distributed on the continent.

Poisonous Look-Alikes: None.

Comments: If you are on the West Coast, compare *Suillus granulatus* with *Suillus pungens* (edible; p. 225). There are several similar species of

Focus Point
Glandular Dots

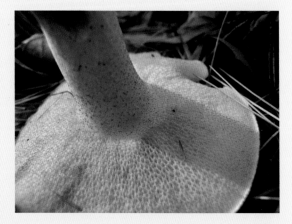

Suillus granulatus is an excellent representative for a physical feature that can be confusing for beginners: glandular dots on the stem. The presence or absence of glandular dots is often important in bolete identification, but the dots can be confused with reticulation (see the Focus Point "Reticulation," p. 125) and scabers (see the Focus Point "Scabers," p. 184). Unlike scabers, glandular dots are not composed of tiny tufts of fibers that are visible, individually, to the naked eye. Glandular dots are small and "smearable" and occur near the apex of the stem or over its entire length. Glandular dots are sometimes whitish or pale yellow and can be difficult to see if they do not darken to cinnamon brown as they do in *Suillus granulatus*. Advanced *Suillus* identification can take one farther into glandular dot hell than ought to be legal, since some species (not the ones treated in this book) don't read mycology texts and don't know when they should be displaying their dots proudly. Drying can help in these cases, since glandular dots sometimes become more visible in the process—but true suillusologists confirm reticent glandular dots with a microscope (where they appear as little clumps of pigmented cells).

Suillus, some of which have pore surfaces and/or flesh that is yellow from the first; flesh that stains pinkish when sliced; or a stem that is, on average, shorter and thicker than the "typical" *Suillus granulatus* stem. Since these species are edible—and since recent DNA analysis has begun to knock them off the taxonomic totem pole, folding at least one of them back into *Suillus granulatus*—I will not waste your time with the gory details except to say that some mycologists are beginning to suspect that specific mycorrhizal affiliation may be a more informative character for separating species within the "*granulatus* complex" than many of the observable physical differences.

In the Woods: (John David Moore) You can find this mushroom under pine trees, where it tends to appear over a more extended period—from midsummer to late fall—than most boletes, at least in eastern North America. Like *Suillus luteus* (edible; p. 221), it can be found right up to the first frosts, long after other boletes have stopped fruiting. Apart from trimming the stems and checking for larvae, field cleaning this glutinous species is pointless. Everything sticks to the slimy cap, so it's best to clean your finds in the kitchen where the messy job of peeling the cap skin can be more easily managed.

In the Kitchen: (John David Moore) The slimier species of *Suillus* have a record of upsetting some digestive systems. The problem seems to mainly result from consuming the skin of the cap. Hence your first task should be to peel off this glutinous feature along with whatever has stuck to it. Tubes also should be removed; they're a source of sponginess in most boletes. What will remain is a rather attractive, pure white, mushroom-shaped morsel that is ready for rinsing and draining. Sliced— not too thinly—and sautéed for two to three minutes, *Suillus granulatus* reveals a delicate flavor and, surprisingly, a lack of the "sluggishness" featured in *Suillus pictus* (edible; p. 223). The delicate flavor may not suit delicate digestive systems, however, so try only a small amount if this is your first experience with a glutinous species of *Suillus*. The mushroom lacks any firm, meaty qualities and is thus best combined with more substantial mushrooms in a sauce or other accompaniment to a meat dish. Dried and reconstituted in warm water, *Suillus granulatus* becomes a bit more chewy and flavorful.

Recommended Recipes: Mushroom Quiche (p. 307); Mushroom Ravioli (p. 307); Porcini Sauce for Pork Roast (p. 309).

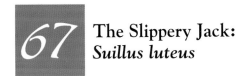

The Slippery Jack:
Suillus luteus

Edibility Rating: Fair.

Distinguishing Features: The slippery jack grows under conifers across North America. Its thickly slimy cap is dark brown to reddish brown but often fades with age. The surface is smooth, and the edge of the cap sometimes features hanging remnants of a partial veil. The pore surface, which is covered with the veil when the mushroom is in the button stage, is white or pale yellow. The pores are fairly small, and the pore surface does not change color when bruised. The substantial stem is whitish overall but becomes yellowish near the apex, where its surface is covered with darkening glandular dots (see the Focus Point "Glandular Dots," p. 220). A prominent ring sheathes the upper stem. It, too, is whitish, but it often develops purple shades, as well as a gelatinous

Above: photo by George Barron

texture. The flesh is white or pale yellow and does not change color when sliced. The surface of the cap turns gray when a drop of ammonia is applied. The spore print is brown.

Ecology: *Suillus luteus* is a mycorrhizal partner with conifers, especially pines, but also apparently with spruces. In Illinois it favors white and red pine (though it curiously seems to stick to one or the other tree in mixed plantations), and it is reported under (introduced) Scots pine across the continent. It usually grows gregariously, but "lone soldiers" are sometimes encountered. It prefers cool temperatures, appearing in fall.

Poisonous Look-Alikes: None.

Comments: Edible look-alikes include *Suillus corthunatus* (not treated in this book), which has a bandlike (rather than sheathlike) ring that turns brownish rather than purplish; and *Suillus subluteus* (not treated in this book), which has a less prominent ring and a more slender stem. Mycologists theorize that *Suillus luteus* is a fairly recent addition to the North American mushroom world. Recent DNA studies show that our North American slippery jack differs very little from the European version genetically, supporting the idea that human activity (probably the planting of trees) introduced the species to our continent.

In the Woods: (John David Moore) In the late fall, when other mushrooms are dwindling, a trip to the nearest white pine plantation should reward you with enough *Suillus luteus* to satisfy any slime lover's taste. As with *Suillus granulatus* (edible; p. 218), cleaning of any sort is best saved for the comfort of your kitchen.

In the Kitchen: (John David Moore) Follow the same cleaning procedure you use for *Suillus granulatus*—but also take care to remove this mushroom's slimy veil and other sticky material from the stem. The tubes are best removed by cutting off the stem and peeling off the tubes from the center toward the cap margin. Sautéed about three minutes over medium heat this mushroom yields a mild flavor and a more chewy substance than *Suillus granulatus*. It is, however, slimy—or perhaps the

Focus Point
Slimy Caps

Yes, I promised I would not patronize you by creating Focus Points to explain things that any reader with a tenth-grade education could figure out. But a "slimy cap" ("viscid" in Mycologese) is not always slimy since mushrooms often dry out after a few hours of exposure to sun and wind.

When this happens, one can often still ascertain that the cap *was* slimy before it dried. Adhering debris is often a clue, especially if it is tightly affixed to the surface of the cap. Additionally, dried but formerly slimy caps often have a glossy or metallic sheen—and some will become slimy again with a drop or two of water. Advanced mushroom identifiers can confirm former sliminess with microscopic analysis (the cell walls of a slimy surface become gelatinized).

better word is *slippery*. Its flavor is improved with the addition of some lemon and herbs, but there is no avoiding the glutinous quality. We once made the mistake of running it through a blender to make a soup. The result was a substance recommending itself for use when hanging wallpaper. If okra is your favorite vegetable, this may be the mushroom of your dreams since it's the equivalent of an okra concentrate. If such substances don't figure into your personal food pyramid, you can redeem *Suillus luteus* with the same preparation recommended for *Suillus pictus* (edible; below). Slice it thin and fry it over high heat until crisp. After you drain it on some paper towels, you'll have a slime-free food with an appealing nutty flavor. Dried *Suillus luteus* can be reconstituted to provide a bit more flavor, but the glutinous quality is still detectable.

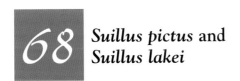

68 *Suillus pictus* and *Suillus lakei*

Edibility Rating: Mediocre.

Distinguishing Features: These beautiful boletes are sometimes called the eastern painted *Suillus* and the western painted *Suillus*. *Suillus pictus* grows under eastern white pine in eastern North America, and *Suillus lakei* is found under Douglas-fir in the west. The caps are fairly dry (a rare but pleasant change in the realm of slimy *Suillus*) and covered with soft, pinkish to brick-rose scruffies. The edge of the cap is tucked under when the mushroom is young; later it often features hanging remnants of a whitish partial veil. The pores are covered with the veil when

Suillus pictus

the mushroom is young. At maturity the exposed pore surface is yellowish, and often bruises brown or cinnamon brown. The stem features a whitish, yellowish, or pinkish ring. Above the ring the stem is fairly smooth; below it the surface is streaked with reddish fibers and scruffies. The flesh is pale yellow and often turns slowly pinkish when sliced. In *Suillus lakei* the flesh in the base of the stem is usually blue-green. A drop of ammonia on the cap of *Suillus pictus* produces a black reaction; the reaction of *Suillus lakei* is not documented (and I have neglected to perform the test when I have collected it). The spore print is brown or cinnamon brown.

Ecology: *Suillus pictus* is a mycorrhizal partner with eastern white pine, but it seems to be rare or absent in the southwestern range of the tree. It appears in summer and fall. *Suillus lakei* is a mycorrhizal partner with Douglas-fir in western North America. It appears in summer and fall in the Rocky Mountains and in fall and winter on the West Coast. Both species grow alone, scattered, or gregariously.

Poisonous Look-Alikes: None.

Comments: With their scruffy reddish caps and partial veils, these species are fairly easy to distinguish from other species of *Suillus*—and from each other, simply by means of their ranges and mycorrhizal hosts (though the blue-green flesh in the stem base of *Suillus lakei* would also serve to separate the two).

In the Woods: (John David Moore) Look for *Suillus pictus* in late summer and early fall under white pine, its exclusive habitat, in northern regions of the East and Midwest. It has the virtue of a dry, feltlike cap—unlike the slimy and sticky caps found in most members of this genus. Young mushrooms are preferable and can be recognized by the darkness of the red caps. As the cap expands, the color is dulled by the stretching of the red cap scales. When field cleaning this mushroom, cut the stems to look for critters and brush off any attached needles or moss.

In the Kitchen: (John David Moore) Although the cap skin of this species is a bit tacky, there's no need to remove it, as is recommended with most other mushrooms in this genus. A rinsing with water to remove any attached dirt or needles and a further check for larvae should be sufficient preparation for cooking or drying. Although *Suillus pictus* is frequently listed as among the best edibles, I find its texture rather off-putting unless one is fond of snails. *Suillus pictus* may have a future as mock escargot, but I find its sluglike consistency has all the palatability of unflavored gelatin. If such is not to your taste either, there is a solution: take your pan of sliced *Suillus pictus* beyond the realm of sauté into the region of serious frying. Slice your mushrooms very thinly and fry them in butter and oil until crisp. Add salt and pepper and any other seasonings you may prefer. You will have overcome both the bland flavor and glutinous texture, creating in effect a mushroom chip, which I find makes a palatable garnish for a baked potato.

 Suillus pungens

Edibility Rating: Bad.

Distinguishing Features: This slimy, medium-sized bolete is found only on the West Coast, under Monterey pine and occasionally under other pines. Its convex cap is thickly slimy through all stages of development. The color is *extremely* variable, changing from nearly white when the mushroom is very young through stages of gray or olive to reddish brown, cinnamon, or tan (or yellow) at maturity. Mottled specimens are

Left and upper right: photos by Chris Ribet

frequently encountered that combine these colors and often appear streaked underneath the slime. The edge of the young cap features a white to yellowish roll of tissue that is *not* a partial veil remnant but simply a soft extension of the cap's edge. The pore surface is not covered with a partial veil when young, but it does usually feature milky, whitish droplets of liquid. The pores are small and not arranged in radial patterns. The pore surface is white at first, but it becomes yellow with maturity; it does not change color when bruised. The stem is white at first but soon begins to develop yellow areas and stains. Its surface is adorned with glandular dots (see the Focus Point "Glandular Dots," p. 220) that are pale or reddish at first but darken to brown with maturity. There is no ring on the stem. The flesh is white, later becoming yellow, and it does not change color when sliced. The odor is strong and unpleasant. The spore print is brown.

Ecology: *Suillus pungens* is a mycorrhizal partner with Monterey pine, which exists as a *natural* tree in only three West Coast locations (two in California and one in Baja California). However, Monterey pine (along with its mycorrhizal partner) has been introduced in various locations on the West Coast, and *Suillus pungens* is also found under other West Coast pines. It grows alone, scattered, or gregariously in fall and winter.

Poisonous Look-Alikes: None.

Comments: Compare *Suillus pungens* with *Suillus granulatus* (edible; p. 218), which is very similar but lacks the roll of tissue on the young cap edge, lacks the strong odor, and usually features tan to reddish-brown colors (without gray or olive shades) that break up into a mosaic when the cap is mature. Several other western species of *Suillus* (all edible; not treated in this book) differ on minor characters.

In the Woods: (Darvin DeShazer) *Suillus pungens* is addicted to Monterey pine and can be found worldwide wherever the tree has been introduced. Pine needles usually stick to the slimy cap, which undergoes a remarkable color change as the mushroom matures. It starts off dirty white, then turns gray to greenish, and eventually turns yellowish to reddish brown—so use the pungent odor and the mycorrhizal tree to help with identification.

In the Kitchen: (Darvin DeShazer) The harsh odor does not disappear upon cooking but rather becomes the taste of your dish. Although some like it, most do not. The texture of this mushroom is poor as soon as it reaches a mature size. The flesh becomes waterlogged and soggy, thus limiting its usefulness to survival food!

70 *Tylopilus alboater*

Edibility Rating: Good.

Photo by Dianna Smith

Distinguishing Features: This bolete grows under hardwoods in eastern North America. Its distinctive cap is black when young and is often covered with a whitish dusting. As it matures the cap fades to grayish or grayish brown and the dusting disappears. The surface is finely velvety and often begins to crack with age. The pore surface is whitish throughout most of the mushroom's development but turns pink in old age as the spores mature. It bruises red, then brown or black, when scratched with a knifepoint. There is no partial veil covering the young pores. The stem is colored like the cap or a little paler. Its surface is smooth, but faint hints of a netlike covering may appear at the extreme apex. There is no ring on the stem. The flesh is white and firm. When sliced, it turns pinkish then slowly gray. The taste is mild and not at all bitter. A drop of ammonia on the cap surface produces no color change. The spore print is pink.

Ecology: *Tylopilus alboater* is a mycorrhizal partner with hardwoods, especially oaks. It grows alone or scattered in summer and fall throughout eastern North America.

Poisonous Look-Alikes: Poisonous boletes (p. 53).

Comments: Other blackish species of *Tylopilus* in eastern North America differ fairly substantially on one or more of the characters emphasized here. Some have brown pore surfaces, flesh that turns blue when sliced, an extremely bitter taste, and/or a stem surface that develops blue-green colors near the base. None of these mushrooms should be eaten. Beginners should compare *Tylopilus alboater* with the old man of the woods (edible; p. 76).

In the Woods: (John David Moore) This firm and durable mushroom can be found in hardwood forests that feature oak (William Chambers Coker, however, records finding it in cow pastures). Keep an eye out for it in mid- to late summer when other boletes are abundant. It tends to grow alone, so it may take some time to gather enough for the kitchen. Although it is fairly free of maggots and other vermin, collect young specimens and check the stems of older ones for infestation. Brush your finds clean in the field and don't be put off by any color changes when trimming and cleaning them since they have nothing to do with edibility.

In the Kitchen: (John David Moore) If your collection has been cleaned in the field, wiping the mushrooms with a damp cloth should be sufficient to prepare *Tylopilus alboater* for the pan or the dryer. This robust mushroom will also keep well for a few days in the refrigerator. Frying for two minutes reveals this mushroom's delicate, earthy, nutty flavor. The flesh of the caps is tender, and the stems are somewhat more meaty. With slightly longer frying, the skin of the cap becomes pleasantly crisp. *Tylopilus alboater* is certainly one of the better boletes for the table, by itself or prepared with fresh herbs and a squeeze of lemon.

Recommended Recipes: Mushroom Quiche (p. 307); Mushroom Ravioli (p. 307); Porcini Sauce for Pork Roast (p. 309).

71 *Tylopilus ballouii*

Edibility Rating: Mediocre.

Distinguishing Features: This striking, medium-sized bolete grows under hardwoods in eastern North America, especially in the Southeast. Its cap is bright orange when fresh—but it usually fades to orangish tan or pale cinnamon brown. The surface is smooth or very finely velvety and often develops pockmarks. The pore surface is creamy white or pale yellowish at first but becomes pale brown with age. It bruises brown

Photo by Roy Halling

when scratched with a knife. The young pores are not covered with a partial veil. The stem is orangish when young but soon fades to yellow or eventually whitish. It is often discolored brownish with age. Its surface is smooth, though it may feature a fine, netlike covering of raised ridges near the apex. It lacks a ring. The flesh is white and soft and may turn a little pinkish or brownish when sliced. The taste is mild or somewhat bitter. A drop of ammonia on the cap surface produces a yellow reaction. The spore print is brown, reddish brown, or purplish brown.

Ecology: *Tylopilus ballouii* is a mycorrhizal partner with hardwoods and occasionally conifers. It is especially fond of oaks and beech. It grows alone or scattered in summer and fall, primarily in southeastern North America (though it has been reported as far north as New York and Massachusetts).

Poisonous Look-Alikes: Poisonous boletes in Group Three (p. 55).

Comments: Although young specimens are strikingly beautiful, middle-aged and older specimens of *Tylopilus ballouii* have usually faded and appear boring and brownish. When all remnants of the former orange glory have disappeared, this species can be difficult to separate from a host of other boletes, though its brown spore print and mature pore surface will eliminate most contenders. Still, I do not recommend eating pale *Tylopilus ballouii* specimens that show no orange color until you are quite familiar with the species (and perhaps not even then since the older specimens are likely to be "splatty"). Be sure to compare *Tylopilus ballouii* with the orange-capped *Leccinum* species in Group Three of the poisonous boletes (p. 55).

In the Kitchen: The one collection of this mushroom I have sampled was bitter—and by all accounts this is often (though not always) the case. In addition, the texture was splatty, so I have serious doubts about whether it is worth your time to search diligently for specimens that lack the bitterness.

 Xanthoconium affine

Edibility Rating: Good.

Distinguishing Features: This bolete is found under hardwoods (and occasionally under conifers) in eastern North America and Mexico. Its cap is brown to dark brown or slightly reddish brown and features a very finely velvety surface. One variety of *Xanthoconium affine* develops small whitish or yellowish spots on its cap with some consistency. The pore surface is white at first but becomes dirty yellow to brownish yellow (*not* olive yellow) as the spores mature. It does not change color dramatically when bruised but may turn slightly darker yellow brown. The pores are small and circular and are not radially arranged. There is no partial veil covering the young pore surface. The stem is whitish toward the apex but is flushed with the color of the cap below. Its surface is fairly smooth, though one variety features a fine, netlike pattern of raised ridges near the apex. The stem lacks a ring. The flesh is white and does not change color when sliced. A drop of ammonia on the cap surface produces a rusty tan color change. The spore print is yellow brown and not at all olive.

Ecology: *Xanthoconium affine* is a mycorrhizal partner with hardwoods (and occasionally with conifers) in eastern North America and Mexico. It grows alone, scattered, or gregariously in summer and fall.

Poisonous Look-Alikes: Poisonous boletes (p. 53).

Comments: Compare this mushroom with *Xanthoconium separans* (edible; p. 232), which has a similarly colored cap when it is young. However, its cap fades much more noticeably with age, is usually somewhat wrinkled, and flashes bright green when ammonia is applied. *Gyroporus castaneus* (edible; p. 167) is also similar but is usually smaller and always features a brittle, hollowing stem. Other look-alikes in the bolete world have olive pore surfaces (when mature) and olive to olive-brown spore prints.

In the Woods: (John David Moore) Look for this often plentiful edible in hardwood forests in northern, southern, or central regions. It often favors woodlands featuring beech, and in northern Michigan it is one of the first summer boletes to appear. *Xanthoconium affine* is a favorite dining spot for maggots and other larvae, so look for the mushrooms with the darkest cap color. They will be young and firm though not necessarily pest free. Trimming about half the stem should reveal how far the larval forces have advanced. The dry caps are generally free of adhering leaf litter, so not much field cleaning is necessary. Avoid collecting the very spongy and paler-capped mature mushrooms as they will undoubtedly carry a full occupancy of maggots, which can quickly migrate to any young specimens you've put in bag or basket.

In the Kitchen: (John David Moore) Clean your collection further by brushing or wiping and check for pests when slicing your finds for the pan or the dryer. Mildly infested mushrooms can be trimmed, and in the dryer a larva or two will shrink to near invisibility. In the end, you will be the best judge of your gastronomic tolerance for formerly wriggling life forms. Whether you're preparing *Xanthoconium affine* for drying or immediate eating, you also may wish to remove the tubes, which, if the mushroom is approaching maturity, may have a spongier texture than the rest of the specimen. Good young specimens sliced and sautéed for three to four minutes have a rich, nutty flavor and slightly chewy texture. Undercooked *Xanthoconium affine* can have a slightly bitter aftertaste, so it's wise to try a bite after four minutes of cooking to see if you need to lengthen the time. The bitterness, however, is not a problem when using this fungus in soups, sauces, or stews. Neither is any bitterness apparent in reconstituted dried mushrooms.

Recommended Recipes: Mushroom Quiche (p. 307); Mushroom Ravioli (p. 307); Porcini Sauce for Pork Roast (p. 309).

 Xanthoconium separans

Edibility Rating: Great.

Distinguishing Features: *Xanthoconium separans* grows under oaks and other hardwoods in eastern North America. The color of the cap is quite variable, but the "typical" specimen is dark lilac brown when young and fades to yellowish brown or pale tan in old age. The surface is dry and is usually a little wrinkled, at least when the mushroom is young. The pore surface is white at first but soon becomes pale yellow to brownish yellow. It does not change color when bruised. The pores are small and circular and are not radially arranged. There is no partial veil covering the young pore surface. The stem is usually shallowly but distinctly wrinkled, and its surface is a little bit harder than the stems of most boletes. In some collections a netlike covering of raised ridges covers the stem near the apex or even over its entire length. The stem is white overall but is flushed with the liver-hued lilac brown of the cap. There is no ring. The flesh is white and does not change color when sliced. A drop of ammonia applied to the young lilac-brown cap or the flushed areas of the stem produces a dark green color change. The spore print is brownish or yellowish.

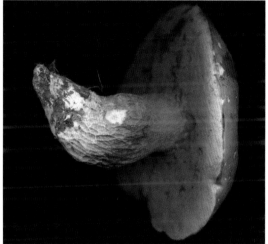

Ecology: *Xanthoconium separans* is a mycorrhizal partner with hardwoods, especially oaks. It is also occasionally reported under conifers. It grows alone, scattered, or gregariously in summer and fall in eastern North America.

Poisonous Look-Alikes: Poisonous boletes (p. 53).

Comments: Edible look-alikes include *Boletus edulis* (p. 123), which is more substantial, grows primarily under conifers, has a white netted stem and an olive spore print, and does not turn green with ammonia; and *Xanthoconium affine,* which is generally browner, doesn't fade as dramatically, has a softer stem, and does not turn green with ammonia.

In the Woods: (John David Moore) Although guidebooks frequently list this bolete as uncommon, in the late summer of 2005 it was a clear contender for Fungus of the Year in central Illinois, where we were practically tripping over *Xanthoconium separans* any time we entered the woods. As with most boletes, it's best to gather the younger ones to eat fresh and older individuals for drying. Don't be deterred by cracking and splitting around the cap edges. This often happens in hot, dry weather and indicates that you'll save dehydrator time for the specimens you want to preserve. Intrusive larvae are mainly found in the stems, which you may wish to check and trim during field cleaning.

In the Kitchen: (John David Moore) If you've cleaned the collection in the field, a quick brushing, wiping, or rinsing will suffice before you sort and slice your mushrooms for the pan or dryer. This is certainly one of the best boletes for fresh consumption. Two to three minutes of sautéing over medium heat produces a mild, meaty flavor and slightly firm texture—especially in the young mushrooms if they are not sliced too thinly. Dried, the flavor of *Xanthoconium separans* is akin to that of the king bolete (edible; p. 123). Fresh or dried, it makes an excellent accompaniment to meat dishes. I'm especially fond of it in a sour cream sauce with shallots served over a good beef filet.

Recommended Recipes: Mushroom Quiche (p. 307); Mushroom Ravioli (p. 307); Porcini Sauce for Pork Roast (p. 309); Spinach Mushroom Ricotta Pie (p. 310).

74 *Xerula* Species

Edibility Rating: Fair.

Distinguishing Features: Members of the genus *Xerula* are tall, medium-sized, gilled mushrooms that grow from the ground near stumps and trees in eastern North America. The caps are bell shaped when young and become flatter with age. The brown to yellowish-brown surface is shallowly wrinkled (especially near the center of the cap) and, when fresh, somewhat greasy or sticky. The gills are white and are attached to the stem, sometimes by a notch. They are fairly well spaced. There is no partial veil covering the young gills. The stem is long and straight and lacks a ring. Its surface is somewhat variable, ranging from fairly smooth and white to finely hairy with brown fibers that stretch to create zones and patterns as the stem lengthens. The most distinctive feature of the stem is its long, tapered "root," which extends deep into the ground (be sure to dig up your specimens with a knife if you want to check this feature). In some collections the rootlike portion of the stem bruises rusty brown when damaged with a knifepoint. There is no sack around the

base of the stem. The flesh is white and thin. The odor is not distinctive. The spore print is white.

Ecology: *Xerula* species are saprobes that decompose woody debris in hardwood forests. They are typically found near stumps and dying trees in hardwood forests, but they are also sometimes attached to dead, buried roots fairly far from any clearly associated, single tree. Occasionally, *Xerula* specimens are found fruiting from well-decayed stumps. They grow alone or scattered from spring through fall in eastern North America.

Poisonous Look-Alikes: Species of *Entoloma* (p. 64) and poisonous members of the *Lepiota* family (p. 51).

Comments: The long "root" at the base of the stem makes species of *Xerula* easy to separate from otherwise similar mushrooms. *Caulorhiza umbonata* (probably edible; not treated in this book) also has a rooting stem, but it grows only under redwoods on the West Coast. Terrestrial species of *Mycena* (some inedible, some poisonous; not treated in this book) will occasionally develop long, rooting stems, but they are usually smaller, have conical caps, and often have distinctive odors. *Xeromphalina tenuipes* (edibility unknown; not treated) is superficially similar to *Xerula* species, but it lacks the rooting stem base and has a dry, velvety cap. There are a only a few, or more than a dozen, species of *Xerula* in North America—depending on which mycologist one consults. All of them are apparently edible, and all conform, more or less, to the basic description offered here. Since microscopic examination and DNA testing are apparently required to separate some of these species, I will leave the gory details to the experts.

In the Woods: (John David Moore) This strikingly tall and slender mushroom, with its unusual rooting base, can be found in hardwood forests throughout summer and fall. Look for *Xerula* species close to and at the very bases of trees. Transporting this rather fragile mushroom is simplified by removing the long, woody stems, which are too tough and fibrous to consume anyway. Brush the caps carefully when field cleaning and place them gills down in your sack or basket. Once dirt gets into the gills, the mushroom will demand a washing in the kitchen, which will only add to the mushroom's tendency to be a bit watery.

In the Kitchen: (John David Moore) Perform any additionally needed cleaning of your *Xerula* caps with a damp cloth, then slice or dice them for a two- to three-minute sauté over low heat. The caps are tender and pleasantly chewy, but the flavor is delicate to the point of lacking distinction. *Xerula* species do, however, absorb flavors well. Broiling the caps gill-side up with butter, herbs, and some good, hard-grating cheese makes an appetizing morsel to serve on toast. Dried and reconstituted, this mushroom gains chewy texture but little flavor.

Difficult

These mushrooms are not easy to identify, and you should not consider eating them unless you are very good at identifying mushrooms and have years of experience under your belt. I can't say it more plainly than that, although I do concede that some of the mushrooms in this section are easier to identify than others. In some parts of the continent, some of the mushrooms *may* stand out from look-alikes better than they do in other geographic areas, but I have not taken this possibility into consideration in putting the section together.

75 The Horse Mushroom: *Agaricus arvensis*

Edibility Rating: Good.

Distinguishing Features: This medium-sized to large gilled mushroom grows from the ground in grassy areas across the continent. Its impressive cap is convex but flattens somewhat with age. The surface is whitish or pale yellowish and soon begins to develop darker, pressed-down fibers and scales. The edge of the cap often features hanging remnants of a partial veil. When rubbed repeatedly the cap edge will usually turn a little yellow. The gills are free from the stem. They are white at first, becoming grayish, then brown without passing through a pinkish stage. When young they are covered with a white, tissuelike partial veil whose surface is usually bumpy. The white stem is rather firm and thick. It features a large whitish ring, and its surface is smooth to finely hairy. There is no sack around the base of the stem. The flesh is thick and white and may turn slightly yellowish when sliced. The flesh in the very base of the stem, however, is *not* strikingly bright yellow and, when crushed between your fingers, does not smell strongly phenolic. The spore print is chocolate brown.

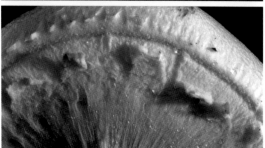

Photos by Pam Kaminski

Ecology: *Agaricus arvensis* is a saprobe found on the ground in grassy areas (lawns, meadows, pastures, and so on). It grows alone, scattered, or gregariously across North America, but it is especially common on the West Coast.

Poisonous Look-Alikes: *Agaricus xanthodermus* and other *Agaricus* species (p. 70)—and, if you have not taken a spore print or collected mature specimens with brown gills, potentially deadly species of *Amanita* (pp. 43–46).

Comments: A "Difficult" rating for the horse mushroom may be a bit of an exaggeration, but since it stains slightly yellow a healthy dose of caution is in order. Be sure to slice open the base of the stem: the flesh should not turn bright yellow and, when crushed between your fingers, should smell pleasant and mild. It is possible that there are several genetically distinct North American species "passing" as *Agaricus arvensis*, some of which may be limited to certain geographical areas. Some people are apparently "allergic" to the horse mushroom; be sure to follow the precautions on page 24 if you are trying it for the first time.

In the Woods: Young specimens are the best, in my opinion. Since the horse mushroom is typically found in areas where the invasive species *Homo sapiens* has influenced the landscape, be sure to consider the possibility of introduced toxins (see p. 20).

In the Kitchen: The horse mushroom is best when fresh and young and can be treated more or less like the common button mushroom sold in stores (*Agaricus bisporus*, p. 28), though it should not be eaten raw.

in the Wild
Agaricus bisporus

Edibility Rating: Great.

Distinguishing Features: The cultivated button mushroom (p. 28) occurs on our continent in both native and "escaped" populations in a variety of habitats (see "Ecology"). The cap is whitish or brownish and usually covered with tiny fibers. It does not bruise yellowish when rubbed repeatedly but may redden somewhat, especially in wet weather. The gills are free from the stem and covered with a tissuelike partial veil when young. They are pale, then pink, then brown. The stem usually features a prominent ring. It is white but may bruise pinkish. There is no sack around its base. The flesh is thick and white and usually turns slightly pink when sliced. The flesh in the base of the stem is not yellow. The odor of the crushed flesh is pleasant rather than phenolic, like almonds, or like anise. The spore print is chocolate brown. The defining feature of *Agaricus bisporus*, however, is microscopic: as its scientific name suggests, its basidia bear two spores each.

Ecology: *Agaricus bisporus* is a saprobe and grows primarily in stacked, underground trays on Pennsylvania mushroom farms. True native populations (not "escapees") have been documented under cypress in coastal

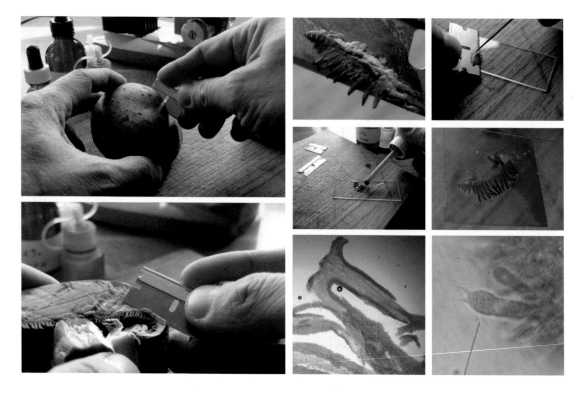

California, under mesquite in desert California, and under spruce in montane Alberta. Populations representing escapes from cultivation exist across the continent, typically in compost areas, gardens, along paths, and in heavily composted or manured soil.

Poisonous Look-Alikes: *Agaricus xanthodermus* and other *Agaricus* species (p. 70).

Comments: Compare *Agaricus bisporus* with the meadow mushroom (edible, p. 114), which grows in grass, has a fragile ring that usually disappears, and features surfaces and flesh that bruise pink less enthusiastically. Although a microscope is not required to determine whether your putative *Agaricus bisporus* is edible (the fact that it is an *Agaricus* that does not stain yellow or smell phenolic will suffice for experienced collectors), I would not bet the house on your species identification without verifying that the basidia bear two spores each. Then again, I have never found *Agaricus bisporus* in the wild; if you live in coastal or desert California you may see it with some frequency and be able to separate it from the many other local *Agaricus* species without a microscope. A 1995 study (Kerrigan et al.) found that *Agaricus bisporus* exists in North America as both a native and an introduced species. Genetically distinct, genuine North American populations are recorded from the areas and habitats I have noted; all other studied North American populations appear to represent "escapees" from mushroom cultivation and consumption and have European genetic roots. The authors speculate that there is a potential biodiversity problem on the horizon.

> The observation that foreign germ plasm of this species apparently outnumbers the native population of coastal California in a 3:2 ratio and has become well established even in native habitat in only about a century is alarming. An esculent weed may still be

Focus Point

Basidia

Microscopic basidia constitute the spore-producing machinery of all mushrooms in the phylum Basidiomycota—the phylum that holds most of the 100 mushrooms in this book (a few, such as the morels, have asci rather than basidia, and belong to the Ascomycota; see p. 194). Basidia cover the spore-bearing surface of the mushroom (the gills in the case of *Agaricus bisporus*), and the spores are produced at their ends on prongs. When mature, the spores are catapulted from the prongs by means of tiny water droplets. The vast majority of basidia in the mushroom world are four-pronged and bear four spores each. Some mushrooms have basidia that bear a different number of spores, usually from two to six. When these exceptions to the four-pronged majority are consistent, mycologists sometimes use the feature to help define species—as is the case with *Agaricus bisporus*. Microscopic examination of basidia is rarely required, for those of us who are not mycologists, in the identification process—though simply determining whether the spore-bearing surface of a mushroom has basidia or asci can narrow identification possibilities when you have no clue what you have collected. A few groups of mushrooms (notably the chanterelles and waxy caps) have distinctively shaped basidia, but the vast majority have basidia with more or less the same, clublike shape. Very rarely, the number of spores borne by each basidium is crucial to identification. Since *Agaricus bisporus* is defined on the basis of its two-pronged basidia, and since it is readily available in grocery stores, it is a good mushroom to use for practicing microscope techniques. While examining basidia is admittedly only rarely important, the same techniques are used to examine cystidia (see the Focus Point "Cystidia," p. 288), which help to define species fairly frequently. Viewing basidia and cystidia is more difficult than viewing spores (see p. 277) or asci (see p. 194) and usually requires a pretty good microscope, as well as special chemicals, stains, and/or reagents. One difficulty involved is that you must create a cross section of the mushroom's gills—a cross section so thin that you can look at it under a microscope at 1000×. Use an extremely sharp razor blade to section the mushroom's cap and use the illustrated method—but if you are as clumsy as I am you should be prepared for disappointing results (again and again) until your sections are thin enough to work. You may be able to see the gill-lining structures of some mushrooms with a water mount and a microscope that falls short of the 1000× goal, but a 2 percent potassium hydroxide mount (stained with something like phloxine or Congo red) and an oil-immersion lens are probably needed to view most basidia and cystidia adequately.

a disrupter of natural ecosystems. A weed that is extensively cultivated and can disperse on 18 wheels, thence from kitchen refuse as well as by microscopic aerospores having great potential range, is not amenable to control. . . . The consequence of these germ plasm invasions is that the native gene pool is diminished both by displacement (competition) and by dilution (interbreeding). (1937)

In the Kitchen: See the entry for the button mushroom on p. 32.

76 *Agaricus* Species (Unidentified)

Edibility Rating: Fair.

Distinguishing Features: This relatively small gilled mushroom grows on the ground in grassy areas near the edges of hardwood forests or tree lines. Its cap averages about 6 cm across and often has a blocky, squarish appearance when young—though it eventually becomes broadly convex or flat. The dry surface is covered with tiny, golden-brown to brown fibers laid over a whitish to tan background, resulting in an over-

all color of brown, though the center is usually slightly darker. The edge of the cap does not turn yellow when rubbed repeatedly. The gills are free from the stem and go through three distinct color stages: white, then pink, and finally brown. When young they are covered with a whitish, membranous partial veil that eventually detaches from the cap edge and leaves a white to pale brown ring on the upper stem. The stem is fairly long and slender, averaging 6 to 7 cm long and 1 cm wide. It occasionally has a very small swollen bulb at its base but more often is completely straight. Its surface is white and features scattered brown fibers below the ring. There is no sack around the base of the stem. The flesh is white and does not change color when sliced. The flesh in the base of the stem is also white—never yellow. The odor of the mushroom is mild, as is the odor of the flesh in the stem base when crushed. The spore print is chocolate brown.

Ecology: This *Agaricus* species is presumably a saprobe. I have found it primarily in grassy areas at the edges of hardwood forests or tree lines, but I have also collected it in the disturbed ground of a path side in a hardwood forest. It grows alone or gregariously and appears in July and August in central Illinois.

Poisonous Look-Alikes: *Agaricus xanthodermus* and other poisonous species of *Agaricus* (p. 70).

Comments: I have not yet identified this *Agaricus*, though it appears in my area almost every year. I have yet to study my collections of it with a microscope, but for the time being, at least, it does not seem to completely match any of the species descriptions in field guides or my (admittedly thin) folder of technical *Agaricus* literature. It has the appearance of a miniature *Agaricus augustus* (p. 112) or *Agaricus subrufescens* (discussed with *Agaricus augustus*), but lacks the strong odor of almonds and the erratic yellow bruising of those species. Since it is an *Agaricus* that does not bruise yellow or smell phenolic when the stem base is crushed, I considered it a safe mushroom for experimentation—though John David Moore (see "In the Kitchen") definitely followed the precautions on page 24 when he tried it!

In the Kitchen: (John David Moore) If your collection checks out according to the traits noted here, you can clean it and eat it—though you may never name it. Don't clean it with water unless your specimens are very dirty in the gills; the texture of this mushroom is slight and watery enough without adding more liquid. Brush or wipe your specimens clean with a damp cloth and sauté whole or coarsely chopped for about two minutes. This mystery mushroom does not have much to recommend it in the way of texture, but it does have a pleasant grassy flavor akin to that of the meadow mushroom (p. 114), though significantly milder.

77 Honey Mushrooms: *Armillaria* Species

Edibility Rating: Good.

Distinguishing Features: The honey mushrooms of North America are medium-sized gilled mushrooms that grow on wood (although several of the species tend to grow on buried wood or roots, appearing terrestrial),

Below: photo by Dianna Smith

usually in dense clusters. The caps are convex at first, expanding to flat with maturity. The surface is fairly smooth or somewhat scaly, depending on the species. The colors vary between species, and are even fairly variable within the limits of each species, but range between yellowish, tan, olive brown, orangish brown, and reddish brown. The gills are attached to the stem or begin to run down it; they are whitish to pale yellowish or pale tan. When young the gills are covered with a tissuelike or cobwebby partial veil. The stem is long and well developed. There is a ring on the upper stem, or there is a fairly prominent "ring zone" of adhering fibers. In many *Armillaria* species the stem bases are narrowed due to the tightly packed, clustered growth of the mushrooms. The faux terrestrial species that fruit alone or in small clusters from roots have thicker—or even swollen—stem bases. There is no sack at the base of the stem. The flesh is whitish and does not change color appreciably when sliced and exposed to air. The spore print is white.

Ecology: Many *Armillaria* species are forest pathogens—parasites that kill trees by causing a white, pulpy rot in the wood. Honey mushrooms spread through wood (and often from tree to tree) by means of black, stringlike "rhizomorphs" (see the Focus Point "Rhizomorphs," p. 246), which one can often discover with a little searching. The presence of rhizomorphs should not be used as an identification character, however, since other mushrooms might easily share the log and rhizomorphs are absent in some honey mushroom species. Several *Armillaria* species are apparently not parasites, subsisting instead as benign saprobes on deadwood. Honey mushrooms fruit prolifically after late summer and fall rains, and the dozen or so recognized species combine their ranges to span more or less the entire continent.

Poisonous Look-Alikes: *Omphalotus* species (p. 65), *Galerina marginata* (p. 46), *Gymnopilus* species (p. 72), and others; see "Comments."

Comments: A host of mushrooms, many of them poisonous, can be confused with honey mushrooms on casual inspection. A spore print is a must, as is inspection of the gill attachment and verification of the clustered growth on wood. These three characters, if truly matched, will eliminate all of the dangerous look-alikes except *Omphalotus* species, which have orange caps, stems, and flesh and lack a partial veil. Most other white-spored, densely clustered wood lovers with attached gills are much smaller than honey mushrooms. Until you have learned to identify the *Armillaria* species in your area with certainty, avoid the ones that fruit from roots or buried wood and thus appear terrestrial, since they open a whole new can of look-alike worms. Also, "lone soldiers" are not uncommon in the honey mushroom army, going AWOL and fruiting alone without the rest of the troops in their clustered units. These specimens can be particularly baffling and should also be avoided. Separating the individual species of *Armillaria* (for those who care) can be accomplished, in some cases, with close inspection of physical features and reference to geographic range—but a few species require microscopic examination or, worse, "mating compatibility" studies in petri dishes (don't ask; you won't be doing it in your kitchen) for reliable identification. Be sure to follow the precautions on page 24 when you try honey mushrooms for the first time; there are occasional reports of "allergic" reactions in some individuals. Some authors caution against collections of honey mushrooms harvested from the wood of various trees (hemlock, buckeye, eucalyptus, and locust; see p. 20).

Focus Point

Rhizomorphs

Many honey mushroom species have long, cord-like "rhizomorphs" that extend through the wood, twisting and turning, often near the surface of the log. The rhizomorphs represent the mycelium of the honey mushroom, and it is easy to see how such tough little cords can wreak havoc on a soft, woody substrate. Rhizomorphs occur elsewhere in the mushroom world as well—though they are typically smaller and white and extend only a few inches from the base of the stem—and their presence can be a valuable identification character (see *Stropharia rugosoannulata*, p. 213, for an example).

In the Woods: (John David Moore) In the Midwest, honey mushrooms can be prolific in the fall. They are mostly found on trees, at the bases of trees, on logs and stumps, and on nearby buried roots. You will usually see them in clusters, some quite dense. Their tough stems can be cut away from the host wood with a knife; then the mushrooms can be kept in a clump or separated, trimmed, and brushed one by one before bagging. The young specimens are the most tender, though some people prefer to discard the tough stems on all specimens.

In the Kitchen: (John David Moore) If you have already removed the stems from your collection and inspected it for invasive larvae, wiping the mushrooms with a damp cloth should suffice for cleaning. Some collectors recommend parboiling honey mushrooms for one minute before slicing and cooking. This not only removes the bitterness in some of the species but also may rid the mushrooms of any gastrointestinal irritants. Sautéed for two to three minutes or until slightly browned, these mushrooms, particularly *Armillaria mellea,* have a slightly sweet and nutty taste, as well as a pleasant, chewy, and sometimes crunchy texture. They are a particularly good addition to a French onion soup. Reconstituted dried honey mushrooms can be tough, though flavorful. It's best to powder the dried ones for use as a flavoring.

Recommended Recipe: Shaggy Mane Soup (p. 310), substituting honey mushrooms for shaggy manes.

78 *Armillaria tabescens*

Edibility Rating: Fair.

Distinguishing Features: *Armillaria tabescens* is a long-stemmed gilled mushroom that grows in dense clusters at the bases of hardwood trees—and from roots, appearing terrestrial. It is found in eastern North America. Its cap is broadly convex, flat, or even shallowly depressed and has a smooth to very finely scaly surface. The color ranges from tan to pale brown or cinnamon brown—or, in one fairly common form, yellow. The gills run down the stem and are *not* covered with a cobwebby or tissue-like partial veil when the mushroom is young. They are whitish, faintly brownish, or pinkish. The stem is quite long, and tapers to the base. It lacks a ring or "ring zone" of adhering fibers. Its surface is whitish to brownish and can be smooth or finely hairy. There is no sack around the stem's base. The flesh is whitish to watery tan and does not change color when sliced. The spore print is white.

Ecology: *Armillaria tabescens* is apparently a harmless saprobe, unlike many of the closely related honey mushrooms (edible; p. 244), which are parasites and attack living trees. It fruits in dense clusters at the bases of dead or dying oak trees or from dead roots. It is almost always found under oaks, but I have seen it on maples and other hardwoods occasionally. I have searched in vain for the black, cordlike rhizomorphs that typify many species of *Armillaria* (see the Focus Point "Rhizomorphs," p. 246). Its range extends southward from the southern edge of the Great Lakes region and westward to Texas and Oklahoma. The yellow-capped form appears to be more southerly in its distribution.

Poisonous Look-Alikes: *Omphalotus* species (p. 65), *Galerina marginata* (p. 46), *Gymnopilus* species (p. 72), and others; see "Comments."

Comments: This species is often called the ringless honey mushroom, and it is indeed the only *Armillaria* species that lacks a partial veil. This makes it fairly easy to separate from the other honey mushrooms (which can be *very* difficult to identify), but it also means that one identifying feature has been removed when comparing *Armillaria tabescens* to all the *other* gilled mushrooms, so caution is in order. Avoid "lone soldiers" and specimens in small clusters of two or three mushrooms since picking them would remove yet another crucial identifying feature (the densely clustered growth). Compare *Armillaria tabescens* with the stockier, shorter-stemmed *Lyophyllum decastes* (edible; p. 275).

In the Woods: (John David Moore) If you're not in the woodland mood, you can hunt the ringless honey mushroom in urban or suburban neighborhoods in the wet days of mid- to late summer. Look around the bases of oak trees but also on open lawns, where this mushroom will appear terrestrial but is actually growing on buried wood. The often large, dense clusters will offer more than enough for the kitchen. Cut off what you can use, preferably discarding the tough stems, and save your cleaning for the kitchen. You may wish to avoid gathering from lawns that show signs of being too well treated with weed killers.

In the Kitchen: (John David Moore) Even if you're sure that your gathering spot is free of chemical additives, it's best to wash your collection well in running water and drain it until dry. This species tends to be more bitter than other "honeys," so parboiling is recommended even if you are using dried specimens. Sautéed for three to four minutes, *Armillaria tabescens* has a taste and flavor distinguishable from other honey mushrooms only in the traces of slight bitterness that tend to persist. When used in soups and stews with a variety of seasonings, the bitterness disappears amid the other flavors.

79 *Boletus* Species (Unidentified)

Edibility Rating: Great.

Distinguishing Features: I find this large bolete under white oak and shagbark hickory in Douglas County, Illinois, in June and July. Its convex cap can reach 20 cm across and has the texture of well-worn leather. Its surface is whitish or pale brown and often becomes cracked with age. The pore surface is initially white and remains so for a long time until finally turning olive brown when the spores mature. It sometimes bruises faintly brownish when scratched with a knifepoint. There is no partial veil covering the young pores. The stem is large and thick and is often swollen in the bottom half, especially when the mushroom is

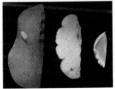
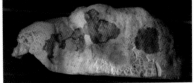

young. Its surface is whitish and features a fine, netlike covering of ridges at the apex or over the entire length of the stem. There is no ring on the stem. The flesh is white and thick and does not change color when sliced. The cap surface turns pale orange or watery tan when a drop of ammonia is applied. The spore print is olive.

Ecology: This *Boletus* species is presumably mycorrhizal with the white oaks and/or shagbark hickories under which it grows. I have found it only in one picnic area in a central Illinois state park, but it has appeared there nearly every summer for over ten years. It grows alone or gregariously and appears in June and July.

Poisonous Look-Alikes: Poisonous boletes (p. 53).

Comments: I have not been able to identify this bolete, which is reminiscent of *Boletus edulis* (edible; p. 123) but differs on several important characters. An unpublished DNA study found it to be fairly close to (but not identical with) *Boletus aestivalis* (aka *Boletus reticulatus*), a European species whose presence in North America is debatable. However, that species is described by most European authors as having a browner cap and a brownish stem—and European authors appear to agree that under the microscope *Boletus aestivalis* has substantially longer spores than the spores of the unidentified species described here. Other potential matches include *Boletus variipes* (edible; not treated in this book) and *Boletus atkinsonii* (edible; not treated), but, like *Boletus edulis,* these species differ on important characters. Regardless of its precise identity, I consider the species described here to be a safe culinary experiment since it is a *Boletus* species that does not have a red or orange pore surface and does not bruise blue.

In the Woods: Because this mushroom is incredibly delicious when dried (see "In the Kitchen"), I collect nearly every specimen I find that has not passed the Bolete Point of No Return and become, in technical mycological parlance, "splatty." Firm young buttons make the best drying material, but I am willing to peel the tube layer from a mature cap in order to make use of older specimens.

In the Kitchen: I am not a fan of fresh boletes, but I think they are better than just about anything else when dried and reconstituted. In texture and taste this bolete is indistinguishable from *Boletus edulis*, and it requires similar cooking strategies.

Recommended Recipes: Mushroom Quiche (p. 307); Mushroom Ravioli (p. 307); Porcini Sauce for Roast Pork (p. 309).

80 *Catathelasma* Species

Edibility Rating: Bad.

Distinguishing Features: These very large gilled mushrooms grow under conifers in northern North America, the Rocky Mountains, and the montane areas of the West Coast. Their caps measure 10–40 cm across when mature; they are convex, with a whitish to grayish or brown surface that often becomes finely scaly or cracked with age. The pale gills run down the stem or begin to do so. When young the gills are covered by a tissue-like, white partial veil. The stem is quite large and long. Its base is tapered, and often rooted several centimeters into the ground. A large, flaring, *double* ring sits on the upper stem. The whitish to brownish stem surface has a dirty appearance. There is no sack around the stem's base. The flesh is white, thick, and hard. It does not change color when sliced and exposed to air. The odor is unpleasant or mealy, but *not*

Photo by George Barron

strongly spicy or fragrant. The taste is mild, mealy, or slightly unpleasant. The spore print is white.

Ecology: *Catathelasma* species are probably mycorrhizal. Their range is apparently limited to areas of northern North America, the Rocky Mountains, and the mountains of northern California and the Pacific Northwest. They grow alone or scattered in late summer or fall, and are not common.

Poisonous Look-Alikes: Species of *Amanita* (p. 43).

Comments: The two species of *Catathelasma* most commonly found in North America are *Catathelasma imperiale* and *Catathelasma ventricosum* (spelled "*imperialis*" and "*ventricosa*" by some authors). There is some debate about how these species should be separated. As I am treating them, *Catathelasma imperiale* has a brownish cap and a mealy taste, while *Catathelasma ventricosum* has a whitish cap and a mild or slightly unpleasant (but not mealy) taste. *Catathelasma imperiale* may be limited to the West; *Catathelasma ventricosum* is best represented in northeastern North America, though it may occur in western ecosystems as well. Edible look-alikes for *Catathelasma* species include the matsutake (p. 297), which is smaller, has gills that do not run down the stem and a ring that is not double, and features a distinct, spicy odor; and several species closely related to the matsutake which also lack double rings or gills that run down the stem.

In the Woods: (Darvin DeShazer) *Catathelasma ventricosum* forms a massive button that expands into a very large cap with an extra long, tapering stem. Be sure to dig up the entire stem for an accurate identification. It fruits consistently for years in the same location, occurring in northern California from the Pacific Coast to the high mountains, but it is not commonly encountered.

In the Kitchen: (Darvin DeShazer) The dirty gray color never cleans up well in the sink—and this stinker still stinks when cooked! The mealy odor and dirty color make it unappetizing. The texture is tough and chewy, and cooking does not seem to help. To make matters worse, it can produce digestive gas (which must pass!) for those who eat it. This large mushroom rates at the bottom of the edibility scale and is better excluded from your basket. Several books rate it as a good edible, but I have yet to meet a single person who has eaten it twice and is proud of it.

81 The Shaggy Parasol: *Chlorophyllum rhacodes*

Edibility Rating: Fair.

Distinguishing Features: The shaggy parasol is a large, terrestrial gilled mushroom that grows in disturbed-ground settings. Its cap is nearly round when young but expands to broadly convex or nearly flat (though it usually retains a central bump). The dry surface is at first smooth and brownish but soon begins to break up so that the center remains smooth and brown but the rest of the surface consists of prominent shaggy scales with brownish tips over a whitish background. The gills are free from the stem and white. When young they are covered with a tissuelike partial veil. The long stem is fairly thick, averaging about 2 cm in width. It features a ring that can be fairly easily detached and moved up and down. The base of the stem is bulbous, but there is no sack surrounding it. The flesh is whitish but typically turns pinkish orange then slowly

Above and lower right: photos by Tim Zurowski; *lower left:* photo by Pam Kaminski

brown when sliced—especially in the upper stem. The spore print is white—and this is a crucial feature, since the poisonous *Chlorophyllum molybdites* (p. 50) can be a dead ringer for the shaggy parasol but has a greenish spore print.

Ecology: The shaggy parasol is a saprobe and typically grows in troops or fairy rings in disturbed ground areas such as roadsides, gardens, the edges of fields, and so on, often in the vicinity of conifers, though it is probably not mycorrhizal. It appears nearly year-round in California when moisture is present; elsewhere it typically appears in the fall. It is widely distributed in North America.

Poisonous Look-Alikes: *Chlorophyllum molybdites* (p. 50), species of *Amanita* (p. 43), and members of the *Lepiota* group (p. 51).

Comments: A spore print is a must. I know experienced mushroom hunters who have poisoned themselves by mistaking *Chlorophyllum molybdites* for the shaggy parasol. Beginners should avoid the shaggy parasol entirely since it features a white spore print, gills that are free from the stem, a ring, and a bulbous stem base—all of which are common *Amanita* features. *Chlorophyllum rhacodes* is also easily confused with other members of the *Lepiota* group, of which it is a member. The lepiotas known to be *deadly* poisonous, however, are smaller, woodland species and do not demonstrate the combination of features emphasized here. The parasol mushroom (*Macrolepiota procera*, p. 281) is sometimes confused with the shaggy parasol, as one might guess from the common names. The "true" parasol, however, is never used as an umbrella by Scooby Doo's owner, who obviously prefers to use the umbrella named after him. Ruh-roh. More to the point, *Macrolepiota procera* has a more slender stem, a cap that is less shaggy, and flesh that does not turn pinkish orange when sliced. Also compare your putative shaggy parasol with *Macrolepiota americana* (p. 278), which bruises yellow then reddish on its surfaces. The shaggy parasol is one of those species often reported as causing "allergic" reactions and minor gastric distress in some individuals. Whether these reactions represent confusion with *Chlorophyllum molybdites* is debatable—but be sure to follow the safety precautions on page 24 if you are trying the shaggy parasol for the first time.

In the Woods: (John David Moore) This hefty mushroom, which looks like a parasol mushroom on steroids, prefers shady areas, often under conifers, where it sometimes will fruit annually—and more than once in a season. Look for it in late summer and fall. Cut away the earthy base, brush it clean, and place it in your bag or basket gills down. Like the parasol mushroom, it is most often free of larvae, but you will probably prefer specimens whose caps are not yet fully open. You may also prefer to remove the stems, which can be tough if not chopped and cooked a bit longer than the caps. Don't be put off by the color changes (pinkish orange to reddish brown), which have no effect on edibility.

In the Kitchen: (John David Moore) Wipe your collection clean with a damp cloth or wash the mushrooms if the gills contain dirt and debris. Since "allergic" reactions to the shaggy parasol have been recorded, sample only a small amount when first trying this mushroom. Chopped or sliced and sautéed for two to three minutes (longer for stems if you're using them) the shaggy parasols I have eaten had a strong earthy taste with a slightly chewy texture. Besides lacking the rich, nutty taste most mycophagists describe, my specimens had a rather unpleasantly bitter aftertaste. This has led me to suspect influence from the area where they grew: shaded by fir trees on frequently windy parkland and closely bounded by playing fields, heavily sprayed corn and soy fields, and a highly fertilized golf course. This is mere speculation about the source of my collections' apparent aberration in taste. The shaggy parasol normally merits high praise for its nutty taste—richer than in the parasol mushroom—and its substantial texture. Like the parasol, it recommends itself to grilling or broiling with or without a seasoned stuffing. It can also be chopped and used effectively in a soup. Fresh specimens will keep up to a week in the refrigerator and dried shaggy parasols retain much of their flavor when reconstituted.

82 The Blewit: *Clitocybe nuda*

Edibility Rating: Good.

Distinguishing Features: Blewits are medium-sized gilled mushrooms that grow on the ground or on woody debris in woods and urban areas. The cap is broadly convex or nearly flat but features a rolled-under edge when young. The surface is characteristically sticky and smooth and is purplish or lavender—though it usually fades to pale tan. The gills are purplish or lilac when fresh and young, but they often fade to creamy white or turn very pale brown with age. They are not covered with a

Bottom left and right: photos by Dianna Smith

cobwebby or tissuelike partial veil when the mushroom is young. They are attached to the stem, usually by a notch, or in rare cases begin to run down it. The stem is fairly thick (1 to 3 cm wide) and is pale purple or whitish, though it may discolor a little brownish with age. It lacks a ring or ring zone of adhering, rusty brown fibers. Its surface is smooth or very finely hairy. The base of the stem usually features the finely fuzzy coating of mycelium that is typical of litter-decomposing mushrooms (see the Focus Point "Litter-Decomposing Saprobes," p. 257), and the mycelium can often be found binding together the surrounding needles, leaves, or debris. The flesh is whitish or pale lilac and does not change color when sliced. The odor is sweet and fragrant but never mealy. The spore print is pale pinkish, or nearly white in a thin print—but never brown, rusty brown, or *deep* salmon pink.

Ecology: *Clitocybe nuda* is a cosmopolitan saprobe, decomposing many types of woody litter. It is found in both hardwood and conifer forests, as well as in urban areas (in brush piles, compost heaps, and so on). It fruits alone, scattered, or gregariously—often in arcs or fairy rings—

throughout North America. It seems to prefer cool temperatures but is also frequently found in summer. Blewits will often produce several "crops" in one season, so be sure to return to your patch if you enjoy this mushroom. Many such patches can be found in San Francisco's Presidio—but you may *not* pick blewits legally in this park, so Bay Area collectors should visit the Golden Gate Blewits for study and admiration rather than pot collecting.

Poisonous Look-Alikes: Species of *Cortinarius* (p. 62) and *Entoloma* (p. 64).

Comments: Blewits demonstrate considerable variability in their colors, depending on their geographical location and (perhaps) the substrate. They also change fairly dramatically over the course of their development, and mature specimens often lack many of the features emphasized here, including the purple colors. Thus, whitish and brownish specimens are often encountered. They are considerably more difficult to identify than their purplish counterparts and should be avoided. The list of potentially dangerous look-alikes gets longer when they lack purple shades, and a microscope may be required for certain identification. Be sure to get a good, thick spore print to avoid confusion with species of *Cortinarius* (rusty brown spores) and *Entoloma* (*dark* pink rather than pale pinkish spores).

In the Woods: (John David Moore) Look for the blewit anywhere organic matter is decomposing. This variably violaceus mushroom inhabits compost piles, heavily mulched gardens, leaf duff in hardwood

Focus Point

Litter-Decomposing Saprobes

Blewits are classic litter decomposers, and since they are larger and easier to identify than many they make a perfect representative species for the group. The ecological role played by these mushrooms is to break apart organic debris: fallen leaves, needles, sticks, and so on. The mycelium often binds forest debris together and can be found with a little searching. Look for whitish fuzz and threads weaving through the debris near the base of the mushroom. In many litter-decomposing species, including the blewit, the whitish mycelial fuzz continues onto the base of the stem itself. The importance of litter decomposers to ecosystems cannot be understated; imagine what would happen if leaves, sticks, and needles never decayed and piled up, intact, year after year. Fortunately, animals, bacteria, and litter-decomposing fungi work tirelessly to process this debris and return it to soil.

forests, and needle piles under pines. Moreover, it has been reported growing on piles of decomposing newspapers. In needles or leaves, it often remains under cover, so look for telltale humps in the duff. The blewit is often plentiful, sometimes appearing in fairy rings. This mushroom's tendency to hide beneath organic litter necessitates some cleaning in the field. More mature specimens should be avoided; though relatively free of parasites, they can be more watery and less flavorful in cooking—and they have often lost their lilac color, making them more difficult to identify.

In the Kitchen: (John David Moore) Brush or wipe off any dirt or debris not removed in the field. Blewits will keep well in the refrigerator for one or two days. Slicing, sautéing, and freezing will keep them flavorful for two to three months. For longer preservation, slicing and drying is recommended, though it tends to intensify an already strong flavor in this mushroom. Blewits can also be thickly sliced, blanched, and then preserved in wine vinegar or olive oil. The strong flavor of the blewit blends well with onions and leeks. Sautéed in butter and perhaps some white wine, it makes a good topping for steak. Used sparingly, either fresh or dried, it works well when added to soups and stews. It should be noted, however, that the attractive but variable violet hues of this mushroom tend to be lost or dulled in cooking.

Recommended Recipe: Portuguese Steak with Mushrooms (p. 309).

 Clitopilus prunulus

Edibility Rating: Great.

Distinguishing Features: *Clitopilus prunulus* is a medium-sized gilled mushroom found on the ground in hardwood and conifer forests across the continent. The cap is whitish or pale grayish, and its surface is finely suedelike (except in variety *orcellus*; see "Comments"). The cap margin is typically somewhat lobed or wavy. The gills, which are pink at maturity, are attached to the stem and usually begin to run down it. There is no partial veil covering the gills when they are young. The stem is smooth and whitish and lacks a ring; it is typically about a centimeter wide. There is no sack around its base. The flesh is white and does not

change color when sliced. The odor of the crushed flesh is mealy or like that of bread dough. The spore print is pink or salmon colored. The spores themselves, under a microscope, are shaped like long footballs and are ridged lengthwise (see "Comments").

Ecology: *Clitopilus prunulus* is a saprobe that grows alone, scattered, or gregariously on the ground in hardwood and conifer forests. It seems to prefer open areas, grassy clearings created by windfalls, and edges of woods. It is widely distributed in North America.

Poisonous Look-Alikes: Species of *Clitocybe* (p. 58) and *Entoloma* (p. 64).

Comments: This is a difficult mushroom to identify with certainty if you have not collected it—and its look-alikes—several times. I acquired my confidence in the species by using a microscope, but perhaps I am too conservative. The pink spore print separates it from the poisonous species of *Clitocybe* in Group Two (p. 60), but there are several species of *Entoloma* (p. 64) of unknown edibility that can be dead ringers until one looks at the spores of *Clitopilus prunulus*, which are distinctive and, combined with the evidence from macroscopic features, definitive. See the Focus Point "Spore Shapes and Sizes" (p. 277) for an introduction to looking at spores with a microscope. A variety of *Clitopilus prunulus* with a slimy, rather than suedelike, cap is called *Clitopilus* *prunulus* var. *orcellus;* it is otherwise indistinguishable from the typical variety.

In the Woods: (John David Moore) You should look for the so-called sweetbread mushroom in late summer among oaks or pines in open areas and on grassy woodland edges. It grows either alone or in groups. Check for a suedelike cap, with the feel of kid leather, and a smell that is mealy or like that of a cucumber. If you get this far, the mushrooms are worth collecting for further investigation, preferably by a mycologist, to be sure they are not *Clitocybe dealbata* (p. 60) or something equally nasty. Pick young specimens—those with the whitest gills and caps—for the table, but also bring along some mature individuals for aid in identification. Field cleaning should involve no more than a quick dusting.

In the Kitchen: (John David Moore) Until you get a positive identification from a trusted authority, you can keep your potential edibles in the refrigerator for a few days. First clean them further with a damp cloth and check the stems for larvae, though they are usually absent in fresh specimens. If your harvest is positively *Clitopilus prunulus*, a few sliced mushrooms sautéed for one to two minutes will have a rich nutty flavor. A longer period in the pan will crisp the edges of the slices nicely and enhance the delicate texture. They are good with garlic, oil, and herbs over pasta, though some people find that the strong flavor recommends mixing this mushroom with other, less assertive ones. The flavor increases in dried specimens, which are best used, perhaps sparingly, in soups and stews.

Recommended Recipe: Pasta with Hedgehogs, Bacon, and Tomato (p. 308), substituting *Clitopilus prunulus* for the hedgehogs.

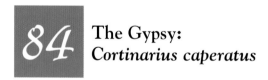

84 The Gypsy: *Cortinarius caperatus*

Edibility Rating: Fair.

Distinguishing Features: The gypsy is a medium-sized, terrestrial gilled mushroom found in hardwood and conifer forests across northern and eastern North America. Its cap is yellowish brown and, when young, features a whitish, filmy coating of fibers—as though someone placed a

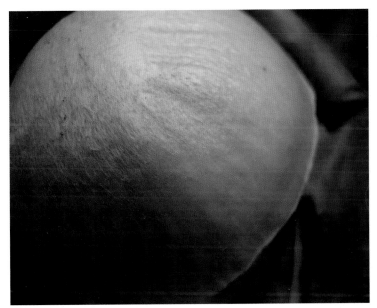

facial tissue on the cap when it was slightly damp. The extreme margin of the cap usually retains this white, pasted tissue appearance into maturity. The gills are attached to the stem and are initially pale, though they become brown or cinnamon brown in age (often going through a "mottled" stage in between). When young they are covered with a white, tissuelike partial veil. The stem is whitish and is usually finely shaggy near the apex. There is a thick, prominent, white ring on the upper stem, and the stem base is sometimes covered with a filmy white coating similar to the tissue material on the cap. There is no sack around the base of the stem. The flesh is whitish, grayish, or pale lilac and does not change color when sliced. The odor is mild. The spore print is rusty brown. The spores are elliptical, measuring 11–15 × 7–10 microns, and are slightly roughened.

Ecology: The gypsy grows on the ground gregariously and is a mycorrhizal partner with hardwoods, conifers, and bushes in the blueberry family. It appears in summer and fall in northern and eastern North America.

Poisonous Look-Alikes: Species of *Amanita* (p. 43), *Gymnopilus* (p. 72), and *Pholiota* (see "Comments").

Comments: Since several of the gypsy's defining features (the ring and the filmy coating on the cap and stem base) could easily lead to confusion with potentially deadly *Amanita* species, be sure that the gills are attached to the stem and the spore print is rusty brown. Some

Gymnopilus and *Pholiota* species can be superficially similar but grow on wood. *Pholiota* species, additionally, have brown (rather than rusty brown) spore prints, caps that are either slimy or scaly, and often scaly stems. Microscopic features are probably not required for successful identification, but I have listed the spore details for those who have microscopes and want extra insurance. Recent DNA testing has consigned the genus *Rozites*, which contained only the gypsy, to the taxonomic trash bin; now the gypsy has returned like a long-lost child to *Cortinarius*, where it was originally placed by Elias Fries (a founding fungal father) in the early nineteenth century.

In the Woods: (John David Moore) This is an abundant late summer fungus in the mixed woods of the northern Midwest. Formerly known as *Rozites caperata*, it now holds the honor of being the only truly reliable edible in the vast, difficult, and gastronomically dangerous genus *Cortinarius*. Any sort of northern forest will do when you are tracking the gypsy mushroom. If you are a huckleberry hunter as well as a fungus follower, you'd be wise to look in your favorite woodland berry spots, since the bushes often appear near *Cortinarius caperatus*. Young mushrooms are preferred for the table since the larger the cap, the more watery the meal. They require little if any cleaning in the field, and young specimens are usually free of intrusive larvae.

In the Kitchen: (John David Moore) If you must clean your collection, avoid washing it if possible since these mushrooms tend to be naturally watery. If you must wash them, be sure to drain them well on paper towels. Larger mushrooms can be chopped or sliced; small ones are best left whole. Sautéed for one to two minutes (don't overcook them) over medium heat, *Cortinarius caperatus* has a mild, earthy flavor and tender texture. The stems are more chewy, and some people prefer to discard them. Dried specimens reconstituted in water or wine have a more substantial texture and more concentrated flavor. The gypsy will provide good fortune in a sauce for steaks or in soups combining other mushrooms of different textures and flavors.

 Flammulina velutipes

Edibility Rating: Good.

Photo by Pam Kaminski

Distinguishing Features: *Flammulina velutipes* is a medium-sized gilled mushroom that grows on the wood of hardwoods in cool (and down-right cold) weather. The wood may be buried, however, and then the mushrooms appear terrestrial. The caps are smooth and reddish brown to orangish or yellowish brown and have a moist, thick "skin." The gills are whitish or pale yellow and are attached to the stem. They are not covered with a partial veil when young. The stem is the most distinctive feature; it is colored like the cap but develops a prominent, velvety, brown or blackish covering from the base up. There is no ring or sack. The flesh is whitish to yellowish and does not change color when sliced. The spore print is white.

Ecology: *Flammulina velutipes* is a wood-rotting saprobe found on hardwood logs and trees. It is especially fond of elms, willows, and poplars (well, not the poplars if we are being strict in our species concepts; see "Comments"). It grows alone or, more often, in gregarious clusters. It prefers cooler temperatures and appears in fall, winter, and spring. It is widely distributed on the continent.

Poisonous Look-Alikes: *Galerina marginata* (p. 46); species of *Pholiota* (see "Comments"), and species of *Gymnopilus* (p. 72).

Comments: A spore print is essential since the deadly *Galerina marginata* is a look-alike that also grows on wood in cool weather. Its cap colors are sometimes similar, its trademark ring often falls away, *and* it can develop a blackish stem base in old age. Mycologist Tom Volk wisely recommends that beginners who are collecting *Flammulina velutipes* for the table take a spore print for *each mushroom* they plan on eating since the two species can share the same log. *Gymnopilus* and *Pholiota* species also grow on wood and can appear somewhat similar but have orange-brown and brown spore prints, respectively. Mycologists have recently separated several North American species of *Flammulina* that are virtually identical in their physical features on the basis of mating studies (which I will leave unexplained except to say that it's the mushrooms, not the mycologists, that are under consideration). Fortunately, these "biological species" (the term for species defined on the basis of whether they can mate) can be separated ecologically, despite the fact that they are pretty much indistinguishable otherwise: *Flammulina populicola* grows on quaking aspen and other poplars from the Rocky Mountains westward; and *Flammulina mexicana* grows in Mexico on the wood of *Senecio cineraroides*, a high-elevation, woody plant. See the entry for the enoki (edible; p. 34), the cultivated version of *Flammulina velutipes*, which looks nothing like the natural version.

In the Woods: (John David Moore) Look for *Flammulina velutipes* on dead or decaying wood, particularly oak or elm. A good time to look for clusters of *Flammulina* is after the first frosts. Indeed, it is speculated that the mushroom may require frost to produce fruiting bodies. Some collectors claim that solidly frozen specimens return to quite palatable normality when thawed. Test this yourself if you're lucky enough to find some. When you are able to harvest these mushrooms, cut through the stems with a knife to avoid pulling away any of the wood and debris. Brush them clean and bag them for further cleaning—or thawing—in the kitchen. Since the caps are sticky, they may pick up debris not easily removed in the field.

In the Kitchen: (John David Moore) Remove the stems from your collection as they can be tough. If you've been careful in the field, a light brushing should suffice to prepare the caps for the pan. If they are very dirty specimens, clean them carefully (they're quite fragile) under running water and let them dry on paper towels. Some people recommend washing in any case to remove the sticky cap coating. Indeed, some even suggest removing the sticky "skin" entirely, though this seems like a great deal of trouble for such a small and fragile mushroom. Moreover I don't find the flavor or texture improved by such painstaking procedures. Sauté the mushrooms briefly (no more than two minutes). *Flammulina velutipes* has a delicate woody, nutty flavor but a rather rubbery texture that's not to everyone's taste. This problem can be avoided if you dry and powder the mushrooms for use as a flavoring in soups and sauces. Used fresh, the caps add a suitable texture to stir-fried dishes.

Recommended Recipe: Five-Spice Beef with Enokis (p. 305), substituting wild *Flammulina* for the enokis.

Hygrophorus russula

Edibility Rating: Bad.

Distinguishing Features: This medium-sized gilled mushroom, found under hardwoods across the continent, is a *Hygrophorus* species with the stature of a *Russula*. Its cap is initially convex with the margin curled

under, but as it matures the margin unrolls and the cap shape becomes flat or centrally depressed. The surface is sticky and smooth or somewhat roughened. The color is pink or pinkish red, but the overall appearance is often somewhat streaky or patchy. In many collections the cap develops yellow stains in age or when handled, especially along the margin. The gills are thick and waxy, moderately spaced, and somewhat fragile; they are initially whitish but soon develop pink and reddish discolorations and are pinkish overall at maturity. They are not covered with a partial veil when the mushroom is young (but see *Hygrophorus purpurascens* in "Comments"). The stem is fairly short in proportion to the cap and is whitish or pinkish. It lacks a ring, and there is no sack around its base. The thick flesh is whitish or pinkish and somewhat stringy (not crumbly). It does not change color when sliced. The spore print is white.

Ecology: *Hygrophorus russula* is a mycorrhizal partner with hardwoods—especially oaks—and grows alone, scattered, or gregariously. It is often found in arcs or fairy rings. It prefers cool temperatures, appearing in late summer and fall (and winter in coastal California). It is widely distributed in North America.

Poisonous Look-Alikes: Species of *Russula* in Group Three (p. 69).

Comments: As its Latin name suggests, this *Hygrophorus* can look a lot like a species of *Russula*. However, its flesh is pliant and a little bit stringy, not crumbly like the flesh of russulas, and its overall appearance when mature is, well, too *messy* for a russula. *Hygrophorus russula* has several closely related (edible) look-alikes that grow under conifers, and these can be very tough to separate with certainty when the host trees are unknown or unclear. *Hygrophorus erubescens* (not treated in this book) is a little smaller, has well spaced gills, bruises yellow with a little more gusto, and differs on microscopic characters. *Hygrophorus purpurascens* (not treated) is nearly identical to *Hygrophorus russula* but does not bruise yellow; it features a cottony or cobwebby covering over the young gills that disappears so quickly you will be lucky to find a specimen young enough to display the feature.

In the Woods: (John David Moore) Hunt for this *Russula* look-alike in late August into September in central and northern regions. It often appears in oak glades, sometimes in rings. Its slight sliminess, which is more pronounced in wet weather, sometimes makes it hard to spot beneath adhering dirt and leaf debris. Do what you can to brush it clean in the field and save the rest of the job for tap water. Check for larvae, which seem to be encouraged by this sticky mushroom's leaf cover.

In the Kitchen: (John David Moore) Now that you've got a collection on the counter, I'll have to say I find this mushroom quite unpleasant. My samples have been notably bitter, and the ones sampled with Michael Kuo, though not bitter, could be described as insipid. On the other hand, all the guidebook descriptions I've encountered describe *Hygrophorus russula* as meaty, excellent, and highly valued (for what?) in Japan. A couple of guides note bitterness in some collections, but the word *insipid* is absent. I am willing to try it again—perhaps in Japan— and if you want to test the opinions of some of the best guidebook authors clean it well with water and drain, slice, and sauté it for two to three minutes. If it's only insipid, try adding some lemon and herbs. If it's bitter, toss it and maybe hope for better luck next time.

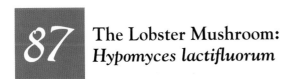

87 The Lobster Mushroom: *Hypomyces lactifluorum*

Edibility Rating: Good.

Distinguishing Features: The common name of this "mushroom" is a bit deceiving since *Hypomyces lactifluorum* is not really a mushroom but a moldlike fungus that *covers* a mushroom—specifically, a species of *Russula* or *Lactarius*. Look on the ground under hardwoods or conifers for a bright orange Frankenstein so deformed that you must use your imagination to "see" the former cap and stem. The surface of the lobster mushroom is a thin, hard crust adorned with tiny, pimply dots. Specimens in the halfway stage are often found, and with these the mushroom underneath is more clearly a (gilled) mushroom.

Ecology: *Hypomyces lactifluorum* is a parasite that attacks species of *Russula* and *Lactarius*, primarily the white species (among them *Russula brevipes* and *Lactarius piperatus*—both inedible when not parasitized). The host mushrooms are mycorrhizal partners with various hardwoods and conifers. The lobster mushroom is found across North America in summer and fall.

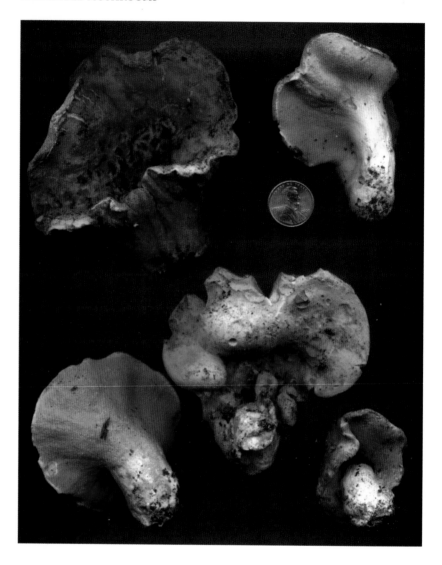

Poisonous Look-Alikes: None for the parasite, but a few for the hosts; see "Comments."

Comments: A "Difficult" rating for such a distinctive fungus requires an explanation. All field guides caution mushroomers that the lobster mushroom should only be eaten *when the host's identity is certain.* To be honest, I have never found a lobster mushroom for which the host could be identified with certainty—though I admit I have never put much effort into it. First of all, *Russula* and *Lactarius* species are not particularly easy to identify even when they're not covered with a fungus that distorts (or completely eradicates) their features. And even when one finds a lobster mushroom growing gregariously among identifiable mushrooms it is not a certainty that the fungus did not parasitize the one poisonous *Russula* in the woods that decided to grow near its edible comrades. The good news is that none of the *Russula* or *Lactarius* hosts will kill you, though a rare few will make you good and sick. There is anecdotal evidence that these minor toxins are reduced in lobster mushrooms —perhaps through the parasitism or the cooking process—but to my knowledge no scientific study has lent credence to this idea. The better news, however, is that the lobster mushroom is sold commercially in grocery stores. Presumably, the distributors know what they're doing. One last note: according to the U.S. Department of Agriculture's *Hypomyces* Web site, the lobster mushroom's hosts include *Lactarius* and *Russula* species, *as well as* "unidentified agarics."

In the Woods: (John David Moore) The lobster mushroom can be found in late summer and early fall in woods where *Russula* and *Lactarius* species appear. It's often buried or partially concealed in leaf litter but is readily detected by its bright red-orange hue. It tends to pick up dirt and debris, so take some care trimming and brushing it in the field.

In the Kitchen: (John David Moore) Clean your finds thoroughly in running water. There's no danger of them becoming soggy since the crustlike exterior and dense body of this monstrosity are virtually impermeable. The palatability of the lobster mushroom is evident in its increasing appearance in dried form on supermarket shelves. Chopped into small pieces and sautéed in butter for three to four minutes, it has a firm, meaty texture and earthy flavor, though it is slightly acrid in some collections. Longer cooking yields more tenderness, and drying concentrates the flavor a bit. It's best combined with other mushrooms in soups or stews.

Laccaria ochropurpurea

Edibility Rating: Mediocre.

Distinguishing Features: This medium-sized gilled mushroom is a common feature in early fall in many eastern forests. Its cap is fairly smooth, and is quite variable in color. Typically, it is very pale brown or lilac brown, but silvery, whitish, or grayish caps are also common. The gills are the most distinctive feature of *Laccaria ochropurpurea*, and they are likely to surprise you when you turn over the bland, boring cap: they

are a beautiful deep purple. They are well spaced, have a thick and waxy appearance, and are attached to the stem. They are not covered with a tissuelike or cobwebby partial veil when the mushroom is young. The stem is quite long in proportion to the cap and about half the time features a somewhat swollen base. Even when it is more or less straight, its width is almost always somewhere between 1 and 2 cm. It is colored more or less like the cap, and its surface is smooth. It does *not* have a faint zone of rusty fibers or a ring on its upper half, and its base is not enclosed in a sack. The flesh is thick and white or very pale lilac and does not change color when sliced. The spore print is white.

Ecology: *Laccaria ochropurpurea* is a mycorrhizal partner with various hardwoods and conifers. It grows alone, scattered, or (more frequently) gregariously in late summer and fall. It is common and abundant in many eastern forests and is often reported under oaks and beech. In my area (central Illinois) it can appear in stunning numbers in white pine plantations after fall rains.

Poisonous Look-Alikes: *Cortinarius* species (p. 62).

Comments: A spore print is essential if you are going to eat *Laccaria ochropurpurea*. It mimics several potentially poisonous species of *Cortinarius* so closely that it is frequently used by field guide authors and mycologists as an example of why spore prints are so important. I have seen *Cortinarius* and *Laccaria* slides placed side by side that baffled everyone in the audience—including the mycologists. *Cortinarius* species feature a cobwebby "cortina" over the young gills, which later can become a rusty zone of fibers on the upper stem, but the cortina often disappears quickly, and the stem often lacks the zone. The white spore print, however, will easily separate *Laccaria ochropurpurea* from the rusty-spored species of *Cortinarius*. Two other common species of *Laccaria* with purple gills are frequently found. In eastern North America *Laccaria amethystina* can be distinguished by its much smaller size and slender proportions. It is edible but too small to be worth considering. In the west, *Laccaria amethysteo-occidentalis* is quite common under conifers. It has a skinnier stem that is shaggy, brownish, and quite tough. The caps are edible but not particularly good.

In the Woods: (John David Moore) Apart from *Laccaria trullisata,* which is so sand covered that it's not worth bothering with, *Laccaria ochropurpurea* is the most robust edible in this genus in eastern North America. Look for it in midsummer through early fall in dry oak and/ or pine woods. To avoid the inherent toughness of this mushroom, select only young individuals, which also have the most attractive violet/ purple gill color. Check the cut stems for critters—they, too, like the color purple—and brush the mushroom clean before bagging.

In the Kitchen: (John David Moore) Wipe your collection clean with a damp cloth and check more closely for larvae while slicing the mushrooms thinly. You may wish to discard the tougher stems, but unfortunately young specimens of *Laccaria ochropurpurea* are often mostly stem with dwarfish caps. Slow and lengthened cooking, as well as chopping rather than slicing the stems, helps to defeat toughness. Sadly, the purple color is lost in cooking. Although this mushroom is spoken of highly for its robust, meaty quality, I have found it to be flavorless. It is best mixed with other, more flavorful mushrooms and/or added to stews, where its substantial texture is more important than taste. Drying does not enhance the flavor, but neither does it increase the toughness. I would say there are better mushrooms with which to fill your pantry.

 Lactarius deceptivus

Edibility Rating: Good.

Distinguishing Features: *Lactarius deceptivus* is a medium-sized (or sometimes quite large) gilled mushroom that grows in eastern North America. Its whitish cap is shallowly to deeply vase shaped at maturity, and it usually develops brownish areas and stains. When the mushroom is young, the edge of the cap is distinctively rolled under and soft—like well-worn kid leather. The surface is smooth at first but is soon roughened and cracked. The gills begin to run down the stem and are fairly well spaced (*not* crowded tightly together). When damaged with the point of a knife, they exude a thick white "milk" that does not change color on exposure to air and does *not* become greenish when it dries on the gills. There is no cobwebby or tissuelike partial veil covering the young gills, though the rolled cap margin can hide them. The stem is hard and white, and it is fairly short in proportion to the cap. It lacks a ring. It may develop brownish stains or become somewhat roughened as the mushroom matures, but it does not feature little potholes on its surface. There is no sack around its base. The flesh is white and fairly hard when the mushroom is fresh; it also exudes white milk when sliced. The taste of the mushroom is unbearably hot and acrid, though it may take several moments to develop. The spore print is white or very pale yellow. A drop of potassium hydroxide on the cap produces a red reaction.

Ecology: *Lactarius deceptivus* is a mycorrhizal partner with hardwoods, especially oaks, and conifers. It grows alone, scattered, or gregariously on the ground. The most impressive fruitings I have seen have been in sandy soil near the coast of Lake Michigan. The species is widely distributed east of the Rocky Mountains, and its range extends as far south as Costa Rica. It fruits in summer and fall.

Poisonous Look-Alikes: Species of *Clitocybe* (p. 58) and a variety of *Lactarius piperatus* that may be poisonous (see "Comments").

Comments: *Russula brevipes* (probably inedible; not treated in this book) is very similar in appearance, but does not exude milk. It is often found growing alongside *Lactarius deceptivus*, so you will need to slice your mushrooms open to check for the copious white milk. Readers may be familiar with warnings regarding white *Lactarius* species in field guides. Documentation of poisonings from these mushrooms is uneven, and many of the cases of upset stomachs may simply represent a reaction to the strongly acrid taste when the mushrooms were not boiled repeatedly (see "In the Kitchen"). However, there is fairly strong evidence that at least one species, *Lactarius piperatus*, is mildly poisonous to some people. Unlike *Lactarius deceptivus*, *Lactarius piperatus* has extremely crowded gills; it also lacks the cottony young cap margin and the brownish scales and discolorations of *Lactarius deceptivus*. In one variety of *Lactarius piperatus* (the variety suspected of poisonings), the juice dries greenish on the gills. Species of *Clitocybe* have soft rather than brittle flesh and do not produce milk when sliced.

In the Woods: Since *Lactarius deceptivus* is fairly large, you will only need to collect a few mushrooms—especially since the cooking process is long and tedious (see "In the Kitchen"). Be sure to return to your collecting area a few days later if you are a fan of the lobster mushroom (edible; p. 267) since *Lactarius deceptivus* is often a host for this edible parasite (but be sure to read my warnings about eating wild lobster mushrooms).

In the Kitchen: Since *Lactarius deceptivus* is so peppery-acrid that it makes your mouth hurt, the strong taste has to be conquered in the cooking process. Three boilings (throw out the water each time) are enough to render a pleasantly peppery flavor. Fortunately, *Lactarius deceptivus* is a sturdy mushroom, and its consistency is such that it remains crunchy and palatable after this abuse. Slice the mushrooms into bite-sized pieces before boiling. Place them in a canning jar, alternating layers of mushroom pieces and salt, and fill the jar with water. You may want to weigh the mushroom pieces down with something so they do not

Focus Point

Taste

The taste of a mushroom—raw, before cooking—is occasionally a feature that aids in the identification of mushrooms. But tasting unidentified mushrooms is obviously dangerous and not, to be honest, nearly as important as some mushroom authors would have you believe. Consider the following.

- Some (though admittedly not "all") strong and distinctive odors correspond unfailingly to tastes, including the frequently encountered mealy (farinaceous) odor. See the Focus Point "Odors" (p. 206).
- Taste is a subjective experience. While such extreme tastes as the burning acridness of *Lactarius deceptivus* are pretty much universally recognized, more subtle gradations in taste are not—and some people are even "taste blind."
- The detection of bitterness can help separate groups (and occasionally species) of boletes—but anyone whose experience with mushrooms warrants tasting them can probably tell a *Tylopilus* from a *Boletus* anyway, especially if multiple specimens have been collected, representing all stages of development.
- Most distinctive tastes are unpleasant—which means that the mushrooms are not likely to be good edibles (absent a long and involved cooking process like the one described here for *Lactarius deceptivus*).

- Any two "species" that differ on taste alone are not likely to be two species (recall that dachshunds and Dobermans are both *Canis familiaris*, and while they may have tasted the same to some of my Asian ancestors they certainly demonstrate that a certain amount of variability in individual features can occur within a species).
- The playing field where taste is most likely to suit up for the game while amateur mushroomers are in the stands contains *Russula* and *Lactarius*—two genera in which hundreds of North American "species" have been described on the basis of subtle differences in variable characters and which, between them, can only muster up a handful of good (though not great) edibles, most of which appear in this book and are easily distinguished without tasting them.
- If you screw up while tasting the wrong *Amanita* or little brown mushroom, you could die.

If you are an experienced mushroom hunter and, regardless of the points listed here, you want to taste mushrooms anyway, at least promise me that you will take a bye on tasting any mushroom you suspect, on the basis of other features, could be poisonous. Take a small section of the cap (including both flesh and pores or gills), and chew it for a few seconds near the front of your mouth. Stay away from falling pianos. Some tastes take a few moments to register, but spit out your sample soon and wash your mouth out with water before allowing your swallow reflex to do anything.

float to the top. When refrigerated, the mushrooms will last at least over the winter. Before adding the mushrooms to any recipe, rinse them thoroughly to wash away the salt. In *Star Trek II: The Wrath of Khan*, Ricardo Montalban quotes a Klingon proverb: "Revenge is a dish best served cold." The same is true for *Lactarius deceptivus*. Scandinavian recipes for similar peppery milky caps—such as Annikki Rintanen's recipe for Salted Mushroom Salad—are served cold.

Recommended Recipe: Salted Mushroom Salad (p. 309).

 Lyophyllum decastes

Edibility Rating: Great.

Distinguishing Features: *Lyophyllum decastes* is a medium-sized gilled mushroom that grows in dense clusters, primarily in disturbed-ground areas (on paths, in ditches, and so on) but also in the woods. The

smooth, individual caps are brown, grayish brown, yellowish brown, or tan and often have a somewhat streaked appearance. The edge of the cap is rolled under when young but later straightens out. The gills are attached to the stem (sometimes by a notch) or begin to run down it. They are white but may discolor a little yellowish in age. There is no partial veil covering the young gills. The smooth stem is white or slightly brownish with age, especially toward the base; it is about 1 to 2 cm thick and lacks a ring. There is no sack around its base. The flesh is white and firm and does not change color when sliced. The spore print is white. Under a microscope, the spores are inamyloid (not bluing in Melzer's Reagent), smooth, and more or less round.

Ecology: This mushroom is a saprobe that usually grows in dense clusters in disturbed soil—though it occasionally fruits alone, without clustered companions, and is not infrequently encountered in woods. The lone soldiers and woodland clumps, however, should not be considered for the table, since the clustered growth in disturbed soil is an important factor in eliminating potentially poisonous mushrooms. *Lyophyllum decastes* can be found across North America, appearing in summer and fall (or in winter in warm climates).

Poisonous Look-Alikes: Species of *Clitocybe* (p. 58) and *Entoloma* (p. 64).

Comments: *Lyophyllum decastes* not only grows in clusters but is probably a cluster of closely related species, all of which share the features emphasized here. A whitish version, sometimes called *Lyophyllum connatum*, should be avoided, since it differs very little in macroscopic features from the poisonous *Clitocybe dilatata* (which also grows in clusters on disturbed soil) and other species of *Clitocybe*. *Lyophyllum decastes* is difficult to identify with certainty, even for experienced mushroom hunters (John David Moore and I used a microscope and called three professional mycologists before eating it for the first time), and I urge you to exercise caution with this species. In many field guides *Lyophyllum decastes* is given the common name fried chicken mushroom.

In the Woods: (John David Moore) Once you are certain that you have identified the so-called fried chicken mushroom, it is a prize worth hunting in late summer and early fall. Look for large, closely packed clusters of *Lyophyllum decastes* in the disturbed ground of waste places, along roads and paths, and in woods. Look closely, for these clusters are often hidden by grass or leaves. It is best to check your first finds of this

Focus Point
Spore Shapes and Sizes

Microscopic examination, while not necessary to identify many edible mushrooms, is absolutely crucial to advanced mushroom identification. The most basic of the many microscopic features assessed by mycologists is the morphology of a mushroom's spores: their shapes, textures, and dimensions. Amateur mushroom hunters who have access to microscopes can easily master the routines necessary for basic spore analysis with a little practice. Use a spore print as the source of your spores. There are several reasons for this. First, the spore print is already necessary in the identification process, so you will have a print on hand. Second, the spore print gives you a gazillion spores to work with, and you will not have to waste time searching for spores on your slide. Last, and most important, you will need to look at mature spores in order to assess their features accurately—and spores, like all the other parts of a mushroom, can change dramatically in the course of their development. By definition, the spores in a print are mature, since they have been rolled off the assembly line by the spore-producing machinery on the gills, pores, or teeth of your mushroom. Scrape some spore dust from the print with a razor blade and tap it onto your slide. If you are only going to check the shapes and sizes of the spores, a tap water mount may suffice. If you have difficulty seeing the spores in a water mount, try adding a drop of drugstore iodine to provide contrast. (If you are going to attempt to assess the *texture* of the spores' walls or whether or not the spores are ornamented with tiny projections, you may need to mount them with special chemicals, stains, or Melzer's Reagent—which you will have to obtain from a mycologist.) Move through your microscope's

stages, from low to high, in order to keep your spores in focus. Spore shapes can be seen with many microscopes—even old, long-forgotten, ten-dollar, garage-sale microscopes that use mirrors for illumination—but if your microscope cannot magnify to about 400× (figure this out by multiplying the magnification number on the lens by the magnification number on the eyepiece), you will have trouble seeing most mushroom spores. Spore shapes range from more or less round—like the spores of *Lyophyllum decastes*—to elliptical, bean shaped, sausage shaped, or truly funky, like the spores of many species of *Entoloma*. I should add at this point that I do *not* recommend you decide to eat your putative *Lyophyllum decastes* after viewing its spores in a water mount at 400× with a science-kit microscope; if for no other reason, the low magnification may make it difficult to view the spores well enough to truly ascertain whether they are round or elliptical. While many mushrooms' spores can be fairly adequately *seen* without an oil immersion lens, 1000× magnification is a necessity if you are going to do much spore analysis and take accurate measurements. To measure spores, your microscope must have a properly calibrated micrometer in the eyepiece; you may be good to go if you are using a microscope in your local school's biology department as a guest, but if you have pulled an old science-kit microscope out of your basement this may be your stopping point until you have purchased a used or new oil-immersion microscope with a micrometer (mine cost $150.00) and boned up a little on microscopy through other sources. Measure as many spores as you can stomach measuring (be sure to measure at least ten) and assess both width and height. Mushroom guides and mycological texts express spore sizes as ranges, accounting for variation (10–14 × 4–5 microns, for example), and you will need to assess the size ranges of your mushroom's spores for comparison. There is much more to be said about using a microscope to view spores, but my goal here is only to whet your appetite if you are developing an interest in advanced mushroom identification. See the Focus Points "Basidia" (p. 241), "Cystidia" (p. 288), and "Asci" (p. 194) for more about mushroom microscopy.

mushroom with an authority. It's worth taking the trouble to get a positive identification. When collecting for identification, remove a clump with the attached substratum. Later, when you are collecting for the table, cut the clump off at the base and brush off what debris you can in the field. Remember your spot since *Lyophyllum decastes* will often fruit there again the next year.

In the Kitchen: (John David Moore) With a knife, separate the individual mushrooms from the clump, trim off any dirty areas around the bases, and discard any specimens that are overly mature. Clean them with a brush or damp cloth. If you're waiting for culinary clearance from your local mycologist, your collection will keep well in the refrigerator for several days. Once you're certain of their edibility, slice some of your finds and try a small amount (allergic responses have been noted) sautéed. Contrary to some authors who take issue with the common name, I've found this mushroom does indeed taste a bit like fried chicken. Cooking time will vary according to how tender you want it. I like to cook it until it's slightly golden brown. It has an excellent meaty texture reminiscent of another chicken, the chicken of the woods (edible; p. 79). Reconstituted dried collections can be a bit chewier but also have a more intense, nutty flavor. *Lyophyllum decastes* is highly versatile; use it in soups, stews, and sauces; with pasta; or on its own sautéed with butter and herbs.

Recommended Recipes: Artichoke Shiitake Pizza (p. 303), substituting *Lyophyllum decastes* for shiitakes; Asparagus Garnish with Mushrooms (p. 303); Shaggy Mane Soup (p. 310), substituting *Lyophyllum decastes* for shaggy manes.

 Macrolepiota americana

Edibility Rating: Good.

Distinguishing Features: This medium-sized to large gilled mushroom grows on wood or woody debris and in disturbed-ground settings. It is often found in urban areas (in wood chips, on stumps, or growing from buried wood and appearing terrestrial). Its cap is oval at first but expands to broadly convex or nearly flat. The surface is pale underneath a layer of brown to reddish-brown scales—but the center of the cap is smooth and brown or reddish brown. When rubbed, or with age, reddish areas appear. The edge of the cap often becomes ragged with maturity. The white gills are free from the stem and stain pinkish to reddish brown as they mature. They are covered with a white, tissuelike partial veil when the mushroom is young. The stem is long and usually distinctively swollen in its bottom half. It features a collarlike ring that is not easily detached to slide up and down the stem. The whitish stem surface is finely hairy and bruises yellow when rubbed. With time, the yellow areas turn reddish, and older stems are often reddish brown nearly overall. There is no sack around the base of the stem. The flesh is white and changes to yellowish or orangish (eventually reddish) when sliced. The spore print is white.

Ecology: *Macrolepiota americana* is a saprobe that prefers to decompose woody debris. It is often found in wood chips and on hardwood stumps, but it can appear to be terrestrial when growing from buried deadwood. Disturbed-ground settings such as paths and ditches are also in its repertoire, however, as is an occasional, good old-fashioned dead log. I once found *Macrolepiota americana* growing fifteen feet above ground in rotting debris in the crotch of a standing, healthy tree (you don't want to know how I picked it). It appears in summer and fall, growing alone or gregariously. Its range apparently spans the continent, but it is much more commonly encountered in eastern North America.

Poisonous Look-Alikes: *Agaricus xanthodermus* and other *Agaricus* species (p. 70); species of *Amanita* (p. 43); *Chlorophyllum molybdites* (p. 50); and members of the *Lepiota* group (p. 51).

Comments: A spore print is a good way to distinguish this mushroom from the green-spored *Chlorophyllum molybdites* (p. 50), which causes more cases of mushroom poisoning than any other North American mushroom. It does not bruise yellow and red, and it grows in grass—though *Macrolepiota americana* can also grow in grass and in some collections the bruising is not pronounced. Also compare it very carefully with species of *Amanita* (p. 43), the poisonous species of *Agaricus* (p. 70), and the poisonous members of the *Lepiota* group (p. 51). Edible look-alikes include the parasol mushroom (edible; p. 281) and shaggy parasol (edible; p. 253), which have detachable rings. The former has a skinny stem, a softer cap, and does not bruise. The latter has a shaggier cap, and, while the interior flesh changes to pinkish orange when sliced, its surfaces do not bruise yellow then red. *Macrolepiota americana* has apparently caused "allergic" reactions with some frequency, so be sure to follow the precautions on page 24 if you try it.

In the Woods: Older specimens of *Macrolepiota americana* are not very good for the table (their caps are too soft and their stems too tough), so collect only fresh buttons with oval or convex caps. As always, slice or brush away any adhering debris. Be sure of your identification before slicing off the stem base and discarding it, however, since the stem bases of look-alike *Amanita* species are crucial in identification. If you are in an urban area, be sure to consider the possibility of introduced toxins and pollutants.

In the Kitchen: *Macrolepiota americana* is best consumed fresh. Clean your mushrooms with a mushroom brush or paper towel and slice them thinly. I think this mushroom is best in scrambled egg dishes—but it should be sautéed thoroughly and separately before being added to the eggs.

92 The Parasol Mushroom: *Macrolepiota procera*

Edibility Rating: Good.

Distinguishing Features: The parasol is a tall gilled mushroom found primarily in eastern North America, where it grows from the ground in woods or at the edges of woods. Its distinctive cap is rather soft for its size and features soft, brownish scales over a pale brown or nearly white background color. At the very center of the cap is a dark brown, nipple-like bump. The gills are free from the stem and are white—though they sometimes turn a little pinkish or brownish in age. When young they are covered with a white, tissuelike partial veil. The stem is slender and beautiful. It is usually about 1 cm wide but up to 20 or more cm long. It tapers gracefully to the apex. Its surface is brownish at first but

as it grows the brown breaks up, creating tiny scales that may form zones or eventually disappear entirely. On the upper stem there is a distinctive, double-edged ring, which can be fairly easily loosened so that it slides up and down the stem. There is no sack around the stem's base, and its bottom portion is not substantially enlarged or swollen. The flesh is white and quite soft in the cap. It may develop faint pinkish hues as the mushroom matures, but it does not turn prominently pinkish orange at the stem apex when sliced open and exposed to air. The spore print is white.

Ecology: *Macrolepiota procera* is a woodland saprobe that grows from the ground in hardwood and conifer forests. It is especially fond of open areas and the edges of woods and is often found growing in disturbed ground such as paths, roadsides, and clearings. It grows alone, scattered, or gregariously in summer and fall throughout eastern North America; it has also been reported, rarely, in California and the Southwest.

Poisonous Look-Alikes: Species of *Amanita* (p. 43); *Chlorophyllum molybdites* (p. 50); and members of the *Lepiota* group (p. 51).

Comments: Compare this mushroom carefully with the poisonous *Chlorophyllum molybdites* (p. 50)—which has a green spore print and a stockier stem and grows in grass—and species of *Amanita* (p. 43), which have "nonsliding" rings and stem bases that are usually swollen, covered with a sack, or otherwise distinctive. Other poisonous members of the *Lepiota* group, to which the parasol mushroom belongs, are smaller mushrooms that lack the distinctive combination of features listed here. The parasol mushroom's closest look-alike is the shaggy parasol (edible; p. 253), which has a shaggier cap, a stockier stem, and flesh that turns pinkish orange (at least in the stem apex) when sliced.

In the Woods: (John David Moore) Look for the famous parasol mushroom from midsummer to mid fall. Its preference for open areas—woodland glades and parklands—and its tall stature make for easy spotting. Note the area where it is growing, since it can appear there in subsequent years. Pick the parasol mushroom when its cap is just starting to open and discard the fibrous stalks, which acquire a woody toughness with cooking. Brush the caps free of any dirt or debris and place them in your bag or basket gills down. The parasol mushroom is free of larvae unless you've selected ones so old that they will not be palatable anyway. Some people avoid any individuals that are starting to dry, but there's no reason why they can't be picked and taken back for the dehydrator to complete the job. However, these more leathery individuals will cook up with a chewier texture than you might prefer.

In the Kitchen: (John David Moore) Finish cleaning the parasol mushroom's cap surface with a damp cloth. Avoid washing it under the tap unless there is debris among the gills that can't be removed any other way. The best way to prepare fresh parasols is grilling or broiling with butter or olive oil and herbs and seasonings of your choice. Simply sautéed for two to three minutes, the parasol mushroom has a delicate, nutty flavor and a texture akin to that of shaggy manes (edible; p. 148). In some specimens I've tried, however, the flavor has been rather nondescript, although other parasol eaters have described some harvests as very strong and rich in nutty flavor. Dried parasols tend to be chewy when reconstituted, and they lose some of the flavor of fresh specimens; they are best used in stews or sauces combined with other mushrooms.

Recommended Recipe: Stuffed Mushrooms (p. 311).

93 *Marasmius oreades*

Edibility Rating: Good.

Distinguishing Features: This small to medium-sized gilled mushroom grows densely gregariously in grass—often in arcs or fairy rings (but see "Comments"). Its cap is thin and usually has a broad central bump or knob. The surface is fairly smooth. As the mushroom matures, the cap dries out and changes color fairly dramatically, going from brownish to pale tan or nearly whitish—and often, along the way, through a two-toned stage. The gills are white or very pale tan and are attached to the stem but do not begin to run down it. They are well spaced, and not at all crowded. They are not covered by a partial veil when the mushroom is young. The stem is tough but bendable. It is fairly thin (about half a centimeter wide at most), and its surface is more or less smooth. There is no ring and no sack around the base. The flesh is whitish and tough, especially in the stem. The spore print is white.

Ecology: *Marasmius oreades* is a saprobe that grows from the ground in grassy areas—including lawns, playing fields, meadows, and sandy back

Upper left: photo by George Barron

dunes covered with beach grass. Lone specimens occasionally appear, but it is more often found growing densely gregariously, almost in clusters, in arcs or fairy rings. Evidence of its mycelium can often be seen, even when mushrooms are not present, as darker areas or rings in the grass. *Marasmius oreades* is widespread on the continent, appearing in summer and fall (or in winter in warm climates).

Poisonous Look-Alikes: Species of *Clitocybe* (p. 58), *Entoloma* (p. 64), and *Inocybe* (p. 60).

Comments: This mushroom is often called the fairy ring mushroom in field guides, but the name ought to be dropped because, believe it or not, some folks hear the name and assume it is the *only* fairy ring mushroom— a potentially tragic error, since both *Chlorophyllum molybdites* (poisonous; p. 50) and *Amanita thiersii* (*very* poisonous; see p. 44), among others, often grow in fairy rings. "one among many fairy ring mushrooms, some of which are deadly," while more strictly accurate, would not make much of a name. A spore print is a must, as well as careful comparison with descriptions in field guides, since this mushroom very

Focus Point
Distant Gills

The gills of *Marasmius oreades* are well spaced, corresponding to what is called "distant" or "sub-distant" in Mycologese. Compare this spacing to the "close" gills of the button mushroom (edible; p. 30 and the "crowded" gills of the shaggy mane (edible; p. 150).

Focus Point
Fairy Rings

Some fungi, when growing in evenly composed substrates, expand outward from a central location at a regular rate as the mycelium grows and searches for new food. The result is a circular area in the substrate, and the outer edge of the circle is the growth region. When mushroom-producing fungi grow like this, the mushrooms appear at the edge of the circle, and the resulting ring of mushrooms can astonish those who are unaware that they are only looking at the spore factories of a larger organism. Without this knowledge, the mushrooms appear to be magically arranged, perhaps by fairies (hence the term *fairy ring*). The mushrooms, however, do not have to be present for the fairy ring to be evident; in well-tended lawns, the outer area of mycelial growth is often represented by a circle several inches wide in which the grass is darker than the surrounding vegetation. Saprobic mushrooms are regularly found growing in rings or arcs, and *Marasmius oreades* is one of many. When mycorrhizal mushrooms appear to be growing in arcs, it is the result of the fact that the host tree's tiny rootlets have grown through evenly composed soil and are more or less equidistant from the tree's base. In this way I have seen a faux fairy ring of *Suillus luteus* (edible; p. 221), a mycorrhizal bolete, in a nearly complete circle under the drip-line of a young white pine. "True" fairy ring mushrooms, however, rely on their own mycelial magic, expanding every year. Some scientific studies have assumed even growth rates and calculated that the subject mycelia must be hundreds of years old. An ongoing Norwegian study of *Marasmius oreades* rings in coastal grasslands is attempting to determine whether new rings are cloned from old rings or result from spores falling in new locations and germinating new mycelia (Abesha, Caetano-Anolles, and Hoiland, 2003).

Focus Point
Hygrophanous Caps

The term *hygrophanous* is one of the few mushroom descriptors in Mycologese that does not irritate me, since there is really no plain-language translation that can be accomplished in a word or two. So, while I am willing to knock mycologists for saying "pileus" and "stipe" when they could just as easily say "cap" and "stem" and be understood by the rest of us, I wouldn't much like hearing "a cap that changes color markedly as it dries out, going progressively through a dark stage, a two-toned stage, and a light stage"—when "hygrophanous cap" would do. Jargon for the sake of jargon is one thing, but a nice term to sum up a whole bunch of words is another. All mushrooms are subject to fading in sunlight, but some do so in the distinctive way described by the lengthy phrase just given. The fact that a mushroom's cap is hygrophanous can be a useful character in identification. *Marasmius oreades* is not the most dramatically or reliably hygrophanous mushroom in the world, but it does demonstrate the char- acter often enough to make it a good candidate for example status. Incidentally, note that mush- rooms with hygrophanous caps create yet another reason to collect multiple specimens represent- ing all stages of development since the color is different in youth and old age.

nearly qualifies as an LBM (see the Focus Point "LBMs [Little Brown Mushrooms]," p. 61). Species of *Entoloma* and *Inocybe* have differently colored spores (pink and brown, respectively); species of *Clitocybe* usu- ally have gills that begin to run down the stem or, if not, have pale pink spore prints.

In the Woods: (John David Moore) "On the Lawns" would be the more appropriate heading here. Lawns, parks, and cemeteries—or any open grassy area—can be home to *Marasmius oreades*. It will appear again and again on watered lawns from spring into fall—but you should be familiar with neighborhood lawn-care habits. An immaculate, lush lawn may mean that any mushrooms you find there will be nicely seasoned with Roundup or other unsavory chemicals. It's best to restrict yourself to lawns you know about. Discard the tough stems of *Marasmius oreades* unless you enjoy the texture of very soggy toothpicks. Forego field clean- ing since the caps should be washed thoroughly when they arrive in the kitchen. Shriveled, sun-dried caps can be gathered and reconstituted in water or put in the food dryer to remove any remaining moisture before storing.

In the Kitchen: (John David Moore) Wash your *Marasmius oreades* caps thoroughly in water and drain them on paper towels. The caps can then be sautéed, fried, or stewed whole. They are very versatile, and fairy ring fans use them in multiple dishes. Cooked with nothing more than butter or oil they have a grassy, earthy flavor and richness. I find that a little goes a long way and prefer them added sparingly to omelets, soups, and stews. Reconstituted dried collections also have strong flavor and can be powdered as a seasoning.

Recommended Recipe: Shaggy Mane Soup (p. 310), substituting *Maras- mius oreades* for shaggy manes, sparingly.

94 The Deer Mushroom: *Pluteus cervinus*

Edibility Rating: Mediocre.

Distinguishing Features: The deer mushroom is a medium-sized gilled mushroom that grows on wood, usually on fallen logs. Its light brown to dark brown cap is convex and, when fresh, slightly sticky. The streaked-looking surface is fairly smooth but on close inspection may be adorned with very tiny, pressed-down fibers, especially over the center. The gills are free from the stem and are not covered with a partial veil when the mushroom is young. They are initially white but turn pink as the mushroom matures. The well-developed, central stem lacks a ring and is white—but it may have a few tiny brown fibers. It does not bruise blue when handled. There is no sack around the stem's base. The flesh is white and soft and does not change color when sliced. The odor in most collections is at least faintly reminiscent of radishes. The spore print is fleshy pink.

Ecology: The deer mushroom is a wood-rotting saprobe that decomposes the wood of hardwoods and conifers across the continent. It grows

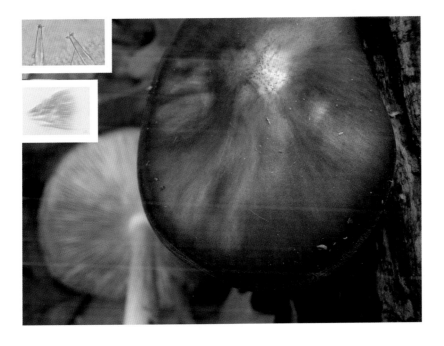

alone frequently but is also found growing scattered or gregariously. It appears from spring through fall and in winter in warm climates.

Poisonous Look-Alikes: *Galerina marginata* (p. 46), and species of *Entoloma* (p. 64).

Comments: The deadly *Galerina marginata* has a rusty brown spore print and usually features a braceletlike ring on the upper stem. The deer mushroom occasionally grows from buried wood and thus appears terrestrial. Avoid these specimens until you are very familiar with the species since they could be confused with species of *Entoloma* (p. 64), which also have pink spores but are truly terrestrial (additionally, they have gills that are attached to the stem and in many cases caps that are somewhat pointed, at least in the middle). Compare the deer mushroom to its close relative *Pluteus petasatus* (edible; p. 289). Several other species of *Pluteus* could easily be confused with the deer mushroom, but none of these is known to be poisonous. A few blue-staining species (rub the stem and the edge of the cap) should probably be avoided since their

Focus Point
Cystidia

Cystidia are special sterile cells that in some mushrooms are found popping up between the basidia (see the Focus Point "Basidia," p. 241). Unlike the basidia, cystidia do not produce spores. Their shapes and sizes vary widely among mushroom species—and many mushrooms do not have cystidia at all. Some mushrooms have boring, club-shaped cystidia that hardly differ from the basidia except for the absence of spore-holding prongs. Others have elaborately ornamented cystidia, thick-walled and enormous cystidia, long and pointed cystidia, and so on. In fact mycologists have given names to many types of cystidia (and they can occur elsewhere on a mushroom—not just on the spore-producing surface). One could spend days learning about the various cystidia found on mushrooms, reading page after page of meticulous descriptions cataloging every conceivable shape and size . . . but no one knows what they are. Don't you love mycology? Um, maybe cystidia hold the gill faces apart so the spores have room to fall? That theory crashes to earth right out of the gate since plenty of gilled mushrooms lack cystidia and manage just fine. Maybe they hold the gills together until the spores are mature? Yeah, and maybe your mail carrier is doing something unproductive on your lawn. I once spent nearly two full days concocting a theory that the little liquid-filled guys are sensors that expand or contract with temperature changes (or changes in humidity) and transmit the information to the basidia so that spores are produced under optimal conditions . . . then I ran out of coffee, thank God. Regardless of what cystidia actually *do*, they are often very important in advanced mushroom identification—and the cystidia of *Pluteus cervinus* are particularly gorgeous under the microscope. They have apical prongs that look like antlers, and, believe it or not, this is the source of the common name deer mushroom.

edibility is not known. The large, wood-loving species of *Volvariella* (some edible, some unknown; not treated in this book) also feature pink spore prints and gills that are free from the stem, but they have a prominent sack around the base of the stem.

In the Woods: (John David Moore) You can hunt this mushroom, given damp conditions, any time from April into October. This may be its only virtue since it does not rank high on most peoples' list of edibles. Look for it on decaying wood of all kinds and harvest the youngest ones, which tend to be less watery. Brush your finds clean with care; they can be rather fragile.

In the Kitchen: (John David Moore) The deer mushroom is perhaps the best edible in the genus *Pluteus*, but that may not be saying much since I've found even the firmest young buttons to be rather watery and insipid. There is a slight earthy flavor but not much beyond that. Cooking over high heat can help dispose of the water content, and a little lemon juice improves the flavor. The deer mushroom can be put to use with other mushrooms with more flavor and substance. Drying can also solve the water problem if you don't let them soak very long when reconstituting them. Drying, however, does nothing to enhance the flavor.

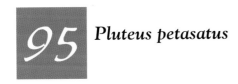

95 *Pluteus petasatus*

Edibility Rating: Mediocre.

Distinguishing Features: This medium-sized to large gilled mushroom grows from deadwood—but often appears to be growing terrestrially (see "Ecology"). Its cap is whitish, grayish, or pale tan overall but features tiny brown scales over the center. The gills are free from the stem and are white throughout most of their development, turning pink with mature spores at seemingly the last possible moment. There is no partial veil covering the young gills. The stem is whitish and straight. It lacks a ring, and there is no sack around its base. It does not bruise blue when handled. The flesh is white and does not change color when sliced. Some collections of *Pluteus petasatus* have a radishlike odor. The spore print is fleshy pink.

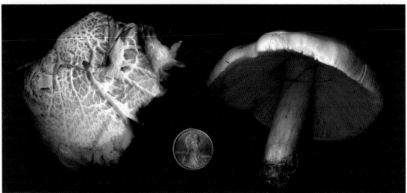

Ecology: *Pluteus petasatus* is a saprobe that prefers the wood of hardwoods. It is often found on stumps, logs, and fallen trees—but its woody substrate repertoire also includes wood chips and dead roots. Even several years after a tree has been removed, *Pluteus petasatus* will colonize the former root system, appearing to grow terrestrially. It is sometimes found growing alone or scattered but is more typically found growing gregariously or in little clusters. It seems especially fond of urban settings but also grows in the woods. It appears in summer and fall (or in winter in warm climates) and is widely distributed in North America.

Poisonous Look-Alikes: Species of *Entoloma* (p. 64).

Comments: Since the gills stay white for so long and the mushroom often appears to grow terrestrially, collectors sometimes have difficulty deciding that *Pluteus petasatus* is a *Pluteus* at all because the genus is characterized by pink spores and growth on wood. A spore print will clear the matter up quickly, however—and then the very features that caused confusion can help determine the species. Compare *Pluteus petasatus* carefully with the deer mushroom (edible; p. 287) and see "Comments" under that species for other look-alikes.

In the Woods: (John David Moore) Look for this white to gray *Pluteus* along roads and trails, where it will appear to be terrestrial but is actually growing on some form of wood chips, sawdust, or buried and decomposing wood. Gather young, firm individuals, taking care to brush them clean without breaking the sometimes easily split caps. You may note a slight radish odor to *Pluteus petasatus* when field cleaning it. Nothing of the radish, however, comes through in the cooked mushroom—not in taste and certainly not in texture.

In the Kitchen: (John David Moore) This mushroom can pick up a lot of dirt and debris, especially under wet conditions. You may have to wash it under running water to clean the gills. If you do so, drain and dry it carefully before chopping or slicing (depending on what condition your collection is in by this time). After you've sautéed *Pluteus petasatus* for two to three minutes, I hope you'll think it was worth the trouble. I find its texture to be unpleasantly gelatinous and its flavor akin to that of unseasoned Styrofoam. It can be made more palatable by making it taste like something else. You might want to start with the spice cabinet and a fresh lemon. As for dried versions of this mushroom, I can't say I've ever found drying it worth the effort.

 Russula claroflava

Edibility Rating: Good.

Distinguishing Features: *Russula claroflava* is a medium-sized gilled mushroom found on the ground in northern and montane forests—primarily in cold conifer bogs or under birch or aspen. Its dull to bright yellow cap is sticky at first, but soon dries out. At maturity it is flat or very shallowly depressed. The surface is fairly smooth, and the edge of the cap develops faint lines by maturity. In old age the cap may discolor

Photo by George Barron

ashy gray. The gills are attached to the stem. They are initially whitish but may develop gray stains. There is no partial veil covering the young gills. The stem is straight and smooth and lacks a ring. It is whitish or pale yellow, but it turns slowly gray when bruised or in age. There is no sack around the stem's base. The flesh is white and crumbly and turns slowly (sometimes *very* slowly) gray when sliced or rubbed. The odor and taste are mild. The spore print is whitish or pale yellow.

Ecology: *Russula claroflava* is a mycorrhizal partner with conifers, birch, and aspen. It is a frequent find in the cold conifer bogs of northern North America and in the aspen elevation zones of the southwestern Rocky Mountains. It grows alone, scattered, or gregariously from the ground in summer and fall.

Poisonous Look-Alikes: *Russula* species in Groups One and Two (p. 69).

Comments: Although yellow *Russula* species are notoriously difficult to identify, the members of the *Russula claroflava* species complex have flesh that ages and bruises ashy gray. This distinction, coupled with their relatively dry caps, mild taste, and ecology, makes them fairly easy to separate from other yellow (and *yellowish*) russulas. For a nonbruising, hardwood-loving yellow *Russula*, see *Russula flavida* (edible; p. 209). Bright yellow *Russula* species with a strong, acrid taste are inedible.

In the Woods: (John David Moore) This is one of the better *Russula* species, though unfortunately it is rarely found in great quantities. It likes wet, swampy conditions around birch, aspen, and conifers, appearing alone or in groups of two or three, mostly in northern regions. Look for gray to blackish staining on the gills and stem, which separates it from other yellow members of this genus. It is not as sturdy as some *Russula* species, so trim the stem (looking for larvae) and brush the mushroom carefully when field cleaning.

In the Kitchen: (John David Moore) Wipe your collection clean with a damp cloth. Don't clean it under running water unless the gills are very dirty. Slice *Russula claroflava* thickly and sauté for three to four minutes over medium heat. It has a sweet, nutty flavor and slightly firm texture. I find there is considerably more flavor here than in *Russula variata* (edible; below) and its kindred species. Drying is advisable when you don't have enough for a meal. Drying also increases the nutty flavor.

Recommended Recipes: Polish Pork Chops with Russulas (p. 308); Salted Mushroom Salad (p. 309).

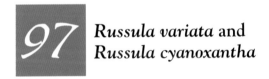

Russula variata and *Russula cyanoxantha*

Edibility Rating: Good.

Distinguishing Features: These medium-sized to large gilled mushrooms grow primarily under hardwoods. Their caps are convex at first but become flat or slightly depressed in age. The surface is fairly smooth, and the colors are extremely variable—and often mixed. Muted greens, purples, and pinks are the "primary colors" for these species, but blues, creamy shades, yellows, and browns are on the palette as well. Specimens that are almost entirely one of these colors are sometimes found, but the more typical cap is a mixture of colors and mottled specimens are more common. The gills are attached to the stem and are not covered with a partial veil when young. In both species they are white, sometimes developing brownish stains with old age. In *Russula variata* they are frequently and conspicuously forked in many places between the stem and the cap edge. In *Russula cyanoxantha* they fork less frequently

Left: photo by Dianna Smith

(if at all) and do so primarily near the stem. The stem lacks a ring. It is white but may develop a few brownish spots with age. There is no sack around the base. The flesh is white and crumbly and does not change color when sliced. The taste of *Russula cyanoxantha* is mild; the taste of *Russula variata* is mild or somewhat acrid. The odor is not distinctive. The spore print is white.

Ecology: These species are mycorrhizal partners with hardwoods, though they are occasionally reported under conifers or in mixed woods. They grow alone, scattered, or gregariously on the ground. Both species are reported from across the continent, but *Russula variata* is more common in eastern North America. They appear in summer and fall. In California, *Russula cyanoxantha* fruits in fall and winter.

Poisonous Look-Alikes: *Russula* species in Groups One, Two, and Three (p. 69).

Comments: *Russula variata*, with its conspicuously forking gills, is the easier of the two species to recognize. In fact this feature, combined with the mottled green and purplish cap colors, is distinctive enough that most *Russula* keys remove the species near the top of the key on this basis and move on to more difficult species. Since variability in cap color is one of the primary distinguishing features of *Russula variata* and *Russula cyanoxantha*, mushroom hunters should identify several collections before experimenting in the kitchen. There are other *Russula* species with greenish, purplish, and/or pinkish caps, and virtually *any* mushroom can appear "mottled" if it has, for example, been covered with leaves during development.

In the Woods: (John David Moore) Look for *Russula variata* in mid- to late summer in hardwood forests, where it will appear alone, scattered, or in troops. Young specimens are best, since they're less likely to be rented out to bugs, but they are often still under the leaf litter, where the dampness encourages slugs. Since recent polls show that 97 percent of all maggots, slugs, and squirrels rate this mushroom as "highly delectable," inspecting your finds carefully for parasites and rodent damage will save you the trouble of littering your yard with *"Russula rejecta"* when you get home. Once you've noted the green to pink and possibly everything-in-between quality of the cap, check for gill forking before finally cutting the stem to see how many maggot diners already have reservations. Brush off your mushrooms and try to remove anything that stuck to the caps when they were wet and slimy.

In the Kitchen: (John David Moore) Young specimens of *Russula variata*, when simply sautéed, have a sweet and sometimes nutty flavor. The flavor in dried specimens is somewhat more pronounced, and the flavor in larger, older specimens can sometimes be peppery. It's best to be aware of this when adding this mushroom to recipes; hold off on the pepper until you've sampled the dish a few times in the process of preparation. Both fresh and dried versions of this mushroom work well in stews and sauces. Cleaning your harvest at home is best managed under cold water since the mushrooms are dense enough that they don't absorb liquids as quickly as many others do.

Recommended Recipes: Polish Pork Chops with Russulas (p. 308); Salted Mushroom Salad (p. 309).

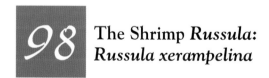

The Shrimp *Russula:* *Russula xerampelina*

Edibility Rating: Good.

Distinguishing Features: The shrimp *Russula* is a medium-sized gilled mushroom that grows on the ground under conifers. Its cap is purplish red to reddish overall, though it may have areas of brown, green, white, or yellow. The center is usually darker than the edge. The surface is smooth, and somewhat sticky when the mushroom is young and fresh. The edge is not lined or is faintly lined in old age. The gills are white

Left and upper right: photos by Tim Zurowski

at first, but become yellow as the spores mature. They are attached to the stem and are not covered with a partial veil when young. With age, they develop brown stains and discolorations. The stem is flushed with the color of the cap. It bruises yellowish then brown. It lacks a ring, and there is no sack around its base. The flesh is crumbly and white but bruises yellow then brown. The odor, which is best detected in older specimens, is distinctively fishy or shrimplike. The spore print is yellow.

Ecology: *Russula xerampelina* is a mycorrhizal partner with conifers—especially Douglas-fir and hemlock. It grows alone, scattered, or gregariously on the ground. It appears in summer and fall across North America.

Poisonous Look-Alikes: *Russula* species in Groups One and (especially) Three (p. 69).

Comments: *"Russula xerampelina,"* as I am treating it here, is a cluster of closely related species, all of which have yellow spore prints and mature gills, stems that are not completely white, tissues that discolor brown, and the distinctive shrimplike odor that gives this species group its common name (as well as a greenish reaction to iron salts on the stem surface). If my experience is indicative, the odor is like fish at first and becomes more and more shrimplike as the mushrooms mature. Keep a specimen in the house for a few days and you'd swear you were on the shrimp boat set of *Forrest Gump.* Yellow and brown species of *Russula* with a shrimplike odor, yellow spore prints, and brown-bruising surfaces are not treated here (although they are edible as far as I know).

In the Kitchen: (Darvin DeShazer) All of the shrimp russulas can be barbecued, broiled, baked, fried, or even roasted over an open campfire. Their crunchy, seafood flavor goes well with many dishes, especially cheese or curry. Old caps will have a stronger fishy taste, and drying and storing them in airtight jars can preserve this odor for future "seafood" meals!

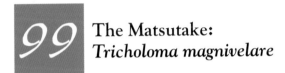

99 The Matsutake: *Tricholoma magnivelare*

Edibility Rating: Great.

Distinguishing Features: The matsutake is a medium-sized to large gilled mushroom that grows on the ground, primarily under pines and other conifers in western North America and Mexico. Its cap is smooth and white at first, with a soft edge that is curled under. The surface soon begins to develop cinnamon discolorations and fibers or small scales; by maturity the center of the cap, at least, is usually cinnamon brown. The gills are attached to the stem, usually by a notch. They are white but

Photo by Taylor Lockwood

develop cinnamon discolorations and stains. They are covered with a white, tissuelike partial veil when young. The stem is white and smooth above the ring but soon develops cinnamon to brown fibers, scales, and discolorations below it. The ring is the flaring, upper edge of a sheath-like covering over the stem that has been stretched and broken apart—but there is no *Amanita*-like sack around the stem's base. The flesh is firm and white and does not change color when sliced. The odor is very distinctive and sweetly fragrant; it is often described as "spicy" or "like cinnamon." It is definitely *not* mealy or foul. The taste is not bitter or unpleasant. The spore print is white.

Ecology: *Tricholoma magnivelare* is a mycorrhizal partner with pines, firs, or Douglas-fir (which isn't really a "fir") in the Pacific Northwest and northern California, often appearing in sandy coastal soil. If your puta-tive matsutake is growing elsewhere, or under different trees, it may still be a matsutake if it is under madrone or tanoak on the West Coast, un-der lodgepole pine in the Rocky Mountains, under pines and oaks in Mexico, or (rarely) under conifers in northern North America. If I still haven't set you up for a matsutake identification, ecologywise, and you have yet to *taste* your mushroom, press 1 now. *Beep.* If you are not wash-ing your mouth out to get rid of a bitter or unpleasant taste, please con-tact a mycologist, who may be very interested in your find. DNA studies support the idea that matsutakes have been found in North American habitats and areas other than those mentioned here (including Ten-nessee and New England), but the tested mushrooms were not ac-companied by thorough ecological information. Other, nonscientific (and fairly rare) reports may be valid—or may represent confusion with several similar species (see "Comments").

Poisonous Look-Alikes: Species of *Amanita* (p. 43).

Comments: Compare the Matsutake with *Catathelasma* species (edible; p. 251). The "Matsutake complex" in North America is confusing and includes many look-alikes for the "true" matsutake. Most (perhaps all) of these lack the fragrant, spicy odor—and many, such as *Tricholoma caligatum* (inedible; not treated in this book), tend to grow under hard-woods and/or are so bitter or otherwise foul tasting that no one would consider eating them. Mycological studies juggle the names of these species with regularity. I will not bore you with the details, except to say that you should match *all* of the characters emphasized here before eating the matsutake, and if you are not in one of the geographic areas mentioned you should proceed with caution.

Focus Point
Notched Gills

The gills of the matsutake are attached to the stem by a "notch." Compare this method of attachment with the free gills of the button mushroom (p. 30), the more broadly attached gills of the enoki (p. 35), and the gills of the oyster mushroom (p. 37), which run down the stem.

Focus Point
Commercial Mushroom Picking

The Japanese are in love with the matsutake, and the result is that an enormous, burgeoning industry has begun to develop wherever the species occurs since it is mycorrhizal and therefore difficult to cultivate. In North America, the matsutake export centers are the Pacific Northwest and Mexico, and in both locations migrant populations of commercial collectors follow the matsutake season, picking mushrooms and selling them for a pittance to middlemen and exporters, who sell them to the Japanese for as much as one hundred dollars a pound, depending on the quality of the mushrooms and the relative scarcity each season. Many of these commercial mushroom pickers scrape out a living by following not only the matsutakes but also the western chanterelles (edible; p. 139), and the black morels (edible; p. 84), which grow in western burn sites in the year following the fire. A 1992 study of the commercial mushroom harvest in Oregon, Idaho, and Washington found that *4 million pounds* of wild mushrooms were being picked by commercial collectors each year, and the number has undoubtedly increased since then (Schlosser and Blatner 1995). Other export markets include Europe, and to a lesser extent, North American restaurants and specialty stores.

This industry is largely unregulated by anyone or any agency concerned about the people involved, though some restrictions have been made to protect the mushrooms and forests. Since commercial picking is obviously competitive and culture clashes are not uncommon among Asian, Latin, and Caucasian collectors (and since the ranks of commercial pickers unfortunately include a disproportionately high number of gun-toting, Unibomber-style, "me against the world" misfits), law enforcement logs and newspaper headlines report violent incidents with some frequency. Mushroom expert David Arora, whose 1986 book *Mushrooms Demystified* is far and away the best guide to North American mushrooms, has admirably become an advocate for commercial mushroom pickers, the overwhelming majority of whom are wonderful people whose hard work ought to be rewarded with more than a Dickensian wage and a cold shoulder from middle-class society. Mushroom pickers of the world, unite! You have nothing to lose but your chains, and a good union could hold the market hostage until you see some decent cash.

Quite a controversy has been stirred up over whether removing 4 million pounds of mushrooms from an ecosystem each year has detrimental environmental effects. Before outlining the contours of this controversy, however, I ask you to reread that last sentence and tell me what your gut instinct says. Hello? Have we not already gone over this debate, time and time again, with other organisms? And have we not discovered our mistakes when it was too late almost every time? Keep your answers in mind when I tell you that there is no scientific proof that harvesting mushrooms in such quantities has detrimental effects on the mushrooms or the forests. Various government agencies have put some limits on mushroom collecting in the Pacific Northwest, issuing permits and licenses and sometimes limiting the number of mushrooms that can be taken from a given location. But these restrictions have not been made on the basis of any indisputable proof that the environment may suffer. Mycologists who have addressed this issue, with the recent exception of Nicholas Money (see "Suggested Readings"), generally say that commercial harvesting is not likely to have adverse effects based on what we know about mushrooms, spore dispersal, and so on.

But studies are few and far between and prove nothing; they generally consist of careful observation of the number of mushrooms that pop up in a relatively small area and completely ignore a gazillion potential influencing factors and considerations. What if weather cycles are producing unrepresentatively high numbers of mushrooms during the time period under study? What if mushroom fruitings are on some long-term cycle we don't know about and the researcher studied a twenty-year peak, rather than a valley, without knowing it? What if the organism's goal is to get out of there rather than stay? What if the matsutake population two hundred miles downwind is not what it's supposed to be? What if we don't even understand geographic spore dispersal very well (what if, in fact, all we really know is based on a few people holding up petri dishes in the wind somewhere) and the mushrooms' "goal" isn't what we thought it was? And so on. As we all learned in junior-high science class, a scientific experiment controls all variables but the one under consideration—and none of the "studies" has come close; in fact it is probably impossible to design such an experiment. All of which means, in my humble opinion, that mycologists should stop stumbling over themselves to serve the money-grubbing mushroom exporters and middlemen and instead figure out a way to cultivate matsutakes, morels, and chanterelles so that commercial mushroom pickers can have decent jobs on mushroom farms—and the mushrooms can be produced in numbers that will help feed more than European and Japanese delicacy seekers. (You don't, of course, have to agree with me on any of this; most of my mushrooming friends—and certainly most mycologists—don't.)

In the Woods: (Darvin DeShazer) Often the spicy odor of the matsutake can be detected long before you spot the first mushroom. Under the two-needle pines along the sandy coast of California and Oregon it stands tall and proud above the reindeer lichens and bearberry, but under the madrone and tanoaks of the inland mountains it remains hidden and visible only as mushrumps (bulges in the leaf litter), with only an occasional tall specimen standing to release its spores. The pines in the Cascade Range offer a unique glimpse of this mushroom: smiling white crescents as the cap breaks the duff and stays half buried. After you find one, be sure to get down on all fours and pat the duff for more mushrumps in order to locate mushrooms that can't be seen.

In the Kitchen: (Darvin DeShazer) Thin slicing is the rule for this massive mushroom. Buttons can yield hundreds of paper-thin slices and add flavor to any dish. A West Coast favorite is a green salad with matsutake cut so thinly that only one gill remains on a slice. No cooking is necessary because this odoriferous mushroom is fantastic raw (but be sure to follow the safety precautions on page 24 when trying it the first time). Specimens from the sand dunes may require a garden hose to blast the sand from the crevices of the gills—though the result is waterlogged mushrooms. Matsutakes can be used in soups or casseroles, and they stand up well to oven heat. They retain most of their odor and spicy flavor when frozen but not when dried.

Recommended Recipes: Matsutake-Persimmon Casserole (p. 307); Candy Cap or Matsutake Waffles (p. 304).

 Tricholomopsis rutilans

Edibility Rating: Mediocre.

Distinguishing Features: This medium-sized gilled mushroom grows from dead conifer wood in fall or winter. The cap is convex at first, but

soon becomes flat or even uplifted. Its surface is dry and yellow beneath a healthy covering of dark red to purplish red scales and fibers. The yellow gills are attached to the stem, often by a "notch." They are not covered by a tissuelike or cobwebby partial veil when young. The stem is dry and yellow, but its surface is also covered with red scales, at least when the mushroom is young. There is no ring on the upper stem, and the base is not enclosed in a sack. The flesh is yellow, and does not change color when sliced. The odor is mild and the taste is mild or somewhat unpleasant. The spore print is white.

Ecology: *Tricholomopsis rutilans* is a wood-rotting saprobe that helps to decay fallen conifer logs. It grows alone or, more frequently, in small clusters. It prefers cooler weather, appearing in fall in most areas of the continent and over winter in warmer climates. Occasionally it appears in spring, as well.

Poisonous Look-Alikes: Species of *Pholiota*, some of which are superficially similar, have brown spore prints. *Tricholomopsis decora*, for which edibility is unknown, is also similar; see below.

Comments: *Tricholomopsis decora* (edibility not documented) is very similar but is generally more yellow and has less prominent, less red scales and fibers on its cap and stem. In most collections the scattered scales are pale brown, especially over the center of the cap.

In the Woods: (Darvin DeShazer) Snags, downed conifer wood, and mossy woodchips are good locations to look for *Tricholomopsis rutilans* on the Pacific Coast. The purplish scales and bright yellow gills can often be seen from a distance.

In the Kitchen: (Darvin DeShazer) Cleaning this beautiful mushroom is never an issue since it grows on wood and almost never requires more than a quick rinse before being tossed into the frying pan. Very few insects seem to like it. The thin flesh cooks quickly—and the cook quickly tires of its bland taste and lack of appeal. The texture is semisoft and adds little to an omelet. I once served it on a pizza, but the meat overpowered the taste of the mushrooms.

Recipes

*M*ost of these recipes could be used for almost any of the 100 edible mushrooms in the book. However, some are particularly suited for certain mushrooms; these are referenced in the entries for the mushrooms themselves under "Recommended Recipes."

Artichoke Shiitake Pizza
by John David Moore

Prepared dough for one 12-inch pizza crust
2 tablespoons olive oil
2 medium garlic cloves, slivered lengthwise
1/2 medium sweet onion, sliced in thin rings
1 small red or yellow sweet pepper, thinly sliced
4 canned, whole artichoke hearts, drained and chopped
1 cup thinly sliced shiitake mushroom caps
1/3 cup pitted and chopped kalamata olives
8 ounces shredded mozzarella cheese
1/3 cup shredded parmesan cheese

Prepare the pizza crust according to package instructions. Brush it with the olive oil and arrange all the ingredients, except the cheese, evenly on the crust. Cover the pizza with the mozzarella and then the parmesan. Bake at 400 degrees for 8 to 10 minutes or until the cheese is melted and the crust edges are brown.

Asparagus Garnish with Mushrooms
by Michael Kuo

1 cup fresh mushrooms
About 20 asparagus spears
1/4 cup cream cheese
2 tablespoons whipping cream or sour cream
2 tablespoons butter
(Immersion blender)

Trim the bottom few inches (the tough part) of the asparagus spears. Discard about half of the "butts," and boil the others for 15 to 20 minutes until mushy. Meanwhile, sauté the mushrooms over low heat in butter. Remove the mushrooms from heat and set aside. Remove the asparagus butts from boiling water, drain them, and start boiling the spears. Place the butts in a large bowl with the cream cheese and the whipping cream or sour cream. Use an immersion blender to puree the mixture until it is smooth and creamy (it will look like guacamole). I have tried using normal blenders and traditional mixers, but the results are not satisfactory; use an immersion blender. Remove the asparagus from the boiling water when it is cooked to your preference (I like mine fairly stiff, so the spears are "done" after 5 or 10 minutes). Ladle the puree over the asparagus and arrange the mushrooms on top. Serve immediately.

Beef Stroganoff with Wild Mushrooms
by John David Moore

4 pounds lean round steak, cut into 1/4 inch strips about 2 1/2 inches long
1 tablespoon olive oil
2 large garlic cloves, minced
1 bay leaf
1 teaspoon sweet paprika
Salt and pepper to taste
8 tablespoons (1/4 pound) butter

3 medium yellow onions, quartered and sliced

3 cups sliced fresh chanterelles, boletes, or
morels

3 tablespoons flour

3/4 cup tomato juice

1 quart sour cream

In a large skillet, brown the meat quickly in the olive oil on all sides with the bay leaf and garlic. Sprinkle the meat with salt, pepper, and paprika; set aside. In another skillet fry the onions in 5 tablespoons of the butter until translucent and golden. Add the mushrooms, cook for two minutes, and set aside. In a saucepan, melt the remaining 3 tablespoons of butter and stir in the flour to make a roux. Stir in the tomato juice and sour cream and add the mixture, together with the onions and mushrooms, to the meat. Cover and simmer for 30 minutes, stirring frequently. Serve over wide noodles.

Bigos (Polish Stew)
by John David Moore

1 tablespoon cooking oil

1 pound polish sausage, sliced in 1/4 inch pieces

1 pound beef stew meat, cut into 1/2 inch
chunks

1 small sweet onion, coarsely diced

1 large carrot, peeled and sliced thin

1/2 medium-sized green pepper, cut into
1/4 inch wide strips

2 medium tomatoes, coarsely chopped

2 1/2 cups sliced fresh mushrooms

About 21 ounces (1 1/2 cans) sauerkraut,
drained

6 to 8 prunes, coarsely chopped (optional)

1/2 teaspoon caraway seeds

2 tablespoons sweet hungarian paprika

Salt and pepper to taste

Sour cream

Fresh dill

In a large frying pan or Dutch oven, brown the sausage and beef in the oil. Add the onion and carrot and cook for 2 minutes or until the onions are soft. Add the remaining ingredients. (If you are using dried mushrooms, add them without rehydrating.) Simmer the stew for 1 hour. Serve with or over potato pierogi, kluski, or wide egg noodles. Top with sour cream and a sprinkling of fresh dill.

Candy Cap or Matsutake Waffles
by Darvin DeShazer and Michael Kuo

1/2 to 1 cup fresh *Lactarius rubidus* or
matsutakes

2 cups flour

1/4 teaspoon baking soda

1 1/2 teaspoons baking powder

1 tablespoon sugar

1/2 teaspoon salt

2 eggs

1 1/4 cups milk or buttermilk

6 tablespoons melted butter

(Waffle iron)

Shred mushrooms with a cheese grater and squeeze the mushroom pulp so that the watery liquid falls into a small bowl. Set the liquid and the pulp aside. Sift the flour, baking soda, baking powder, sugar, and salt into a large bowl. In a separate bowl, combine 2 egg yolks (save the whites) with the melted butter, the mushroom liquid (up to 1/2 cup), and the milk or buttermilk. Beat the mixture thoroughly, then pour it into the large bowl with the flour mixture; add the mushroom pulp. Combine with a fork. Beat the two egg whites until they are stiff, then fold them into the batter. Use the batter in a waffle iron, following the manufacturer's directions.

Chanterelles in Brandy Cream Sauce
by Vincent Ferraro

This scrumptious recipe comes from Vincent Ferraro, owner of Ariano's restaurant in Durango, Colorado. If you are in the Four Corners area in August, be sure to visit Ariano's for this heavenly dish.

2 tablespoons butter
Shallots to taste
Fresh chanterelles
1 tablespoon brandy
1/2 cup heavy cream
1/4 cup grated Parmigiano-Reggiano (imported Italian parmesan cheese)
Salt and pepper
2 slices of white sandwich bread
Parsley

Melt the butter in a skillet over medium heat. Add the shallots and a good handful of fresh chanterelles and cook, stirring, until the shallots brown (about 3 minutes). Add the brandy. Let the alcohol cook off, add the heavy cream, and bring to a boil. Cook for 3 minutes. Add the grated Parmigiano-Reggiano, reduce heat, add a pinch of salt and ground white pepper, and simmer. Remove and discard the crusts from the bread slices and toast them. Cut them diagonally and arrange on 4 small plates. Spoon the mushrooms and sauce over the toast. Garnish with finely chopped parsley.

Chicken of the Woods with Lemon Cream
by John David Moore

1 cup chicken of the woods cut in 1/2 inch squares
1 1/2 tablespoons butter
1 medium shallot, minced

1 teaspoon chopped fresh tarragon
1 generous squeeze lemon juice
1/3 cup whipping cream
2 thick slices of french bread, toasted
Fresh parsley for garnish

Slowly sauté the mushrooms and shallots in butter over medium heat for 5 minutes. Add the lemon juice, tarragon, and whipping cream. Cook until heated through. Serve over the toast and garnish with chopped parsley.

Five-Spice Beef with Enokis
by John David Moore

1 pound eye of round steak cut into 1/4 inch strips
1 tablespoon peanut or vegetable oil
2 cloves garlic, minced
2 teaspoons five-spice powder
1/2 cup water
1 medium onion, coarsely chopped
1 medium sweet red pepper, cut in wide strips
15 snow peas
4 ounces enoki mushrooms in small clusters
1 tablespoon sesame seeds, toasted
Soy sauce (optional) to taste

Brown the meat strips quickly in oil at high heat. Reduce the heat to medium and add the garlic and five-spice. Cook for about 3 minutes and add the water. Cook the mixture down to a thin sauce. Add the onion, pepper, and snow peas and cook briefly so vegetables are still somewhat firm. Add the enoki mushrooms and stir them into the mixture just enough to heat them through. Sprinkle with toasted sesame seeds and serve with basmati rice. Add soy sauce to taste.

Glazed Duck with Cranberry and Mushroom Stuffing
by Michael Kuo

1 young duck
1 pound fresh cranberries
Honey
1 cup fresh mushrooms
Salt and pepper

Wash the cranberries and add the mushrooms. Wash the duck and stuff its cavity with the cranberry and mushroom mixture. Brush the duck with honey and sprinkle with salt and pepper. Bake the duck according to the directions on its package (something like 40 minutes at 325 degrees for a small duck), but cover it with aluminum foil about halfway through, after the skin has browned (the honey will brown it sooner than expected).

Jaeger Sauce for Schnitzel or Steak
by Michael Kuo

1/3 pound chopped bacon
1/2 of a medium-sized onion
1 to 2 cups sliced, fresh mushrooms
1 tablespoon tomato paste
1/2 cup water
1/2 cup dry red wine
Salt and pepper
Paprika
2 tablespoons sour cream

Fry the bacon and onions until the bacon is crisp and the onions are golden. Drain, leaving 2 or 3 tablespoons of bacon grease. Add the tomato paste and mushrooms and sauté until the mushrooms are thoroughly cooked. Add the water, wine, and spices and simmer for 5 to 10 minutes. Add the sour cream and stir thoroughly. Simmer the sauce over low heat, stirring occasionally, until time to serve. Ladle it over schnitzel, pork chops, or steaks.

Lamb with Mint and Mushrooms
by John David Moore

1 tablespoon olive oil
2 leg of lamb steaks
2 garlic cloves, minced
2 cups fresh *Lactarius thyinos* or chanterelles
    (1 1/2 cups if using rehydrated mushrooms)
1 1/2 cups fresh mint leaves, chopped
1 small lemon, juiced
1/4 cup whipping cream
Salt and pepper to taste

In a large frying pan, brown the lamb quickly on both sides in the olive oil over high heat. Reduce heat, add the minced garlic, cover, and cook over low heat for 2 minutes or until the lamb is cooked through. Remove the lamb and keep it warm in foil. Add the mushrooms to the pan juices and cook for 2 to 3 minutes. Add the lemon juice and mint, reserving some mint for garnish. Cook the sauce uncovered for 1 minute. Add the whipping cream and cook for 2 minutes, stirring constantly. Return the lamb to the pan and heat through. Serve topped with sauce and fresh mint.

Marinated Mushrooms
by John David Moore

1 cup small, whole or halved button mushrooms
2 tablespoons white wine or cider vinegar
1/4 cup olive oil
2 tablespoons sweet hungarian paprika
1 tablespoon lemon juice
1/4 to 1/2 teaspoon chili powder
1 tablespoon chopped parsley

Put the mushrooms in a bowl. Mix the wine or vinegar, oil, paprika, chili powder, and lemon juice in a separate bowl. Pour the mixture over the mushrooms and stir gently to coat. Cover and chill for 45 minutes. Sprinkle chopped parsley over the mushrooms and serve.

Matsutake-Persimmon Casserole
by David DeShazer

Olive oil
Ground cinnamon or pumpkin pie spice
1 can cream of mushroom soup
1/2 cup white wine
2 cups seasoned bread crumbs
8 slices cheddar cheese
1 very large matsutake
8 fuyu persimmons

Grease a casserole dish with olive oil. Slice the persimmons and layer them in the dish, alternating the layers with sliced matsutake. Sprinkle cinnamon or pumpkin pie spice on each layer. Blend the wine and the soup and pour the mixture over the layered slices. Top with cheese and finish with the bread crumbs. Bake at 350 degrees for 40 minutes.

Mushroom Quiche
by John David Moore

1/2 cup butter (at room temperature)
2 cups sifted all-purpose flour
1/2 teaspoon salt
1/2 to 3/4 cup water
1 egg white
1/4 pound sliced bacon
2 cups milk or cream
3 whole eggs
1/4 teaspoon salt
1/8 teaspoon white pepper
Freshly grated nutmeg
1 chopped scallion
3/4 cup diced gruyère cheese
1/3 cup crumbled dried porcini or *Leccinum* slices

Add the salt to the flour and cut the butter into it. Make a well in the middle of the mixture and gradually pour in the water, stirring quickly with your index finger in spiral fashion from inside to outer edge to make a dough. When the dough can be formed into a ball without sticking to the fingers, refrigerate it covered with a damp cloth for about 2 hours. Roll out the dough on a floured board or pastry cloth and transfer it to a 9 inch pie pan. Brush the pie shell with egg white.

Preheat oven to 375 degrees. Slice the bacon into 1 inch pieces, fry it in a skillet until not quite crisp, and drain on paper towels. Scald the milk or cream, cool, and then beat it together with the eggs, salt, pepper, nutmeg, and scallion. Distribute the bacon, cheese, and mushrooms in the bottom of the pie shell. Pour in the liquid mixture. Bake for 35 to 40 minutes until the top starts to brown. Cool slightly or completely and serve.

Mushroom Ravioli
by Michael Kuo

This recipe requires 3 to 4 hours preparation time.

2/3 cup flour
1 egg
1 tablespoon water
1/2 teaspoon salt
1 tablespoon cooking oil

1/2 to 3/4 cup porcini or other dried boletes
Dry white wine for rehydrating
1/2 cup ricotta cheese
1/2 cup grated parmesan cheese

1/4 cup butter
1/4 to 1/2 cup parmesan cheese

Dump the flour on a large cutting board or wooden countertop and make a well in the center. In a small bowl, combine the egg, water, salt, and oil with a few strokes of a fork (do not overmix). Pour the mixture into the well and, using your hands, fold the ingredients together until you create a dough ball of even consistency. Knead the dough for 10 minutes. Cover it and set aside at room temperature for 1 hour. While you are waiting, make the ravioli stuffing. Rehydrate the porcini in dry white wine for 10 to 20 minutes. Remove the mushrooms and dry them on paper towels. In a bowl, combine the rehydrated porcini with the ricotta and parmesan cheeses. Cover and set aside. After an hour has passed, roll out the dough with your hands and a rolling pin, sprinkling flour on everything (the dough, the cutting board, your hands, and the rolling pin) as you go. When the dough is paper thin, use a pizza cutter to slice it into two roughly equal portions. Place one sheet of dough on the cutting board and, visualizing a grid of squares 2 to 3 inches across, put 2 to 3 teaspoons of stuffing in the center of each future square. Place the other sheet of dough over the top, and use your fingers to press everything together; the result will be that the little stuffing piles create humps. Now press harder with your fingertips in the unstuffed areas, sealing the two dough sheets together. Use a pizza cutter to separate the ravioli squares, then score each square's edges firmly with a fork, creating attractive, fluted edges while simultaneously sealing each ravioli square by pressing hard. Put the squares on a rack and dry them at room temperature for an hour. Turn them over, and dry them for another hour. Cook them in boiling water, about 5 at a time, for a few minutes (use a slotted spoon to remove the cooked squares and set them aside). Be sure to keep the water at a rolling boil throughout the process. Melt 1/4 cup of butter, drizzle it over the ravioli, and sprinkle 1/4 to 1/2 cup of grated parmesan cheese over the top. Serve immediately. (Alternatively, use the ravioli in an alfredo sauce.)

Pasta with Hedgehogs, Bacon, and Tomato
by John David Moore

1 large shallot, finely chopped
2 large garlic cloves, minced
1 tablespoon olive oil
6 or 7 thick slices of smoked bacon, cut into 1/2 inch pieces
2 tablespoons bacon drippings
2 cups hedgehog mushrooms
3 medium, ripe tomatoes, chopped
1 medium bell pepper, cut into 1 inch, thin strips
2 tablespoons fresh basil, chopped
Salt and pepper to taste
Pasta of choice
Freshly grated parmesan or romano cheese

Sauté the shallot and garlic in the olive oil for one minute. Set aside. Fry the bacon until almost crisp and drain, reserving 2 tablespoons of the drippings. Add the mushrooms and bacon drippings to the shallots and garlic, and sauté for 3 to 4 minutes or until the mushrooms are suitably tender. Add the bell pepper strips and cook for another minute. Add the tomatoes and basil and simmer for 2 minutes. Add salt and pepper to taste. Serve over pasta and top with cheese.

Polish Pork Chops with Russulas
by John David Moore

4 loin pork chops
3 tablespoons chopped onions
1 1/2 cups sliced fresh russulas or 2/3 cup dried russulas reconstituted in water and drained
1 cup tomato sauce
1/2 cup sour cream
1 medium dill pickle, chopped
3 tablespoons dry sherry
Salt and freshly ground black pepper
Sprigs of fresh dill for garnish

In a lightly greased skillet, brown the chops on both sides over brisk heat. Cover, reduce the heat, and cook slowly until the chops are almost tender, about 20 minutes. Add the onion and russulas, cover, and continue cooking until the chops are tender and onions are soft, about 5 minutes longer. Add the tomato sauce and sour cream and simmer. Do not boil the sauce after the sour cream has been added or it will curdle. Stir in the pickle, sherry, and seasonings. Serve garnished with dill sprigs.

Porcini Sauce for Pork Roast
by Michael Kuo

One pork roast, cooked
1/2 cup pork roast drippings
Butter (if needed)
2 tablespoons flour
1/2 to 1 cup whipping cream
2 tablespoons white wine
1/2 cup porcini or other dried boletes
Paprika
Salt and pepper
Lemon juice

Heat the pork roast drippings over medium heat in a saucepan (add butter if needed to make 1/2 cup). Add the flour and mix with a whisk into a roux. Slowly add the whipping cream and wine, stirring constantly. Add the porcini and reduce the heat to low. Add the spices and lemon juice. Stir gently, adding more liquids if needed. Ladle generously over sliced pork roast and serve immediately.

Portuguese Steak with Mushrooms
by Michael Kuo

Dry white wine to rehydrate dried mushrooms
4 tablespoons butter
2 cloves garlic, minced

4 filets mignons
1/2 cup dried or 1 cup fresh mushrooms
1 cup whipping cream
Salt and pepper
Paprika
2 lemons, juiced, or 3 tablespoons lemon juice

Cheaper steaks can be substituted for the filets— but not rib eyes, T-bones, or thinly sliced cuts. Preheat the oven to 300 degrees. If using dried mushrooms, rehydrate them for 10 minutes in the wine. Heat an iron skillet and melt the butter over high heat. Add the garlic, stirring constantly. While the skillet is noisily popping, brown the filets briefly on each side and add the mushrooms. Reduce the heat to low. Add the whipping cream, spices (don't skimp on the pepper and paprika), and lemon juice. Stir until the sauce is evenly mixed and ladle some over each filet. Put iron skillet in the oven and roast the filets for 5 to 15 minutes, depending on how you prefer your steaks. Remove skillet from the oven, put the filets aside, and cook the sauce down over medium heat for a few minutes. Ladle the sauce over the filets and garnish. Serve immediately.

Salted Mushroom Salad
by Annikki Rintanen

1 cup salted *Lactarius* or *Russula* mushrooms
    (recipe follows)
1 medium onion
2 green onions (scallions)
Pepper
1/2 cup sour cream or whipping cream

Salted Mushrooms: Slice fresh mushrooms into bite-size chunks and boil for 2 to 3 minutes. Drain thoroughly. Repeat the process 3 times if you are using *Lactarius deceptivus* or another strongly acrid species. Put the mushroom pieces in a glass jar, layer by layer, sprinkling each layer with a coating of salt. Place a clean, flat stone over the top layer and add boiling water until the jar is full. The mushrooms must be completely submerged. Close the lid tightly and store in a cool place. Before using the mushrooms, rinse them thoroughly to remove the salt.

Mushroom Salad: Dice the onion and green onions and add 1 cup of salted mushrooms (you may want to chop them into smaller pieces), pepper, and sour cream or whipping cream. Serve cold.

Shaggy Mane Soup
by John David Moore

3 cups shaggy manes, chopped
1 large clove garlic, chopped
1 shallot, chopped
2 tablespoons butter
1 tablespoon flour
1 cup chicken or vegetable stock
1/4 cup white wine
1/2 cup whipping cream
Fresh parsley, chopped
Squeeze of fresh lemon

Sauté the shaggy manes, garlic, and shallots in the butter over medium heat for about 2 minutes. Whisk in the flour and cook over low heat for about 1 minute. Slowly stir in the stock and the wine. Stir the mixture while bringing it to a boil, reduce the heat, cover, and simmer for 20 minutes. Let the soup cool and then puree the mixture in a blender. Return the soup to the pan, add the whipping cream, and heat without boiling. Serve with a garnish of chopped fresh parsley and a squeeze of lemon.

Shrimp-Stuffed Morels
by John David Moore

6 large yellow morels with stems
1 cup medium shrimp, shelled, cooked, and
    cut into thirds
1/2 cup freshly shredded parmesan cheese
2 medium garlic cloves, minced
2 tablespoons fresh basil, chopped
1/2 cup sour cream
Prosciutto slices, cut into 6 strips, 1 inch wide
1 tablespoon butter, melted
1 tablespoon olive oil
Fresh parsley, chopped

Wash the inside and outside of the morels under running water and blanch them in boiling water until pliable. Remove them with a slotted spoon, drain, and cool thoroughly. Cut up the cooked shrimp and set aside. Combine the cheese, garlic, and basil with the sour cream and set aside. Slit open one side of each morel cap lengthwise and insert 3 to 5 shrimp pieces (depending on the size of the morels) into the cap and hollow stem. Fill each mushroom with the cheese and sour cream mixture and wrap with the prosciutto strips. Pour the melted butter and olive oil into a baking dish. Place the morels in the dish, stuffed side up, and bake at 350 degrees for 10 minutes. Drizzle the mushrooms with lemon juice, sprinkle with the fresh parsley, and serve over rice.

Spinach Mushroom Ricotta Pie
by John David Moore

10 to 12 ounces frozen spinach, thawed and
    well drained
2 cups ricotta cheese
1/2 pound fresh boletes, chopped
1/2 cup grated swiss cheese
1/2 cup grated parmesan cheese
1/4 cup onion, finely chopped

1/4 pound pepperoni, sliced
2 teaspoons dijon mustard
1 teaspoon fresh oregano leaves, chopped
    (1/2 teaspoon if using dried oregano)
1/4 teaspoon salt
Pepper
1 egg, slightly beaten
Pastry for one 2-crust, 9-inch pie

1 large (15 ounce) can tomato sauce
1/2 teaspoon garlic powder
Dash of pepper
1/4 cup white wine
1 tablespoon fresh basil, chopped

Drain spinach thoroughly and blend with ricotta, mushrooms, swiss and parmesan cheese, onion, pepperoni, mustard, oregano, salt, and pepper. Stir in the egg. Roll out half the pastry and line a lightly greased pan. Spread in the pie filling. Roll out the remaining pastry and place on top of the pie filling. Seal the edges, pierce the center of the crust, and bake in a 425 degree oven for about 25 minutes or until crust is browned. Combine the tomato sauce, garlic powder, pepper, wine, and basil. Heat and serve over the pie.

Stuffed Mushrooms
by John David Moore

3/4 cup hazelnuts, toasted and finely chopped
1 teaspoon olive oil
1/2 teaspoon salt
8 mushroom caps (2 to 3 inches in diameter)
    sliced
1/4 cup butter
2 yellow onions, chopped
1 large garlic clove, minced
1 tablespoon fresh basil, chopped
1/2 cup crab claw meat
1 cup bread crumbs
Juice and grated peel of 1 lemon
1 cup gruyère cheese, grated
Salt and pepper to taste

Combine the hazelnuts, oil, and salt in a bowl. Remove the stems from the mushrooms. Chop the stems and set them aside. If using boletes, remove and discard the tubes from the caps. Melt the butter in a large frying pan. Brush the mushroom caps with half the melted butter and place them stem-side down on a baking sheet. Reheat the remaining butter, add the onions and garlic, and sauté until the onions are soft and golden (5 to 8 minutes). Add the basil and chopped mushroom stems and sauté for 1 minute. Remove from heat and stir in the nuts, crabmeat, bread crumbs, lemon juice, lemon peel, cheese, salt, and pepper. Broil the mushroom caps for 3 minutes, turning once. Fill caps with the stuffing and broil for 4 to 6 minutes or until the stuffing is very hot.

Photos by Dianna Smith

Suggested Readings

Works Cited

Abesha, E., G. Caetano-Anolles, and K. Hoiland. 2003. "Population Genetics and Spatial Structure of the Fairy Ring Fungus *Marasmius oreades* in a Norwegian Sand Dune Ecosystem." *Mycologia* 95:1021–31.

Coker, W. C., and A. H. Beers. 1943. *The Boleti of North Carolina*. Reprint 1971. New York: Dover.

Horton, T. R., and T. D. Bruns. 2001. "The Molecular Revolution in Ectomycorrhizal Ecology: Peeking into the Black Box." *Molecular Ecology* 10:1855–71.

Kerrigan, R. W., D. B. Carvalho, P. A. Horgen, and J. B. Anderson. 1995. "Indigenous and Introduced Populations of *Agaricus bisporus*, the Cultivated Button Mushroom, in Eastern and Western Canada: Implications for Population Biology, Resource Management, and Conservation of Genetic Diversity." *Canadian Journal of Botany* 73:1925–38.

McIlvaine, C., and R. Macadam. 1902. *One Thousand American Fungi*. Reprint 1973. New York: Dover.

Schlosser, W. E., and K. A. Blatner. 1995. "The Wild Edible Mushroom Industry of Washington, Oregon and Idaho: A 1992 Survey." *Journal of Forestry* 93:31–36.

Stuntz, D. E. 1947. "Studies in the Genus *Inocybe* I: New and Noteworthy Species from Washington." *Mycologia* 39:21–55.

Mushroom Guides and Readings

Arora, D. 1986. *Mushrooms Demystified: A Comprehensive Guide to the Fleshy Fungi*. Berkeley: Ten Speed Press.

Barron, G. 1999. *Mushrooms of Northeast North America*. Edmonton, AB: Lone Pine.

Bessette, A. E., O. K. Miller, Jr., A. R. Bessette, and H. H. Miller. 1995. *Mushrooms of North America in Color: A Field Guide Companion to Seldom-Illustrated Fungi*. Syracuse: Syracuse University Press.

Bessette, A. E., W. C. Roody, and A. R. Bessette. 2000. *North American Boletes: A Color Guide to the Fleshy Pored Mushrooms*. Syracuse: Syracuse University Press.

Evenson, V. S. 1997. *Mushrooms of Colorado and the Southern Rocky Mountains*. Denver: Denver Botanic Press.

Horn, B., R. Kay, and D. Abel. 1993. *A Guide to Kansas Mushrooms*. Lawrence: University Press of Kansas.

Jenkins, D. T. 1986. *Amanita of North America*. Eureka, CA: Mad River Press.

Kibby, G., and R. Fatto. 1990. *Keys to the Species of Russula in Northeastern North America*. Somerville, NJ: Kibby-Fatto Enterprises.

Kuo, M. 2005. *Morels*. Ann Arbor: University of Michigan Press.

Largent, D. L. 1973. *How to Identify Mushrooms to Genus I: Macroscopic Features*. Eureka, CA: Mad River Press.

Largent, D. L., and H. D. Thiers. 1973. *How to Identify Mushrooms to Genus II: Field Identification of Genera*. Eureka, CA: Mad River Press.

Lincoff, G. H. 1992. *The Audubon Society Field Guide to North American Mushrooms*. New York: Knopf.

McKnight, K. H., and V. B. McKnight. 1987. *Mushrooms*. Peterson Field Guides. New York: Houghton Mifflin.

Metzler, S., and V. Metzler. 1992. *Texas Mushrooms*. Austin: University of Texas Press.

Money, N. P. 2002. *Mr. Bloomfield's Orchard: The Mysterious World of Mushrooms, Molds, and Mycologists*. New York: Oxford University Press.

Money, N. P. 2005. "Why Picking Wild Mushrooms May Be Bad Behaviour." *Mycological Research* 109:131–35.

Moser, M. 1983. *Keys to Agarics and Boleti (Polyporales, Boletales, Agaricales, Russulales)*. Edited by G. Kibby, translated by S. Plant. London: Roger Phillips.

Phillips, R. 2005. *Mushrooms and Other Fungi of North America*. Boston: Firefly Books.

Roody, W. C. 2003. *Mushrooms of West Virginia and the Central Appalachians*. Lexington: University of Kentucky Press.

Smith, A. H. 1949. *Mushrooms in Their Natural Habitat*. New York: Hafner Press.

Smith, A. H. 1973. *A Field Guide to Western Mushrooms*. Ann Arbor: University of Michigan Press.

Smith, A. H. 1975. *The Mushroom Hunter's Field Guide*. Ann Arbor: University of Michigan Press.

Smith, A. H., H. V. Smith, and N. S. Weber. 1979. *How to Know the Gilled Mushrooms*. Dubuque, IA: William C. Brown.

Smith, A. H., H. V. Smith, and N. S. Weber. 1981. *How to Know the Non-gilled Mushrooms*. Dubuque, IA: William C. Brown.

Smith, A. H., and H. D. Thiers. 1971. *The Boletes of Michigan*. Ann Arbor: University of Michigan Press.

States, J. S. 1990. *Mushrooms and Truffles of the Southwest*. Tucson: University of Arizona Press.

Weber, N. S. 1995. *A Morel Hunter's Companion: A Guide to the True and False Morels of Michigan*. Lansing, MI: TwoPeninsula Press.

Weber, N. S., and A. H. Smith. 1985. *A Field Guide to Southern Mushrooms*. Ann Arbor: University of Michigan Press.

Tree Guides

Peattie, D. C. 1991. *A Natural History of Western Trees*. Boston: Houghton Mifflin.

Peattie, D. C. 1991. *A Natural History of Trees of Eastern and Central North America*. Boston: Houghton Mifflin.

Preston, R. J. 1989. *North American Trees Exclusive of Mexico and Tropical Florida*. Ames: Iowa State University Press.

Cooking Mushrooms

Grigson, J. 1983. *The Mushroom Feast*. London: Penguin.

Leibernstein, M. 1993. *The Edible Mushroom: A Gourmet Cook's Guide*. Hartford: Globe Pequot Press.

McLaughlin, M. 1994. *The Mushroom Book: Recipes for Earthly Delights*. San Francisco: Chronicle Books.

Rombauer, I. S., M. R. Becker, and E. Becker. 1985. *Joy of Cooking*. New York: Simon and Schuster.

Web Sites

Baroni, T. *Basidiomycetes of the Greater Antilles*. http://www.cortland.edu/nsf/GA.html

CABI Bioscience Databases. *Index Fungorum*. http://www.indexfungorum.org/Names/Names.asp

Halling, R. E. *A Revision of Collybia s. l. in the Northeastern United States and Adjacent Canada*. http://www.nybg.org/bsci/res/col/colintro.html

Halling, R. E., and G. M. Mueller. *Macrofungi of Costa Rica*. http://www.nybg.org/bsci/res/hall/

Kuo, M. *MushroomExpert.com*. http://www.mushroomexpert.com

Lamoureux, Y., and J. Després. *Key to Tricholoma of Quebec*. http://www.mycomontreal.qc.ca/tricho/home.htm

Mueller, G. M. *The Mushroom Genus Laccaria in North America*. http://www.fieldmuseum.org/research_collections/botany/botany_sites/fungi/index.html

Pacific Northwest Key Council. *Keys to Mushrooms of the Pacific Northwest*. http://www.svims.ca/council/keys.htm

Petersen, R. H., K. W. Hughes, and N. Psurtseva. *Biological Species in Pleurotus*. http://fp.bio.utk.edu/mycology/Pleurotus

Petersen, R. H., K. W. Hughes, and S. A. Redhead. *The Genus Flammulina*. http://fp.bio.utk.edu/mycology/Flammulina/default.html

Phillips, R. *Roger's Mushrooms*. http://www.rogersmushrooms.com

Snowarski, M. *Fungi of Poland*. http://www.grzyby.pl

Tulloss, R. E., and Z. Yang. *Studies in the Genus Amanita*. http://pluto.njcc.com/ ~ret/amanita/

Uljé, K. *All about Ink Caps*. http://www.homepages.hetnet.nl/~idakees/index.html

U.S. Department of Agriculture. *Hypomyces*. http://nt.ars-grin.gov/taxadescriptions/ keys/HypomycesIndex.cfm

Volk, T. *Tom Volk's Fungi*. http://www.tomvolkfungi.net

Wood, M., and F. Stevens. *MykoWeb*. http://www.mykoweb.com

Photo Credits and Acknowledgments

Photos and Illustrations

All photos, scans, and graphic compilations are mine unless otherwise noted in captions. The following photographers contributed to this book.

Irene Andersson: 196
George Barron: 166, 201, 222, 251, 284, 292
Mark Davis: iii, 16, 88, 92, 193, 198, 203, 219
Roy Halling: 229
Pam Kaminski: 42, 50, 66, 76, 85, 113, 122, 124, 125, 143, 164, 168, 210, 238, 253, 263
David Lewis: 196
Taylor Lockwood: 113, 139, 297
Emilio Pini: 58
Chris Ribet: 226
Konnie Robertson: 198
Neil Selbicky: 193
Dianna Smith: 54, 62, 64, 76, 80, 88, 105, 147, 160, 182, 227, 244, 256, 294, 312
Hugh Smith: 56, 80, 85, 88, 134, 137, 145, 147, 155, 157
Mike Wood: 162
David Work: 96
Tim Zurowski: 73, 145, 160, 253, 296

Acknowledgments

I wish to thank John David Moore, without whose diligent efforts this book (and my love of mushrooms) would have been impossible; Darvin DeShazer, who has patiently tutored me on western mushrooms and whose contributions to the book were indispensable; all the photographers; Ken Gilberg, Kate Klipp (to whom this book is dedicated), and Shannon Stevens, who all contributed wonderful entries on the edibility of some very odd mushrooms; Carol Schmudde, my mother, for her tireless proofreading (and of course a million other things!); Gary Lincoff; Andy Methven; Dana Ringuette; Jean Toothman; Tom Volk; Bob Zordani; and my wonderful editor, Mary Erwin.

Glossary and Index

Scientific names of mushrooms are indexed by both species and genus name, since mycologists frequently shift genus names around (see p. 8). Italicized page numbers represent illustrations; page numbers in bold type represent full treatments. Glossary entries are included for terms used in this book and for mycological terms frequently encountered in field guides and mushroom literature.

Text design by Mary H. Sexton
Typesetting by Agnew's, Grand Rapids, Michigan
Font: Goudy

Frederic W. Goudy designed Goudy Old Style
in 1915. Flexible enough for both text and display, it is one of the most popular typefaces ever
produced. Its recognizable features include the
diamond-shaped dots on i, j, and on punctuation
marks. Many additions to the typeface family
were created over the next several decades.

—*courtesy www.adobe.com*